ACKNOWLEDGEMENT

My thanks are due to Fiat (England) Ltd. for their unstinted co-operation and also for supplying data and illustrations.

I am also grateful to a considerable number of owners who have discussed their cars at length and many of whose suggestions have been included in this manual.

Kenneth Ball G I Mech E
Associate Member Guild of Motoring Writers

Ditchling Sussex England.

FIAT 1300, 1500 1961-67 AUTOBOOK

Workshop Manual for
Fiat 1300 1961-66
Fiat 1500 1961-67

by

Kenneth Ball G I Mech E

and the

Autopress team of Technical Writers

AUTOPRESS LTD   GOLDEN LANE   BRIGHTON   BN1 2QJ   ENGLAND

The AUTOBOOK series of Workshop Manuals covers the majority of British and Continental motor cars.

For a full list see the back of this manual.

CONTENTS

ISBN 0 85147 214 1

First Edition   1972

© Autopress Ltd. 1972

Printed in Brighton England for Autopress Ltd by G Beard & Son Ltd

INTRODUCTION

This do-it-yourself Workshop Manual has been specially written for the owner who wishes to maintain his car in first class condition and to carry out his own servicing and repairs. Considerable savings on garage charges can be made, and one can drive in safety and confidence knowing the work has been done properly.

Comprehensive step-by-step instructions and illustrations are given on all dismantling, overhauling and assembling operations. Certain assemblies require the use of expensive special tools, the purchase of which would be unjustified. In these cases information is included but the reader is recommended to hand the unit to the agent for attention.

Throughout the Manual hints and tips are included which will be found invaluable, and there is an easy to follow fault diagnosis at the end of each chapter.

Whilst every care has been taken to ensure correctness of information it is obviously not possible to guarantee complete freedom from errors or to accept liability arising from such errors or omissions.

Instructions may refer to the righthand or lefthand sides of the vehicle or the components. These are the same as the righthand or lefthand of an observer standing behind the car and looking forward.

CHAPTER 1

THE ENGINE

1:1 Description

This Chapter deals with the 116.000, 116C.000, 115.000 and 115C.000 engines. All are of basically similar construction; both the 116 and 116C engines are of 1295cc while the 115 and 115C engines have the cylinder bore increased so that the capacity becomes 1481cc. In all cases the stroke and therefore the crankshaft remains the same.

Reference to **FIGS 1:1, 1:2** and **1:3** clearly shows the main constructional features but particularly noticeable is the 'cross-flow' cylinder head design. The crankcase is of cast iron and supports the crankshaft in three main bearings. End thrust of the crankshaft is taken on the centre bearing.

The cylinder head is of aluminium alloy and the combustion chambers are fully machined. Suitable ports carry hot water from the head to the inlet manifold to assist in mixture vaporization. Cast iron valve seat inserts are fitted. The valves are operated by rockers supported on twin shafts so that the pushrods from the single camshaft are kept as short and light as possible.

The camshaft is driven by a duplex roller chain from the crankshaft and is supported by three bearings in the crankcase.

A centrifugal impeller type water pump is fitted and is driven in the conventional manner by a V-belt from the crankshaft pulley. This belt also drives the generator. The crankshaft pulley is not conventional at all, it is in fact an ingenious centrifugal oil purifier and its operation is fully described later in this Chapter under the lubrication system.

The camshaft drives the distributor and gear type oil pump from a skew gear meshing with a gear on the oil pump shaft.

A twin choke carburetter is fitted and a paper element type air filter ensures a supply of clean air to the engine. The carburetter type has been varied to suit the particular engine for which it is intended, both Weber and Solex have been fitted.

The differences between the 115.000, 116.000 and the 115C.000 and 116C.000 engines are in detail only and do not affect servicing procedures. The 'C' engines have had the compression ratio raised by slight alterations to the combustion chambers and piston crown profiles, larger valves are fitted together with a modified inlet manifold and a later type carburetter. The 115C.000 engine has a modified camshaft which provides a different valve timing diagram. Both engines have the crankcase

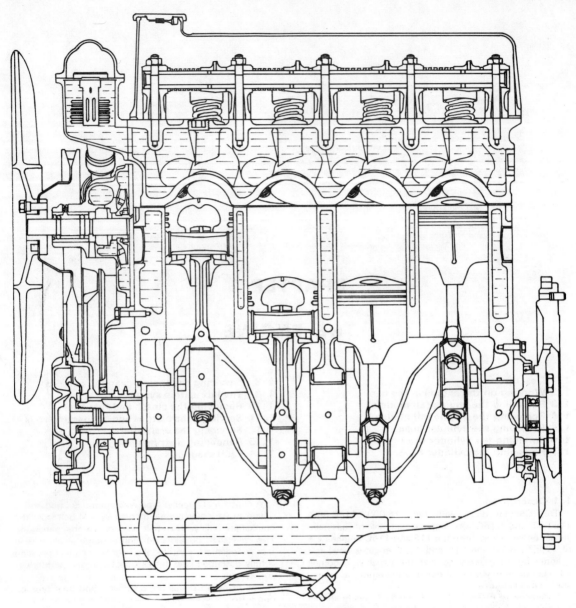

FIG 1:1   Sectional view of engine through crankshaft

breather pipe connected to the air filter casing. Slight alterations have also been made to the distributor to enable the ignition advance curve to be varied.

1:2 Working on the engine in the car

Although all normal servicing can be performed easily without disturbing the engine there is not a great deal of room fore and aft in the engine compartment.

Decarbonization, attention to the water pump, generator, distributor, starter and fuel pump are all straightforward.

Removal of the radiator gives just enough room to work on the centrifugal oil filter but all other operations involve either removing the engine or the gearbox. For work on the clutch, flywheel or rear main oil seal only the gearbox need be removed but any work on the oil pump, camshaft, pistons and connecting rods entails lifting the engine out of the car. This is not a great disadvantage; when any of these items needs attention, the mileage covered will have made a complete overhaul essential in any case. It must be noted that the gearbox will have to be released before the engine will lift out. This is to extract the gearbox first motion shaft from the flywheel.

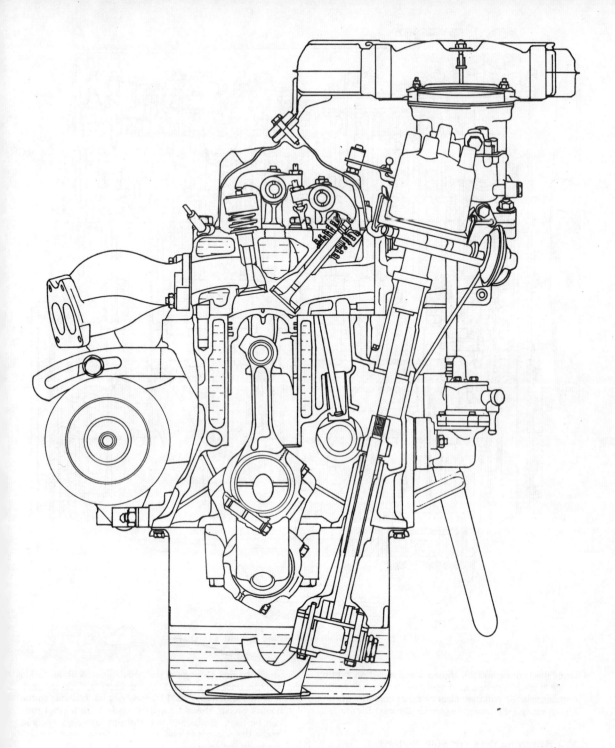

FIG 1:2 Sectional view of engine from front

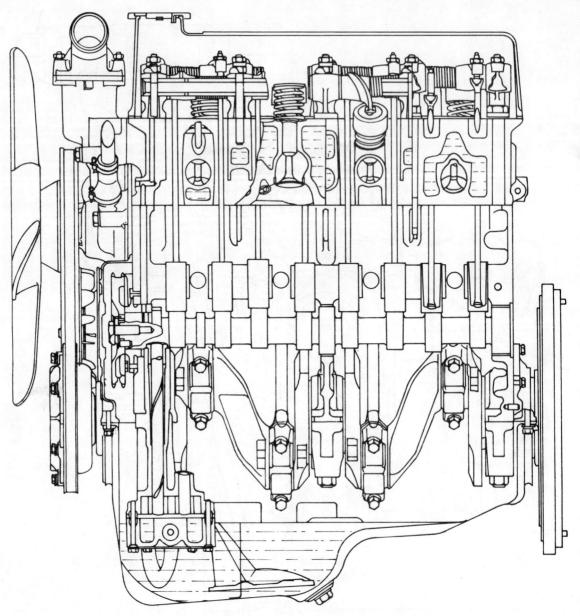

FIG 1:3   Sectional view of engine through camshaft

Once this is done and the engine is supported on a lifting tackle it must be swung diagonally across the engine compartment. It will then clear all other components and lift out easily. Full details are given in the next Section.

1:3 Removing the engine (all models)

It will be necessary to obtain working space under the car either by placing it over a pit or by raising it from the ground. If the latter course is adopted make sure that it is safely supported on substantial wooden blocks placed under the box sections of the body shield. A lifting tackle will be necessary and a lifting bracket. This bracket, which is shown in **FIG 1:4,** may not be available to the private owner, therefore a sling made from a stout rope can be used. Be careful that the sling is safely secured under the sump and cannot slip or damage any accessories on the engine.

If the engine is being removed with the intention of replacing it with a completely new or reconditioned unit the water pump and cylinder head can be left in place. If the existing unit is to be reconditioned and put back again

FIG 1:4 Lifting the engine

FIG 1:5 Transmission flexible joint

Key to Fig 1:5 1 Front propeller shaft   2 Sliding joint
3 Spider   4 Flexible joint   5 Sliding joint bolts
6 Transmission bolts

it is good practice to remove as many components as possible to lighten the lift and reduce the difficulty of handling the suspended weight.

Proceed to remove the engine as follows:

1 Disconnect and remove the battery.

2 Open the radiator drain cock and also the cock situated at the lefthand side of the cylinder block. Remove the radiator cap.

3 Disconnect the radiator hoses then remove the two nuts which secure the bottom of the radiator to the body and take off the rubber pads and spacers. Release the bolt from the top clamp and remove the rubber pads and spacers. The radiator will now lift up and out of the engine compartment.

4 Disconnect and suitably mark all electrical connections to the engine. A good method is to tie labels to the leads, writing on the label the exact function of the cable.

5 Remove the throttle and choke cables from the carburetter and the fuel pipe from the tank at the pump. At this stage removal of the air cleaner will give more room to work. This is easily done by removing the centre wing nut, the cover and the paper element. From inside the casing release the four self-locking nuts which hold it to the carburetter. Remove the bolt and rubber spacers holding the air cleaner casing to the rocker box cover then lift the casing away complete with its gaskets.

6 Undo the four bronze nuts holding the exhaust pipe to the manifold and pull the pipe clear of the manifold.

7 Disconnect the heater hoses.

8 From below the car remove the three bolts which hold the propeller shaft sliding joint to the flexible coupling (see FIG 1:5, items 5). Undo the two bolts holding the propeller shaft centre bearing and the

shafts should be free enough to push to one side to clear the gearbox when it moves back. If not, the rear shaft must be released at the differential and the whole assembly pushed to the rear of the car.

9 Remove the splitpin at the end of the clutch slave cylinder pushrod, release the return spring and unbolt the cylinder from the clutch housing. Pass a piece of wire through the splitpin hole and back through one of the cylinder casting bolt holes to hold the pushrod and piston in the cylinder. Do not disconnect the hydraulic fluid line but tie the cylinder up out of the way without straining the fluid line.

10 Loosen the speedometer drive cable lock ring on the gearbox and remove the cable.

11 Remove the bolts and take off the flywheel cover from the front of the bellhousing and at the same time loosen the exhaust pipe bracket nuts.

12 Disconnect the two gear rods. It will be found easiest to release the one at the side from below the car and the other rod from above the car. This latter is the operating rod and should be released at the relay lever.

13 Remove the starter motor bolts and support the starter motor until it can be lifted up through the engine compartment.

14 Now place a jack with a piece of soft wood packing between its head and the sump and just apply a little pressure. This will prevent the engine swinging inadvertently when the gearbox is removed.

15 Place a second jack under the gearbox then raise it to just support the weight. Remove the remaining bolts between the bellhousing and engine making sure that the gearbox does not slip off the jack. Remove the bolts holding the crossmember supporting the gearbox then with the help of an assistant gently ease the gearbox back and away from the engine. When the

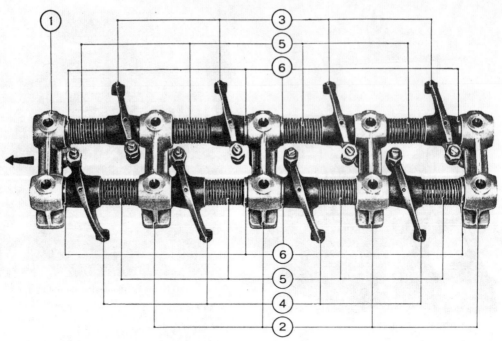

FIG 1 : 6   Rocker shafts, complete assembly

Key to Fig 1 : 6   1 Front pedestal   2 Intermediate and rear pedestals   3 Exhaust rockers   4 Inlet rockers   5 Springs
6 Thrust washers

first motion (primary) shaft is free of the clutch, lower the gearbox and remove from under the car.

16 Fit the sling round the engine, attach it to the tackle and just take the strain. Remove the engine mounting nuts, lift the engine and swing it across the engine compartment as illustrated in **FIG 1 : 4**. It can now be lifted clear of the car. When the engine is supported on a tackle never allow any part of the person to come below it no matter how safe the lifting gear may appear to be. Lower the engine and support on wooden blocks or bolt it to an engine stand if available.

1 : 4 Replacing the engine

This is a direct reversal of the dismantling process and no difficulty should be experienced. It will be easier to connect the gearbox to the engine if the rear of the engine is allowed to tilt slightly downwards and the gearbox to point upwards at the same angle. Put the gearbox into top gear; by turning the output flange the primary shaft can turn thus making it possible to line up the splines with the clutch hub splines.

Tighten the engine mounting nuts to 25.3 lb ft (3.5 kg m) and the rear crossmember bolts to 18.8 lb ft (2.6 kg m).

1 : 5 Removing the cylinder head

This is the most frequent operation that the private owner will undertake in order to decarbonize the engine and attend to the valves. Remember that the head is made from an aluminium alloy and can be easily damaged or distorted. Be particularly careful to undo the head holding bolts in the proper sequence.

1 Disconnect and remove the battery then drain the radiator.

2 Remove the air cleaner as described in **Section 1 : 3** and then release the carburetter throttle and choke cables.

3 Disconnect the sparking plug leads and the coil to distributor cap HT lead. Remove the distributor cap complete with the leads. If it is felt that any doubt may exist when replacing the plug leads, put one spot of paint on the lead for the plug nearest the front of the engine, two spots for the next and so on.

4 Remove the rocker box cover and disconnect both heater hoses. Remove the radiator to cylinder head hose and also the water pump to head hose.

5 Disconnect the fuel pipe, it is best to remove this completely between the carburetter and fuel pump.

6 Disconnect the temperature gauge sender cable and the vacuum advance pipe at the carburetter.

7 Release the exhaust pipe from the manifold.

8 It is easier to remove the carburetter at this stage so that the rocker shaft and cylinder head bolts are more accessible. If this is done a new gasket will be needed upon reassembly.

9 The rocker shafts are mounted on five pedestals. Do not mix these pedestals up as the one nearest the front of the engine carries the oil feed for both shafts. See **FIG 1 : 6** for the complete rocker assembly and **FIG 1 : 7** for a detail of No. 1 pedestal. Bend back the locking tags holding the pedestal nuts and undo them

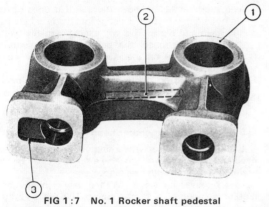

FIG 1 : 7   No. 1 Rocker shaft pedestal

Key to Fig 1 : 7   1 Pedestal   2 Cross drilling   3 Inlet oil recess

FIG 1 : 8   Cylinder head bolt tightening sequence

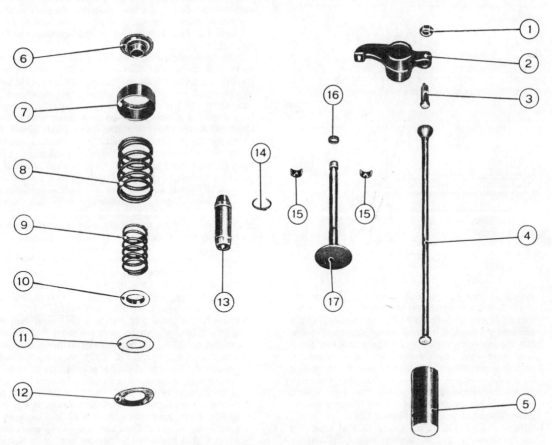

FIG 1 : 9   Complete valve assembly

Key to Fig 1 : 9   1 Adjusting screw nut   2 Rocker arm   3 Adjusting screw   4 Pushrod   5 Tappet   6 Upper spring seat   7 Oil boot   8 Outer spring   9 Inner spring   10 Lower spring seat   11 Lower washer   12 Cushion washer   13 Valve guide   14 Valve guide snap ring   15 Valve cotters   16 Upper oil shield   17 Valve

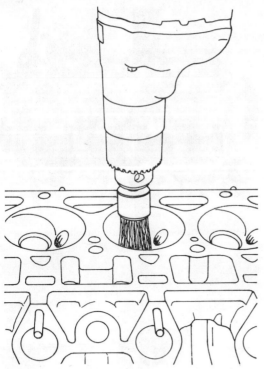

FIG 1:10 Decarbonizing the combustion chambers

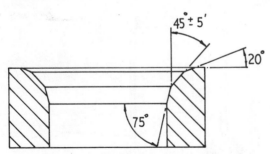

FIG 1:11 Sectional view of valve seat insert

evenly so that no unequal pressure is put on the shafts. Lift the complete assembly gently, moving the rockers so that no pushrod is lifted out because of the oil film between the rod and rocker adjusting screw. Put the assembly down in a clean place and cover with clean rag or newspaper until ready for attention.

10 Lift out and identify the pushrods. Number them 1 to 8 from the front of the engine. A good plan is to push them into numbered holes in a piece of cardboard. Make sure no tappet comes out with a pushrod by giving the rod a quick twist before lifting it.

11 Release the cylinder head bolts a little at a time in reverse order to the tightening diagram shown at FIG 1:8, i.e. begin at No. 9 and work back to No. 1.

12 The head should now lift off. Note that the inlet and exhaust manifolds were left on to give a good hand hold to lift with. Occasionally an aluminium head

will stick but this is most unusual. If it does do so, do not attempt to drive a wedge into the face between the head and block. This will almost certainly wreck the head. Reconnect the battery and momentarily spin the engine on the starter. The cylinder compressions will break the joint.

13 With the head on the bench remove the two manifolds, the plugs and the thermostat housing. Take out the thermostat.

1:6 Servicing the cylinder head

Bear in mind the earlier warning about damage to the head and be sure to work on it on a suitable clean bench, preferably covered with newspaper.

First remove the valves. With a valve spring compressor, compress No. 1 valve spring. This will be on the inlet valve on No. 1 cylinder nearest the front of the engine. When the spring collar is sufficiently depressed the two collets can be withdrawn. Release the compressing tool and the springs, collet holder, oil seal and the valve will be free. Keep all these components together in one place and identify them as No. 1 valve assembly. Repeat for the second valve and identify these components as No. 2 valve assembly. Proceed until all eight valves are removed. Never mix the sets of components up. FIG 1:9 shows all the components of a valve assembly.

Clean the head by first washing thoroughly in paraffin to remove all oil and gum deposits. Dry off and then remove the carbon from the combustion chambers with a wire brush mounted in an electric drill as shown in FIG 1:10. Do the same in the inlet and exhaust ports. Very carefully scrape the head face clean with a very blunt penknife. Check that the valve guide bores are clean and do the same for the oil way which carries the oil to the rocker gear. This oil way is at the front of the head on the mating face of No. 1 rocker shaft pedestal. A pipe cleaner soaked in petrol is useful here. If there is any scale in the water ways remove as much as possible by scraping then flush the head through with clean water. Dry off and carry out the following inspection:

(a) If the engine has a history of blown or leaking cylinder head gaskets check the head face for distortion. To do this a surface plate is essential. Coat the plate with a thin film of engineers blue and slide the head over it. The marking should be completely even over the whole head face. If not, a specialist engine reconditioning firm must be called in to regrind the head, removing as little metal as possible.

(b) Examine the valve seat inserts. If any more than the slightest pitting is to be seen the seats must be reground or recut. Do not attempt to hand lap deep pits out of the seats. FIG 1:11 shows a correctly recut seat. The seating face angle must be 45 deg. + or —5 deg. relieved at the top by a 20 deg. land and at the bottom by a 75 deg. land. If piloted cutters are available the owner can undertake this work but it is usually more economical to entrust the work to a specialist. Do not attempt to work on the seats until assured that the valve guides are not worn beyond serviceable limits.

(c) Clean all carbon and oil from each valve and examine the seating face. If badly pitted it is advisable to renew the valve. If only lightly marked the valve may

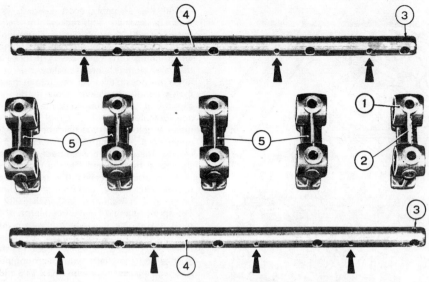

FIG 1:12   Oil feed holes in rocker shafts

Key to Fig 1:12   1 Front support   2 Inlet valve rocker shaft-to-exhaust valve rocker shaft oil delivery passage   3 Oil inlet holes
4 Rocker shafts   5 Intermediate and rear rocker shaft supports

be fit for further service if the stem is not worn below .314 inch (7.985 mm). If the stem passes this check try it in its guide. If the clearance between the stem and guide exceeds .004 inch (.10 mm) the guide must be renewed.

(d) Assuming that the valve stem is not badly worn and the face is suitable for reconditioning, check the concentricity of valve and head seating. Lightly coat the valve seating face with engineers blue and fit it to the head. Rotate it against the seat for two or three revolutions then carefully withdraw it and examine the faces. The valve should have lost some of the blue all round its face and the head insert should have a complete band of blue over its seating. If the insert is only marked in one place the insert is not concentric with the valve guide and must be recut. If the insert is marked all round but the valve has a bright mark over only part of its circumference the valve is bent and must be renewed.

If this examination shows that new guides are needed drive the old guide out from inside the port with a drift which is piloted to the valve stem diameter and drive in a replacement from the top face of the head. Fit a new circlip to the new guide before fitting it. Note that the exhaust valve guides are longer than the inlet valve guides. New guides are supplied finish reamed and no work is necessary on their bores. The clearance between valve and guide should be between .001 and .0024 inch (.029-.062 mm). The valves should be refaced on a valve grinding machine to a face angle of 45 deg. 30′ + or −5′. Make sure that this does not so thin the edge of the valve that it becomes less than .02 inch (.5 mm). Recut the inserts to suit the new guides.

The valves and seats may now be lapped together using a little fine grade carborundum paste. Lightly coat a valve with the paste and insert it in the head. Using a rubber suction cup tool oscillate the valve back and forth half a dozen times over about half a turn. Raise the valve off its seat, redistribute the paste, advance the valve a third of a turn and again oscillate it for a half dozen turns. Repeat this process until a matt grey band shows all round both the face of the valve and the head seat insert. This band of contact should be .03 inch to .06 inch (.8 to 1.5 mm) wide for the inlet valves and .05 inch to .075 inch (1.2 to 1.9 mm) for the exhaust valves.

When this condition obtains remove every trace of lapping compound with a petrol-soaked rag, being sure to destroy every piece of rag contaminated with abrasive. Throughout the lapping process keep the valves numbered to their positions in the head which they will finally occupy.

It is always advisable to renew valve springs at every top overhaul but if existing springs can be tested to show the following figures they may be refitted.

Outer spring:
Free length   1.968 inch (50 mm)
Compressed to .976 inch (24.8 mm), pressure 98 + or — 5 lb. (44.6 + or — 2.2 kg)

Inner spring:
Free length   1.543 inch (39.2 mm)
Compressed to .850 inch (21.6 mm), pressure 56 + or — 3 lb. (25.7 + or — 1.3 kg)

A quick way to check a spring is to compare it with a new one. Any appreciable difference in length should involve rejection of the old one.

The valves may now be refitted to the head by the use of the compressing tool in the reverse order to which they were dismantled. Ensure that all components are scrupulously clean then give each valve stem a light coat of clean engine oil before assembly. See that the collets are properly seated in the valve stems and fit new upper oil seals (see item 16, **FIG 1:9**).

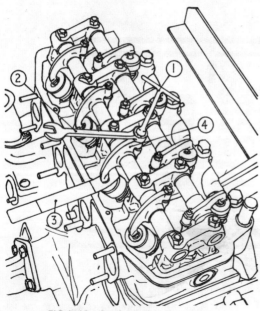

FIG 1 : 13   Setting valve clearances

Key to Fig 1 : 13   1 'T' spanner   2 Ring spanner
3 Feeler gauge   4 Rocker

The rocker gear must now be examined for wear and pitting on the rocker working faces. **FIG 1 : 6** shows the rocker shafts assembled to their pedestals. Note that the inlet shaft (nearest the camera) carries the rockers which have the pad end at the greatest angle to the adjusting screw. The two shafts are identical but are fitted in opposing positions so that the oil feed holes coincide with the position of the rockers. **FIG 1 : 12** clearly shows the arrangement. Holes number 3 must be in line with the oil way cross-drilled in pedestal No. 1.

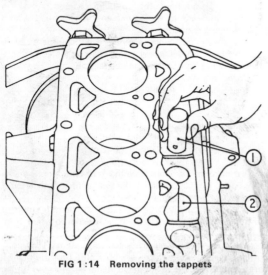

FIG 1 : 14   Removing the tappets

Key to Fig 1 : 14   1 Tappet   2 Tappet bore

Pull the assembly apart keeping pedestals, thrust washers, springs and rockers in their same relative positions with the two shafts. Thoroughly clean all the parts in petrol and dry off. Examine the rocker arm faces which contact the valve stems. If these are indented by the valve stem it is best to renew the rocker since it will never be possible to set the tappet clearance correctly if this condition obtains. Only if the indenting is very slight is it permissible to stone the contact face, any considerable removal of metal will expose the softer material below the case hardened surface and wear will again occur at a high rate. Check the tappet adjusting screws, these seldom wear badly but if scored or pitted they must be renewed. Try the rocker arm on the shaft. If the clearance exceeds .004 inch (.10 mm) renew the rocker arm. New component clearance should lie between .001 inch and .003 inch (.032 and .068 mm). The springs should have a free length of 2.75 inch (69.8 mm), any appreciable reduction means renewal.

Reassemble the rocker gear by reversing the dismantling process, liberally coating the rocker arm bushes and the shafts with clean engine oil. Be careful to check the assembly with **FIGS 1 : 6** and **1 : 12** ensuring that the rocker arm oil feed holes are as shown in **FIG 1 : 12**.

Examine the pushrods by rolling them along a true surface. If bent they can be straightened by gentle pressure between blocks in a vice or under a press. See that both ends are free from pitting, scoring or other damage.

Note particularly that the pushrod length and inlet valve length have been changed. Beginning at engine No. 001303, Type 116.000 (1300 cc) and engine No. 000635, Type 115.000 (1500 cc) the pushrod length was reduced to 8.445 inch (214.5 mm) from 8.543 inch (217.0 mm) and the valve length increased to 4.358 inch (110.7 mm) from 4.200 inch (106 mm). Quote engine number when ordering spares to be certain of obtaining the correct lengths. If an incorrect valve or pushrod is fitted, damage can occur.

The cylinder head and valve gear can now be refitted as described in the next Section.

1 : 7 Replacing the cylinder head

First see that the cylinder block top face is absolutely clean and that all traces of the old gasket have been removed. Plug the water passages and the pushrod bores with screws of newspaper so that no dirt will fall into them. Use a piece of clean strong rag to plug the rocker gear oil feed hole. Turn the engine over until two pistons are at the bottom of their stroke and two at the top. With a blunt penknife, scrape all the carbon from the crowns of the top pistons and blow all loose particles away. Turn the engine a half turn and repeat for the other two pistons. Wipe the bores free of carbon particles, turning the engine over several times to do this. Remove all the screws of newspaper and the rag plug from the oil feed passage. Double check that this has been done. Make sure that no carbon is trapped in the head bolt holes. Carefully clean the threads in the cylinder block and see that the bolts can screw in the full depth.

Position a new cylinder head gasket on the cylinder block and place the head in position. The manufacturers do not recommend greasing the gasket or the use of any type of jointing compound.

Fit the nine cylinder head bolts and tighten them in the sequence shown in **FIG 1 : 8. Do this in two stages.** First tighten them all to 22 lb ft (3 kg m) then, using the same sequence, finally tighten them to 65 lb ft (9.0 kg m). A torque wrench is essential for this operation, guessing just will not do.

Oil the pushrod ends and replace through the head into the tappets. The rods should be in order of removal, check that they are; the inlet valve pushrods are shorter than the exhaust valve pushrods.

Replace the rocker gear on the head studs making sure that the No. 1 pedestal is fitted over the oil feed hole at the front of the engine. See that each pushrod is correctly aligned with the rocker arm adjusting screw then tighten the pedestal nuts down to 16 to 17 lb ft (2.3 kg m). Use new locking tabs and bend up each end to lock the nuts. Tighten the nuts evenly, a little at a time so that the shafts are not unduly strained.

The tappet clearance can now be set. Both inlet and exhaust tappets must be adjusted to .008 inch (.20 mm) with a cold engine. This clearance is correct for all engines **except the 115C.000.** On this engine the inlet tappet clearance is the same but the exhaust clearance must be set to .010 inch (.25 mm).

The best way to set the clearances is to turn the engine crankshaft until the valves of No. 1 cylinder are just 'balancing'. That is to say, the inlet valve is just opening and the exhaust valve is closing. Set the clearances of both valves of No. 4 cylinder. Turn the engine crankshaft until No. 4 cylinder valves are 'balancing' and set No. 1 cylinder valve clearances. Repeat until No. 3 cylinder valves 'balance' and set No. 2 cylinder valves. Finally, 'balance' the valves of No. 2 cylinder and set the clearance of No. 3 cylinder valves. **FIG 1 : 13** shows the method of adjustment using a feeler gauge and spanners.

The rest of the operations necessary to re-assemble the engine are a reversal of the dismantling procedure but clean all carbon deposits from the manifolds before replacing them. See that the joint faces are clean and use new gaskets. Make sure the inlet manifold gasket is correctly positioned with regard to the heating water hole for the manifold. Replace the rocker box cover with a new joint washer and fit new washers to the sparking plugs. Fit new water hoses if the existing ones show any sign of cracking or perishing.

1 : 8 Servicing the timing gear and camshaft

These operations are not possible with the engine in the car since the removal of the timing cover will almost certainly damage the sump gasket at the front thus necessitating the removal of the sump.

Remove the engine as described in **Section 1 : 3,** then remove the cylinder head (see **Section 1 : 5**). Continue as follows:

1 Lift the tappets from the crankcase (see **FIG 1 : 14**) keeping them in order of removal. Remove the fuel pump.
2 Undo the bolt holding the distributor clamp and lift the distributor out. Now release the two nuts holding the distributor mounting to the crankcase and lift off

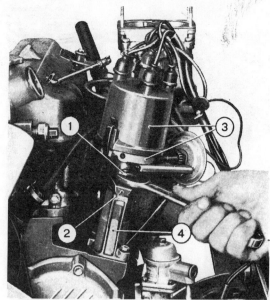

FIG 1 : 15   Removing the distributor

Key to Fig 1 : 15   1 Clamp nut   2 Clamp   3 Distributor   4 Mounting

the mounting (see **FIG 1 : 15**). Reach inside the aperture with a pair of round nose pliers and lift the drive gear away from the oil pump shaft splines.
3 Remove the generator, drive belt and fan blades.
4 Refer to **FIG 1 : 16** and release the six bolts round the face of the centrifugal oil filter. Remove the cover and gasket. Bend back the locking tag and remove the hollow centre bolt (see **FIG 1 : 17**). A heavy ring spanner and some means of preventing the crankshaft from turning will be needed. Remove the lockwasher,

FIG 1 : 16   Removing the centrifugal oil filter, stage 1

FIG 1:17 Removing the centrifugal oil filter, stage 2

Key to Fig 1:17   1 Filter hub   2 Baffle ring   3 Hollow bolt   4 Spanner

FIG 1:18   Removing the camshaft sprocket

plain washer and baffle ring. The main body of the filter can now be pulled away from the crankshaft.

5 Turn the engine upside down and rest it on soft wood packing. Undo the eighteen screws holding the sump and remove the sump.

6 Undo the eight bolts holding the timing cover to the front of the engine and lift it off.

7 Undo the camshaft sprocket holding bolt as shown in FIG 1:18 then pull the sprocket and chain away from the camshaft. It cannot be wrongly reassembled since the parts have a locating dowel in the camshaft face.

8 Remove the two bolts holding the camshaft front bush. These bolts are asymmetrical to prevent the bush being incorrectly assembled. There is thus no need to mark the bush and crankcase face.

9 The camshaft should now slide forwards out of the crankcase just clearing the oil pump shaft. If the

FIG 1:19   Checking camshaft for straightness

tolerances are such that the camshaft fouls the oil pump, undo the two bolts holding the oil pump delivery pipe to the front main bearing and the bolt holding the oil pump body to the crankcase. Lift off the oil pump. When withdrawing the camshaft be very careful that the cam lobes do not scratch the centre bearing as they pass through.

10 Inspect the camshaft journals and the cam faces. They must be smooth, bright and free of scores. Place the shaft on Vee-blocks on a surface plate and set a dial indicator to the centre journal as shown in FIG 1:19. Rotate the shaft; if the maximum to minimum movement of the indicator needle exceeds .004 inch (.1 mm) the camshaft must either be straightened or renewed. Transfer the indicator to each cam in turn and measure the lift. It should be .226 inch (5.73 mm). Any appreciable difference indicates cam wear and the shaft must be renewed.

11 Inspect the camshaft bushes; any scoring or evidence of seizure means renewal. The front bush is easily renewed but the centre and rear bushes are a press fit in the crankcase and must be line reamed very accurately to size. If they are to be renewed this work must be entrusted to a Fiat Service Station. The clearance between a new camshaft and a new bush should not exceed .0035 inch (.089 mm) for the front and .0025 inch (.064 mm) for the centre and rear bearings. When the clearance reaches .006 inch (.15 mm) renewal is necessary.

To rebuild the timing gear proceed as follows:

1 Coat the camshaft journals and cam faces with clean engine oil and carefully slide it home in the crankcase. Fit the front bush and tighten the two bolts. See that the shaft rotates freely.

2 Replace the oil pump, using new gaskets.

FIG 1 : 20 Camshaft timing marks

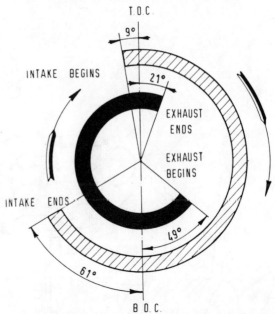

FIG 1 : 21 Valve timing diagram, 116.000, 115.000 and 116C.000 engines

3 Examine the timing chain and sprockets for wear. If the chain can be moved sideways a large amount when laid flat on the bench this indicates worn pins and bushes and the chain should be renewed. When a chain reaches this condition it is usually necessary to renew the sprockets. Examine these carefully, any sign of 'hooking' of the teeth must mean renewal.

4 Place the chain round the crankshaft sprocket then round the camshaft sprocket so that the timing marks are aligned as shown in **FIG 1 : 20.** Rotate the camshaft so that the dowel enters the hole in the sprocket, fit the centre bolt with a new locking washer, check that the timing marks are still properly aligned then tighten the bolt to 50 lb ft (7.0 kg m). Bend up the locking washer as shown in **FIG 1 : 20.**

5 Turn the engine up the right way and refit the tappets, making sure that they are not worn or damaged, particularly on the bottom face. Coat each one with clean engine oil.

6 If any doubt exists, check the valve timing as follows:

(a) Turn the crankshaft until No. 1 piston is at the top of the compression stroke. To find this position fit a dial indicator so that the stem will contact the piston crown. As the crankshaft is turned watch the inlet tappet. When it falls to its lowest point the piston should then be moving up the bore on the compression stroke. The dial indicator stem should contact the piston on the last part of its travel. When the indicator reading is at a maximum this is TDC. Rock the crankshaft back and forth to find the exact spot. The timing marks on the sprockets should now be in perfect alignment.

(b) To check the timing against the makers diagram fit a circular protractor to the crankshaft with a pointer

attached to the crankcase. Adjust the pointer to the 0 deg. mark on the protractor with the engine at TDC on the compression stroke of No. 1 cylinder (see (a)). Continue to turn the engine in its correct direction of rotation until the inlet tappet of No. 1 cylinder has moved up .017 inch (.45 mm). This is easily checked by temporarily fitting a pushrod to operate the dial

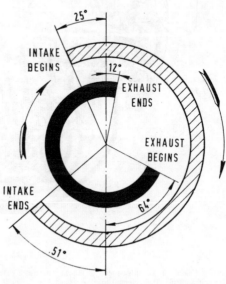

FIG 1 : 22 Valve timing diagram for 115C.000 engine

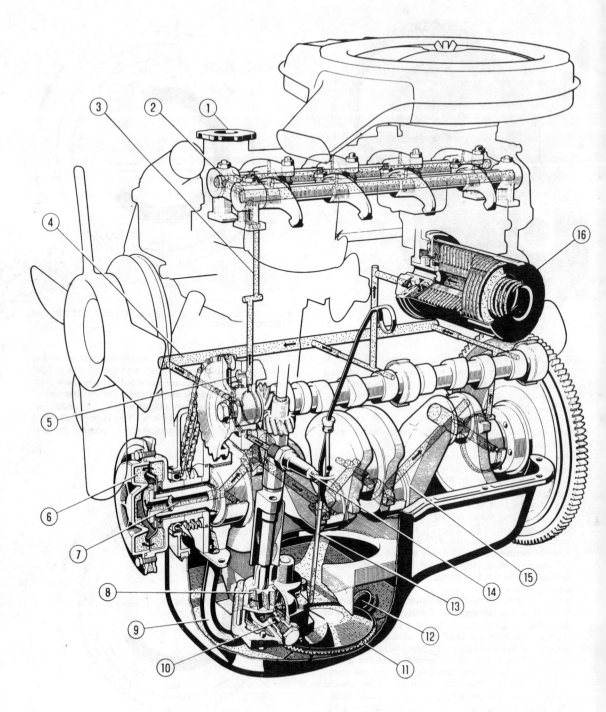

FIG 1:23   Oil circulation diagram

Key to Fig 1:23 1 Oil filler cap   2 Rocker shafts   3 Rocker shaft oil delivery passage   4 Main oil delivery passage   5 Timing chain oil connection   6 Centrifugal oil filter   7 Crankshaft with cutaway of inner oil passage   8 Gear oil pump   9 Pump-to-centrifugal filter oil delivery pipe   10 Oil pressure relief valve   11 Oil pump suction filter   12 Oil pan drain plug   13 Oil dipstick   14 Low pressure indicator sending unit   15 Supplementary filter oil return to pan   16 Bypass, supplementary oil filter

indicator. The .017 inch (.45 mm) movement represents the valve clearance specified for timing checks. The pointer on the protractor should now be at 9 deg. before TDC (see **FIG 1:21**) for the 116.000, 115.000 and 116C.000 engines and 25 deg. before TDC for the 115C.000 engine (see **FIG 1:22**).

7 Replace the skew gear on the oil pump shaft and fit the distributor mounting with the two bolts. Instructions for retiming the distributor are given in **Chapter 3.**

8 Examine the crankshaft oil seal in the timing cover. If worn, press out the existing one and press in a new seal, coating its outer diameter with a non-hardening jointing cement. Support the timing cover round the seal boss while pressing the new seal in. Coat the inner face of the seal with engine oil so that it does not run dry and burn when the engine first starts up. Fit the timing cover to the front of the crankcase with the eight bolts. Use a new gasket coated with jointing cement. Note that the four short bolts have the spring washers and the four long ones have captive washers.

9 Fit the centrifugal oil filter by reversing the order of dismantling. Tighten the hollow bolt to 101 lb ft (14 kg m) and bend up the locking tag. Fit a new rubber seal to the face of the filter and fit the cover, tightening the six bolts securely.

10 Replace the fuel pump and refit the cylinder head and rocker gear.

11 Make sure the sump face and crankcase face are clean then fit a new sump gasket. This is in four sections, make sure they interlock and use a little jointing cement on the faces. Position the sump on the gasket and fit the eighteen screws. Tighten these evenly working round the sump flange.

12 Complete the rebuilding and replacement of the engine as described in earlier sections.

1 : 9 The lubrication system

Before commencing work on the engine lubrication system study **FIG 1:23** so that the circulation can be followed. The pump sucks oil from the sump through a mesh strainer and delivers it via a pipe to the face of the front main bearing. From here it flows forwards along the two flats machined on the crankshaft and into the centrifugal filter. Pressure is maintained by a special sealing disc and ring clamped to the crankshaft by the filter and running in a recess machined in the crankcase. The assembly is shown at **FIG 1:24**, items 7 and 8. Any solid particles in the oil are flung to the periphery of the filter while clean oil flows through the hollow bolt and into the crankshaft. It lubricates the big-end and main journal bearings and then passes out of the crankshaft rear main bearing and up to the camshaft rear bearing. From here it passes through drilled passages to the centre and front camshaft bearings and to the bypass filter. From the front camshaft bearing the oil flows upwards to lubricate the rocker gear, to a jet which sprays oil into the inner face of the camshaft sprocket, to the oil pressure warning light switch and also via a small bleed passage to lubricate the pump shaft. The big-end bearing caps are drilled to provide a direct squirt of oil at the camshaft.

To service the oil pump the sump must be drained and removed. Unbolt the pump from the engine and remove it as described in the previous section.

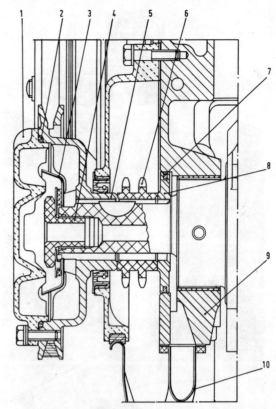

FIG 1:24 Sectional view of centrifugal oil filter

Key to Fig 1:24   1 Centrifugal filter cover   2 Seal ring 3 Baffle ring   4 Pulley hub-to-crankshaft hollow screw 5 Centrifugal filter pulley hub   6 Timing drive drive sprocket 7 Oil shield disc ring   8 Oil shield disc   9 Front main bearing cap   10 Front main bearing cap oil delivery pipe

Proceed as follows:

1 Clamp the pump in a vice as shown in **FIG 1:25** and remove the delivery pipe.

2 Unscrew the pressure relief valve from the side of the pump.

3 Undo the bolts holding the inlet strainer assembly and lift away. The gears can now be lifted out of their housings.

4 Refer to **FIG 1:26** and dismantle the pressure relief valve.

5 Wash all components in clean petrol and dry thoroughly.

Examine the body for cracks or burrs on mating faces and replace or correct as necessary. See that the suction strainer gauge is clean.

Check the gears for wear as follows:

(a) Backlash between gears should be .006 inch (.15 mm). If it exceeds .010 inch (.25 mm) the gears must be renewed.

(b) The clearance between the tips of the gears and the housing must not exceed .010 inch (.25 mm). Use a feeler gauge to measure this. If wear has occurred it is most likely that the whole pump needs renewal.

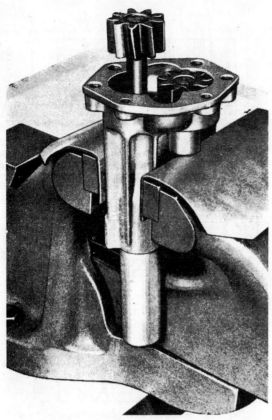

FIG 1 : 25   Dismantling the oil pump

A pump in good condition should produce between 57 and 64 lb/sq. inch (4 and 4.5 kg/sq cm) pressure but this depends on the mechanical condition of the rest of the engine bearings.

The dismantling and removal of the centrifugal filter was described in the previous Section. It should be a routine service function to remove the end cover and clean the interior of the filter. Always refit the cover with a new gasket.

Renewal of the bypass filter is simple provided a strap wrench is used to unscrew and refit the element. The filter must be changed every 6000 miles (10,000 km) but a check on its condition can be made at any time as follows:

After the car has completed a run of some reasonable distance and the engine is thoroughly hot, stop the engine and feel the filter. If it is cold it is blocked and must be renewed immediately. **FIG 1 : 28** shows a new filter being fitted. Coat the rubber seal between the filter and crankcase with oil when fitting.

1 : 10 Removing the clutch and flywheel

This operation can be performed with the engine in the car provided the gearbox is removed as described in **Section 1 : 3**.

Mark the clutch cover and flywheel with a small centre punch so that the cover can be refitted in the same relative position. Undo the six bolts a little at a time, working round the sequence so that the pressure is released evenly then lift the cover and friction plate away.

Mark the position of the crankshaft; a spot of paint on the centrifugal filter and the timing cover is one way. Now mark the position of the flywheel so that it will be refitted to the crankshaft exactly where it came from. Undo the six bolts and lift the flywheel off.

The gearbox first motion shaft bearing in the crankshaft will now be revealed. If this needs renewal a special extractor tool is essential (Part No. A40006/1/3). The new bearing can be gently drifted into place with a drift which seats on the bearing outside diameter only.

If the flywheel ring gear is damaged it can be renewed, but a hydraulic press is recommended by the makers for removal and replacement. It is advisable to entrust this work to a Fiat dealer since the conventional temperatures needed for shrinking a ring gear on would destroy the heat treatment characteristics of this one.

The flywheel is refitted by reversing the dismantling process. Tighten the flywheel to crankshaft bolts to 58 lb ft (8 kg m). Directions for refitting the clutch are given in **Chapter 5**.

1 : 11 Servicing the pistons and connecting rods

Remove the cylinder head and sump as described in earlier Sections.

Before removing the big-end bolts, check that the connecting rods and bearing caps have serial numbers stamped on one side so that no mistakes can be made upon reassembly. If in any doubt, number each assembly from the front of the engine, one centre punch dot on rod and cap then two dots on the next and so on. Undo the bolts and pull the cap complete with its bearing shell away from the rod. Now push the rod and piston up the

(c) Measure the clearance between the gear faces and the pump body as shown in **FIG 1 : 27**. It must not exceed .006 inch (.15 mm). Replace the gears or the body as necessary. New gears are .7076 inch to .7086 inch long (17.973 to 18.00 mm).

(d) See that the driving gear is a press fit on its shaft and the driven gear has not more than .004 inch (.10 mm) clearance on its shaft. The latter shaft must be tight in the pump body.

(e) The drive shaft must be renewed if it has worn so as to give .004 inch (.10 mm) clearance in the pump body.

If any of the pump components has reached the rejection limits quoted above, the owner is advised to obtain a replacement pump from a Fiat dealer if possible since such wear must indicate a very high mileage pump.

Examine the pressure relief valve components carefully. If the valve (see item 4, **FIG 1 : 26**) has .006 inch (.15 mm) clearance in the housing (see item 5), renew the assembly. The spring should have a free length of 1.114 inch (28.3 mm). Any significant reduction means a weak spring and this should be discarded.

Rebuild the pump by reversing the dismantling process using new lockwashers and gaskets. Smear all moving parts with clean engine oil as assembly proceeds. Refit to the engine and replace the sump. Refill with the correct grade of oil.

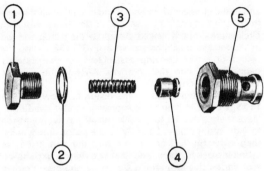

FIG 1 : 26   Oil pressure relief valve

Key to Fig 1 : 26   1 Plug   2 Seal   3 Spring   4 Valve
5 Housing

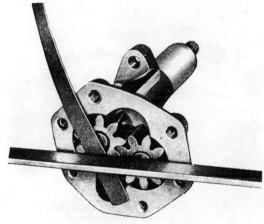

FIG 1 : 27   Measuring the gear to housing clearance

FIG 1 : 28   Fitting the bypass filter

Key to Fig 1 : 28   1 Filter   2 Strap wrench

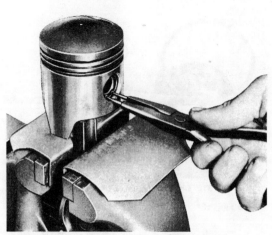

FIG 1 : 29   Removing gudgeon pin circlip

cylinder bore and remove them from the top face of the cylinder block. Repeat for the other three assemblies.

To remove a piston from its connecting rod first remove the circlip as shown in **FIG 1 : 29.** Now heat the piston in very hot, not boiling water and push the gudgeon pin out. Be careful to support the piston on a soft surface if the pin is tight and a drift has to be used. If the piston is to be refitted to the rod, make a scratch **inside** the skirt to identify it with its rod. One, two, three or four scratches to suit No. 1, 2, 3 or 4 rods.

Ease the rings from the piston by slipping three thin pieces of tin between the back of the ring and the piston and arranging them at 120 deg. to each other. The ring can then be slipped upwards and off the piston. A simple three-legged tool can be bought at any accessory shop for this purpose if preferred.

Keep the rings, piston, gudgeon pin, connecting rod, cap and bearing shells in sets. Discard the circlips and big-end bolts. It is bad practice to re-use these last two items since the failure of an overstressed circlip or stretched big-end bolt will wreck the engine.

Remove all carbon from the piston paying particular attention to the bottom of the ring grooves. A broken piston ring makes a good scraper for the grooves but be careful not to remove any metal from the piston. Do not use abrasive cloth to polish the piston and do not touch the bearing surfaces below the rings which are in contact with the cylinder walls.

The pistons and cylinder bores must now be inspected so that any reconditioning such as reboring can be decided upon. Carry out the following checks:
(a) Refer to **FIG 1 : 30.** If a feeler gauge thicker than .008 inch (.20 mm) can be pushed between the piston and cylinder, the cylinder must be rebored.
(b) Check the piston ring to groove clearance as shown in **FIG 1 : 31.** If the clearance exceeds .006 inch (.15 mm) the piston must be renewed. New pistons and rings should not give a clearance greater than .003 inch (.075 mm).
(c) Push a piston ring into an unworn part of the cylinder using the top of the piston to keep it square in the bore. If the ring gap exceeds .024 inch (.60 mm)

FIG 1:30   Checking piston clearance

Key to Fig 1:30   1 Feeler gauge   2 Piston

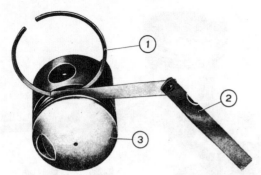

FIG 1:31   Checking ring to groove clearance

Key to Fig 1:31   1 Ring   2 Feeler gauge   3 Piston

renew the ring. The correct gaps for new rings in a new bore are as follows:

Compression rings	.012 inch to .018 inch (.30 to .45 mm)
Stepped oil control ring	.008 inch to .014 inch (.20 to .35 mm)
Radial slotted oil ring	Nil

(d) Try the gudgeon pin in the piston. If it will enter a cold piston either the pin or piston must be renewed.

For all practical purposes, if check (a) reveals the need for reboring, new pistons will be supplied and only the check for ring gap need be considered.

Examine the connecting rods. See that the small-end bush is tight in the rod and the gudgeon pin to bush clearance is between .0002 inch and .0004 inch (.004 and .010 mm). If the rod has been twisted this will have shown up as heavy bearing marks on the piston at opposite sides, top and bottom. Should this have occurred or the small-end bush be oversize, obtain a replacement rod from a Fiat dealer. Check the weight of the rod and cap. This should be 24½ oz (694 gr).

To assemble the piston and connecting rod, first fit a new circlip in one end of the piston gudgeon pin bore. Now heat the piston in hot water, smear oil on the pin

and in the connecting rod bush and push the pin through the piston and rod. Fit the second circlip. Make sure both circlips are properly seated. Assemble the piston and rod in the relative positions shown in **FIG 1:32.** Using the pieces of tin or the ring assembler, slip the correctly gapped rings into their grooves. Arrange the gaps at 120 deg. to each other.

Fit a ring compressor to the piston as shown in **FIG 1:33.** Do not tighten the compressor screws dead tight, leave them a quarter turn slack, this will assist the piston to slide into the bore. Liberally oil the piston and cylinder then enter the rod and piston into the bore from the cylinder block top face. **See that the piston expansion slot faces the camshaft.** Gently tap the piston crown with a wooden block or hammer handle until the piston passes down into the bore. This must occur steadily and without a jerk. Any doubt or unusual noise and the piston should be removed to make sure a ring has not broken. Fit the big-end bearing shells, oil the crankpin and fit the big-end bearing cap, tightening the bolts to 48 lb ft (6.6 mk g).

1:12 Servicing the crankshaft

To remove the crankshaft dismantle the engine as described in previous Sections. The camshaft may be left in place but the oil pump must be removed.

Continue as follows:

1 Remove the rear main oil seal by undoing the bolts and pulling the seal housing from the crankshaft.

2 Mark the main bearing caps so that they can be replaced in their correct locations then undo the bolts. Lift off the caps. When the centre bearing cap is released the thrust bearing top halves will come away and when the front bearing cap is released the oil shield disc and ring can be removed.

3 Lift the shaft out and remove the lower thrust bearing halves and the bearing shells.

Examine the shaft and bearings as follows:

1 Wash thoroughly in clean petrol and allow to dry.

2 If the journals or crankpins are scored or out of round by more than .002 inch (.05 mm) the shaft must be reground and undersize bearing shells fitted. Four undersizes from .010 inch to .040 inch (.254 to 1.016 mm) are available.

The journal standard diameter is 2.478 inch to 2.479 inch (62.962 to 62.982 mm) and the crankpin diameter 2.086 inch to 2.0868 inch (52.983 to 53.004 mm).

To check the crankpin or main journal bearing clearance the use of 'Plastigage' is recommended. Make sure the components are clean and dry then assemble the bearing with a piece of Plastigage laid on the shaft. Tighten the bearing cap bolts to the correct torque then release them and remove the cap. Measure the width to which the Plastigage has been flattened using the scale marked on the packet. This will show the bearing clearance. The main journals should not have more than .003 inch (.069 mm) and the crankpins the same clearance. This is the condemning limit. New assemblies should not have less than .001 inch (.025 mm) clearance. If the upper figure is exceeded either the shaft must be ground or new shells fitted.

Examine the oil shield disc and ring. Any sign of damage must involve renewal.

Always fit a new rear oil seal. Press out the old one and press in the new in the same way that was adopted for the front seal in the timing cover.

Check the end float of the shaft. Lay the top main bearing shells and thrust bearing halves in the crankcase then insert the shaft. Fit the centre main bearing cap complete with shell and thrust bearing bottom halves. Tighten the bolts moderately then push the shaft hard to one end. Measure the clearance between the shaft cheeks and the thrust bearings with a feeler gauge. The end play should lie within .0024 inch to .010 inch (.06 to .26 mm). If greater than this fit oversize thrust bearings.

To refit the shaft, first make absolutely certain that everything is clean and that all foreign matter such as grinding dust is removed from the oilways.

Lay the top half bearing shells and thrust washers in position, coat with clean engine oil and fit the shaft. Slide the oil shield disc and ring on the crankshaft front end and position in the crankcase. Fit the bearing caps and shells not forgetting the bottom halves of the thrust bearing. All components must be liberally coated with engine oil. Tighten the main bearing bolts to 76 lb ft (10.5 kg m) and then fit the rear oil seal carrier with a new gasket. See that the shaft rotates freely.

Fit the big-end bearing shells to their connecting rods and caps and install these on the shaft, again using plenty of oil. Tighten the big-end bolts to 48 lb ft (6.6 kg m).

Continue to rebuild the engine as described in previous Sections.

1:13 Rebuilding a stripped engine

The methods to be used have been described under the appropriate Sections but as a general guide when starting absolutely from scratch proceed in the following sequence.

Fit the camshaft, the crankshaft, rear oil seal and oil shield disc, flywheel, pistons and rods, oil pump, crankshaft sprocket, camshaft sprocket and chain, tappets, cylinder head and rocker gear. Check the valve timing then fit the timing cover, sump, centrifugal oil filter, fuel pump, breather pipe, bypass oil filter, both inlet and exhaust manifolds, the water pump, thermostat and hose elbow. Set the tappets. Fit the distributor and set the ignition timing. Fit the carburetter and connect the pipe from the fuel pump. Fit and centralize the clutch. Fit the rocker cover, plugs and generator. Fit the engine mountings and refit the power unit to the car.

Always use new oil seals, gaskets, locking washers, splitpins, circlips and big-end bolts. Liberally lubricate all appropriate moving parts with the oil on which the engine is intended to run.

1:14 Fault diagnosis

(a) Engine will not start

1 Discharged battery
2 Corroded or loose battery terminals
3 Starter motor defective
4 Ignition fault, moisture, incorrect point gap, etc.
5 Lack of fuel
6 Defective sparking plugs

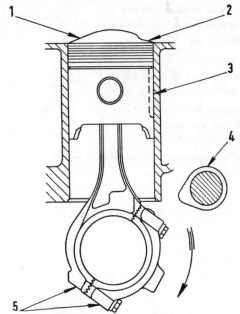

FIG 1:32 Correct assembly of piston and rod, from front of engine

Key to Fig 1:32   1 Piston size mark   2 Cut-out in crown for valve clearance   3 Expansion slot   4 Camshaft 5 Connecting rod and cap marks

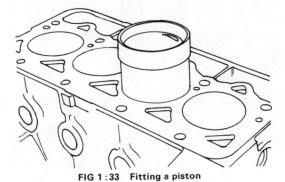

FIG 1:33   Fitting a piston

(b) Engine stalls

1 Idling speed too low
2 Incorrect carburetter setting
3 Lack of fuel
4 Ignition fault
5 Defective sparking plugs
6 Incorrect valve clearance

(c) Engine lacks power

1 Incorrect ignition timing
2 Carburetter jets blocked
3 Binding brakes
4 Incorrect valve clearance
5 Low compression
6 Fuel pump failing

(d) Engine idles erratically

1 Incorrect carburetter adjustment

2 Blocked jets

3 Carburetter flooding

4 Air leaks on inlet manifold

5 Blown cylinder head gasket

6 Incorrect valve clearance

7 Uneven compressions

8 Incorrect ignition timing

9 Defective distributor advance mechanisms

(e) Engine misses at speed

1 Main jet obstructed
2 Incorrect ignition timing
3 Weak coil or capacitor
4 Plug gaps too wide
5 Weak valve springs
6 Worn camshaft lobes

(f) Noisy engine

1 Worn crankshaft bearings
2 Worn cylinder bores and pistons
3 Tappet clearance too great
4 Worn timing chain

CHAPTER 2

THE FUEL SYSTEM

2:1 Description

All models have a mechanically-operated diaphragm type fuel pump driven from the camshaft supplying fuel to a twin choke carburetter. A paper element air filter is fitted. The 115C.000 and 116C.000 engines have either the Weber type 34 DCHD or Solex C34 PA1A2 carburetter. A yellow paint mark on the body identifies the carburetter as being set for the 116C.000 engine and a green mark for the 115C.000. The 116.000 engine has the type 2836 DCD Weber and the 115.000 the type 2836 DCD1 carburetter.

2:2 The fuel pump

Refer to **FIG 2:1** for a view of all the components which make up the pump. If fuel is failing to reach the carburetter first make sure that the pump is bolted securely to the crankcase and that the trouble does not lie with the fuel pipes. If these are in order it is most likely that the pump diaphragm is damaged or a valve is not seating.

Remove the pump by disconnecting the fuel pipes and undoing the two nuts holding the pump to the crankcase. Pull the pump off the studs then pull the pushrod out of the housing. The housing can now also be eased away from the studs. Remember to remove the pushrod before the housing otherwise it might drop into the crankcase. Clean the old gaskets from both faces of the housing, the crankcase face and the pump flange.

Dismantle the pump as follows:

1 Remove the centre bolt from the domed cover and take off the cover, filter gauze and gasket.
2 Remove the five screws holding the halves of the pump body together and separate the halves.
3 From the top of the pump remove the screw 3 (see **FIG 2:2**) lift out the cover **2**, followed by the valve cage, gasket, inlet valve and spring.
4 Turn the pump body upside down and remove the outlet valve in the same way as described for the inlet valve.
5 Press the diaphragm down then rotate it to free it from the yoke lever.
6 Drive out the rocker pin 18 (see **FIG 2:1**) by driving it out towards the serrated end. (Put the drift against the plain end). The rocker arm and washers will now come away.

Wash all parts in clean petrol and blow through the fuel ports and passages. Obtain an overhaul kit and fit all

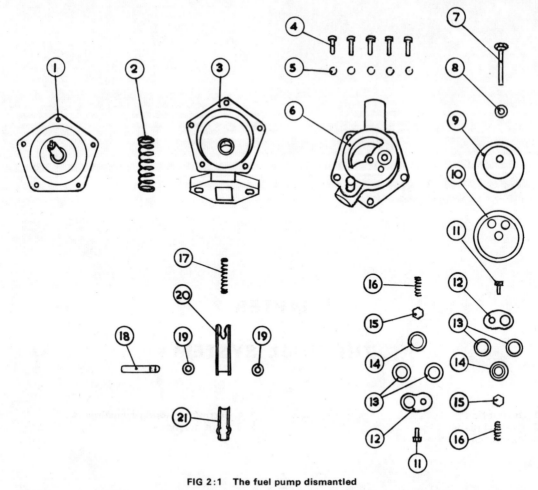

FIG 2 : 1 The fuel pump dismantled

Key to Fig 2 :1   1 Diaphragm   2 Diaphragm reaction spring   3 Lower body   4 Lower body-to-upper body screws
5 Lockwashers   6 Upper body   7 Upper body cover screws   8 Screw gasket   9 Upper cover   10 Filter gauze   11 Valve cage
cover screws   12 Valve cage cover   13 Valve cage gaskets   14 Valve cages   15 Inlet and outlet valves   16 Valve springs
17 Rocker arm reaction spring   18 Yoke lever and rocker arm pin   19 Plain thrust washers   20 Yoke lever   21 Rocker arm

the new parts which it contains even if existing ones appear serviceable.

Rebuild the pump by reversing the dismantling process being careful to tighten the diaphragm screws evenly when the rocker arm is held in the full amount of its travel. Check the pump operation by holding the thumb over the inlet pipe and operating the rocker a few times. If the thumb is then removed a very definite sound of released vacuum should be heard. Repeat for the outlet pipe, a small pressure should be generated here.

Refitting the pump to the engine correctly is important. Refer to **FIG 2 : 3** and continue as follows:

1 Turn the engine until the camshaft eccentric is at the low position as shown.

2 Now fit a gasket 'B' to the crankcase, then the housing, then the gasket 'A'.

3 Slide the pushrod home and check the protrusion beyond the gasket 'A'. This must be between .04 to .06 inch (1 to 1.5 mm). If not, try other thicknesses of gasket until the right protrusion is obtained. These gaskets are supplied in thicknesses of .05 inch (1.3 mm) and .03 inch (.8 mm). Remove the pushrod, the gaskets and the housing. Coat the gaskets with a little jointing cement and reassemble. Fit the pushrod with a smear of oil then replace the pump and tighten the nuts.

2 : 3 The carburetters
Weber 2836 DCD and DCD1:

The operation of these carburetters will be more easily understood if it is remembered that although the instrument has two chokes, most of the engine speed and load range is covered by the primary choke. The secondary comes into operation for high speed or heavy load conditions.

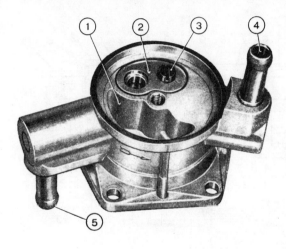

FIG 2:2   Pump inlet valve cage

Key to Fig 2:2   1 Upper body   2 Inlet valve cage cover
3 Valve cage cover screw   4 Fuel outlet connector
5 Fuel inlet connector

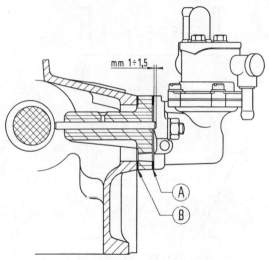

FIG 2:3   Adjusting the pushrod position

Key to Fig 2:3   A Gasket .03 inch (.8 mm)   B Gasket
.05 inch (1.3 mm)   (mm 1 ÷ 1.5, see text)

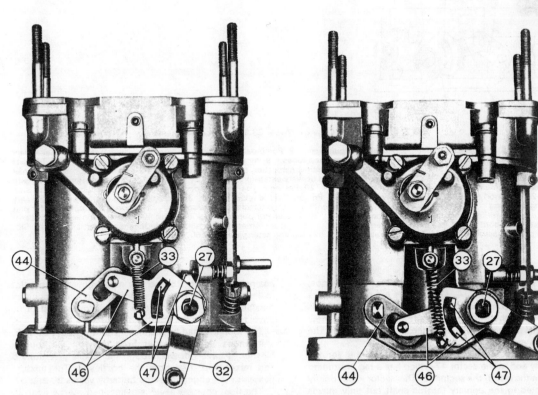

FIG 2:4   Throttle valve differential opening linkage

Key to Fig 2:4   27 Primary throat throttle shaft   32 Throttle control lever, main   33 Primary sector return spring   44 Secondary
throat throttle shaft lever   48 Primary idle sector   47 Lug and stop sector

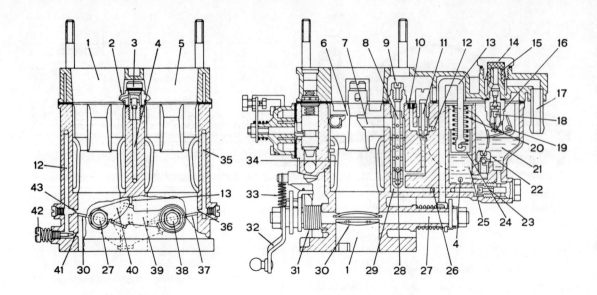

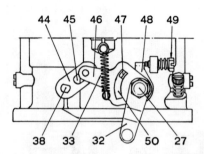

FIG 2 : 5   Sectional view of Weber 28.36 type carburetters

Key to Fig 2 : 5   1 Primary throat   2 Accelerator pump jet   3 Pump delivery valve   4 Pump delivery passage   5 Secondary throttle   6 Auxiliary Venturis   7 Nozzle tubes   8 Emulsion tubes   9 Air bleed jets   10 Idle air metered bushings   11 Idle jets   12 Idle mixture passage   13 Pump control rod   14 Strainer inspection plug   15 Strainer   16 Needle valve   17 Fuel inlet connection   18 Valve needle   19 Float pivot   20 Pump delivery extension spring   21 Fuel bowl   22 Pump suction valve with drain hole   23 Main jets   24 Pump piston   25 Float   26 Passages, jets-to emulsion tubes   27 Primary shaft   28 Emulsion holes   29 Emulsion tube wells   30 Primary throttle   31 Primary throttle return spring   32 Throttle control arm, main · 33 Primary sector return spring   34 Primary venturis   35 Secondary throttle transfer port passage   36 Secondary throat transfer port   37 Secondary throttle transfer port   38 Secondary shaft   39 Accelerator pump control idle arm   40 Accelerator pump control arm   41 Passage idle port   42 Idle mixture metering screw   43 Primary throat transfer port   44 Secondary shaft arm   45 Slot   46 Idle primary sector   47 Lug   48 Stop sector   49 Idle running setting screw   50 Primary sector slot

The working of the throttles in the chokes is most easily seen in **FIG 2 : 4.** Lever 32 is connected to the accelerator pedal and in the lefthand view the pedal is released and the throttle is closed. In the righthand view the pedal is depressed and the throttle is wide open. The action is as follows:

The lever 32 is connected solidly to the throttle butterfly and to the sector 47 which has a tag protruding through the slot in the sector 46. This sector is not rigidly connected to the primary throttle shaft but only moves when the lever 32 has opened the primary throttle far enough for the tag on sector 47 to reach the end of the slot. When this happens the two sectors move as one

against the spring 33 and the roller moves in the slot in lever 44. This lever is connected to the secondary throttle butterfly, and this now opens to the limit of its travel as shown in the righthand illustration.

The fuel flow can be more easily followed in **FIG 2 : 5.** Air enters the carburetter from the top via the air cleaner. It travels down through the auxiliary venturis 6 and mixes with fuel from the nozzles 7. The mixture passes to the engine past the butterfly valves 30 and 37.

The float chamber level is maintained by the float 25 operating the needle valve 18.

From the float chamber the fuel passes through the main jet 23 to the emulsion tube well 29. It is now mixed

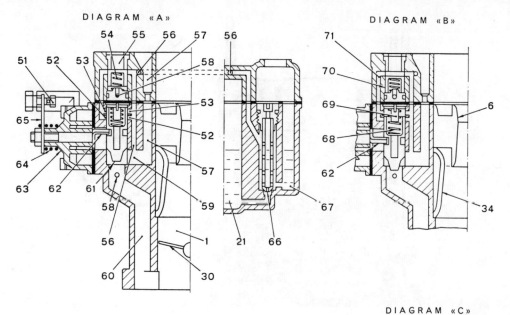

DIAGRAM «A» DIAGRAM «B»

DIAGRAM «C»

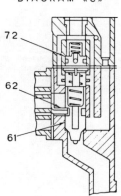

FIG 2:6   The starting device, Weber 28.36

Key to Fig 2:6   1 Primary throat   6 Auxiliary venturis   21 Fuel bowl   30 Primary throttle   34 Primary venturis   51 Choke cable screw   52 Leaning air port   53 Leaning air port   54 Choke valve spring   55 Stop bushing   56 Choke mixture passage   57 Air passage   58 Vacuum passage   59 Mixture recess   60 Choke mixture passage   61 Choke piston   62 Rocker arm   63 Lever with choke cable sheath holder   64 Arm return spring   65 Choke control arm   66 Choke jet   67 Choke reserve supply well   68 Choke piston spring   69 Spring stop   70 Choke valve   71 Leaning air passage   72 Spring stop
Diagram A   Choke all the way in   **Diagram B**   Choke part way in   **Diagram C**   Choke all the way out

with air from the air bleed jets 9 and emulsion ports 28; from here it passes to the nozzles 7 and thus into the venturis.

For slow-running, the fuel passes from the well 29 to the pilot jet 11, where it is mixed with air from the jet 10 and thus to the port 41 which is controlled by the mixture adjusting screw 42.

The long stroke accelerator pump 24 provides a small jet of fuel on sudden throttle openings to balance the air/fuel ratio. At these times, the air tends to leave the fuel behind thus causing a temporary weak mixture and a 'flat spot' in the engine pick up. The pump operates from both throttle spindles so that the transition from

primary to primary plus secondary chokes is also smoothed out. A metered passage in the suction valve 22 bypasses excess fuel back to the float chamber.

The operation of the starting device is shown at **FIG 2:6**. The piston 61 communicates through the recess 59 with the passage 60. The recess 59 is the outlet for passage 56 from the jet 66 and the air bleed 57. The passage 56 communicates with the air intake through the bush 55 which can be blanked off by the valve 70. The valve 70 communicates with the throttle barrels below the butterflies. From the orifices 52 and 53 the top of the piston 61 connects through a drilling 71 to the air intake.

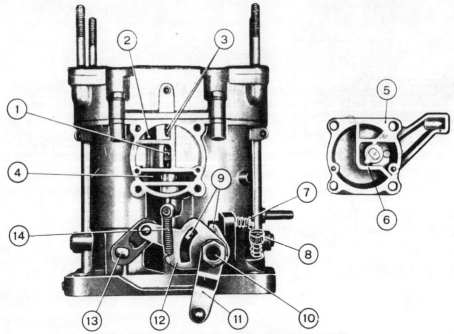

FIG 2:7   Starting device dismantled, Weber 28.36

Key to Fig 2:7   1 Choke piston   2 Choke mixture recess   3 Leaning air ports   4 Mixture recess   5 Choke device cover with choke control cable sheath support   6 Piston rocker arm   7 Idle running setting screw   8 Idle mixture setting screw   9 Secondary throttle control sector and lug   10 Primary shaft   11 Throttle control lever, main   12 Primary idle sector   13 Secondary shaft   14 Primary sector return spring

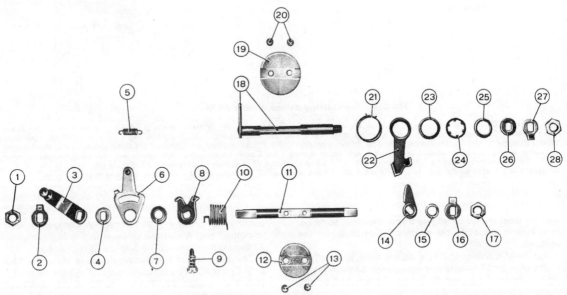

FIG 2:8   Throttle valve assembly, Weber 28.36

Key to Fig 2:8   1 Lever mounting nut   2 Lockwasher   3 Throttle control lever, main   4 Washer   5 Primary sector return spring   6 Primary idle sector   7 Primary shaft bushing   8 Stop sector and secondary throttle control lug   9 Idle running setting screw and spring   10 Return spring   11 Primary shaft   12 Primary throttle   13 Mounting screws   14 Accelerator pump control lever   15 Primary shaft bushing   16 Lockwasher   17 Lever nut   18 Secondary shaft and lever   19 Secondary throttle   20 Mounting screws   21 Return spring   22 Accelerator pump idle control lever   23 Washer   24 Toothed lock ring   25 Washer   26 Space washer   27 Lockwasher   28 Nut

When the choke is operated the piston 61 is lifted to the open position thus closing the orifices 52 and 53. If the engine is now turned, the manifold depression forces the fuel from the jet 66 and the reserve well 67 through the passage 56 to the recess 57 where it is mixed with air from the drilling 57. This rich mixture passes along passage 60 to the engine. When the engine fires and speeds up the vacuum increases and operates the valve 70 through the passage 58. This draws air from the bush 55 to automatically weaken the mixture. However, as the engine warms up, even this mixture will be too rich, therefore the starting device will be moved progressively to the off position by the driver. This will allow the ports 52 and 53 to supply more air until the piston tapered end finally closes off the passage 60. **FIG 2 : 7** gives a good view of the starting device partly dismantled.

Servicing the carburetter consists of making sure that the throttle valves and linkage operate freely, that the jets and ports are clean and unobstructed and that the float level is properly set. If the engine has covered a high mileage it is likely that wear has developed in the throttle spindle bores. If this is so an exchange carburetter is a wise investment. Provided this condition does not appear, proceed to service the carburetter as follows:

1 Unscrew the six bolts holding the top of the carburetter to the main body. Be careful not to drop the float as the top is lifted away.
2 Unhook the spring at the side of the carburetter from the primary throttle sector 33 (see **FIG 2 : 4**).
3 Refer to **FIG 2 : 8**. Release the locking tabwasher 2, unscrew nut 1 and remove items 2 to 8 and item 10. Repeat with items 17 to 14 in that order.
4 Undo the screws 13, remove the butterfly valve 12 and pull out shaft 11.
5 Repeat with items 28 to 21 in that order. Remove the screws 20 and the butterfly valve 19. Pull out shaft 18.
6 Clean all the components and obtain new tabwashers 2 and 27.

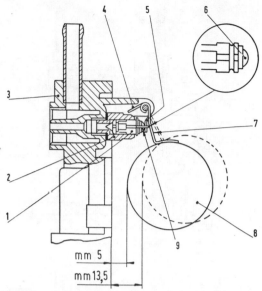

FIG 2:9 Setting the float level, Weber 28.36 and 34 DCHD

Key to Fig 2:9 1 Needle 2 Needle valve 3 Carburetter cover 4 Lug 5 Tang 6 Mobile ball 7 Tangs 8 Float Needle return hook   5 mm=.1969 inch   13,5 mm=.5315 inch

7 Remove all jets carefully noting the position from which they are taken.
8 Undo the four screws holding the starting device to the carburetter and lift off. These screws are shown in **FIG 2 : 4**.
9 Remove the accelerator pump components being careful not to damage the pump piston or the bore in which it operates.

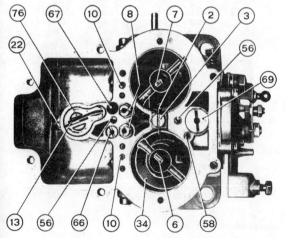

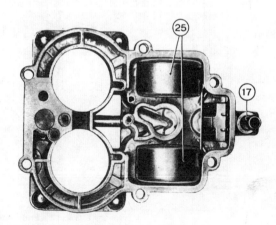

FIG 2:10   Plan view of Weber 28.36 DCD types

Key to Fig 2:10 2 Pump jet 3 Pump delivery valve 6 Auxiliary venturis 7 Nozzle tubes 8 Emulsion tubes with air bleed jets 10 Idle air metered bushing   13 Pump control rod   17 Fuel inlet connector   22 Pump suction valve with drain hole 25 Float 34 Primary venturis 56 Choke mixture passages 58 Vacuum passage 66 Choke jet 67 Choke reserve supply well 69 Spring stop   76 Pump spring retaining plate

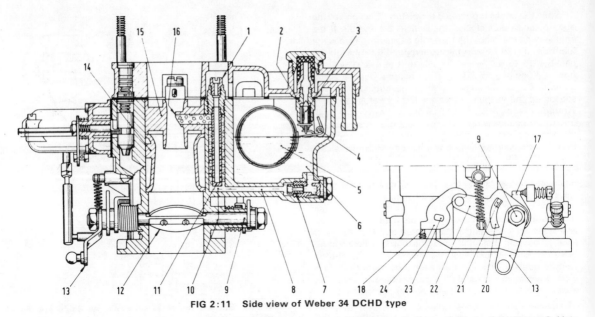

FIG 2:11   Side view of Weber 34 DCHD type

Key to Fig 2:11   1 Air correction jet   2 Needle valve   3 Valve needle   4 Pivot pin   5 Float   6 Bowl   7 Main jet   8 Main jet-to-emulsion well passages   9 Primary throttle spindle   10 Emulsion well   11 Emulsion tube   12 Primary throttle   13 Primary throttle control lever   14 Primary venturi   15 Secondary venturi   16 Discharge tube   17 Lever stop sector   18 Secondary throttle stop adjusting screw   20 Slot for lug (21)   21 Drag lug for sector (22)   22 Sector for release and return of lever (24)   23 Secondary throttle spindle   24 Secondary throttle return lever

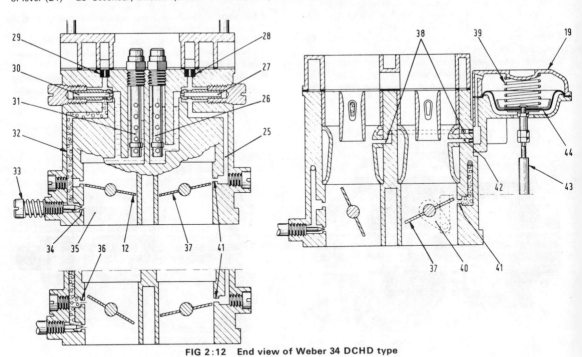

FIG 2:12   End view of Weber 34 DCHD type

Key to Fig 2:12   12 Primary throttle valve   19 Vacuum chamber   25 Secondary throat idle transfer port passage   26 Secondary emulsion tube   27 Secondary idle jet   28 Secondary idling air calibrated bushing   29 Primary idling air calibrated bushing   30 Primary idle jet   31 Primary emulsion tube   32 Idle passage   33 Idle adjusting screw   34 Idling feed orifice   35 Primary throat   36 Primary throat idle transfer port   37 Secondary throttle valve   38 Vacuum device port and passage at primary throat   39 Spring   40 Secondary throttle control lever   41 Secondary throat idle transfer port   42 Vacuum device port at secondary throat   43 Secondary throttle control rod   44 Vacuum device diaphragm

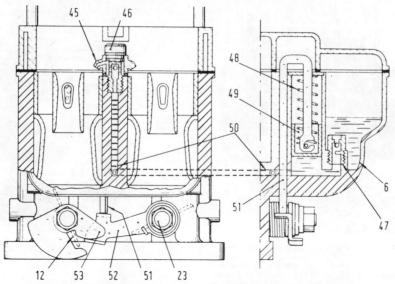

FIG 2:13   View through accelerator pump· Weber 34 DCHD type

Key to Fig 2:13   6 Bowl   **12** Primary throttle valve   **23** Secondary throttle spindle   **45** Accelerator pump jet   **46** Delivery valve   **47** Suction valve   **48** Spring   **49** Accelerator pump plunger   **50** Delivery passage   **51** Plunger rod   **52** Rod control lever, idler   **53** Pump control lever, primary

10 Clean all jets by blowing air through them, never poke pieces of wire or bristle into the orifices as this will destroy the very careful calibration carried out by the manufacturer.

11 Wash all other parts in petrol and blow air through all the drill ways and ports. Dry thoroughly.

12 See that the throttle shafts work freely without binding and that none of the linkage is strained or deformed.

13 Check that the accelerator pump ball valve seats properly. An inoperative pump caused by a defective ball valve will ruin the engine performance by causing flat spots in the speed range.

At this stage the petrol level should be checked by attention to the float setting and needle valve. Proceed as follows:

1 Screw the needle valve body into the float chamber lid using a new seal washer. Refit the strainer gauze and nut to the top of the lid. Replace the needle valve and hold lightly against the seating. Try to suck air past the needle valve from the fuel inlet pipe stub. If air does pass, renew both the needle valve and the body.

2 Refer to **FIG 2:9**. This shows a diagrammatic view of a typical float assembly. Remove the float chamber lid gasket then hold the lid vertically with the float hanging downwards. With the needle valve closed the float should be .2 inch (5 mm) from the lid face. Bend the lug 5 until this distance is correct. Now gently move the float away to the limit of its travel. The gap should now be .53 inch (13.5 mm). If not, bend lug 4 as necessary. Check that the ball 6 moves freely.

Rebuild the carburetter by reversing the dismantling process using all new gaskets and seals. Refer to **FIG 2:10** for a guide to the positions of the various jets not shown in the side views.

Weber 34 DCHD:

This instrument and the Solex described later are similar in construction to the Weber 2836 DCD and DCD1 types except for one important difference. The 2836 DCD and DCD1 secondary throttle is mechanically operated by a link from the primary throttle. The 34 DCHD and Solex secondary throttles are operated automatically by vacuum in the primary choke overcoming the return spring in a vacuum chamber thus moving the diaphragm and thence by a link to the secondary throttle spindle. Provision is made for the secondary throttle to be closed by a mechanical trip from the primary throttle should the vacuum device fail.

The accelerator pump is of the plunger type. Reference to **FIGS 2:11, 2:12** and **2:13** show the fuel and air flow through the carburetter. The servicing instructions are exactly the same as those given for the 2836 type carburetters except for the vacuum device. The only trouble likely to occur here is for the diaphragm to puncture; this is easily replaced by removing the four screws holding the top cover and freeing the diaphragm and link.

FIGS 2:14 and **2:15** show the main external features of the carburetter.

Solex C34 PA1A2:

This carburetter is shown at **FIG 2:16**. The main difference between this and the Weber carburetter 34 DCHD is in the accelerator pump. This is of the diaphragm type operated by a cam from the primary throttle spindle. Reference to **FIG 2:17** will show the method while **FIG 2:18** shows the pump removed from the carburetter. Always renew the pump diaphragm and gaskets if a flat spot develops in the engine speed range.

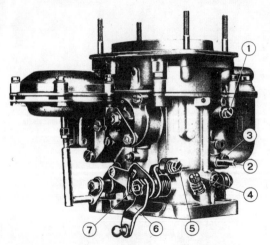

FIG 2:14   Weber 34 DCHD, throttle linkage side

Key to Fig 2:14   1 Idling jet   2 Vacuum advance line connector   3 Main jet   4 Volume control screw   5 Throttle stop screw   6 Primary throat throttle control lever   7 Primary throat throttle spindle

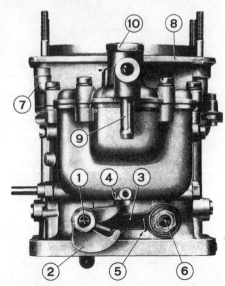

FIG 2:15   Weber 34 DCHD, float chamber side

Key to Fig 2:15   1 Primary throat throttle spindle   2 Accelerator pump control lever, primary   3 Rod control lever, idler   4 Plunger rod   5 Return spring for lever (3)   6 Secondary throat throttle spindle   7 Body side cover   8 Air cleaner mounting flange   9 Fuel delivery line connector   10 Filter inspection cover

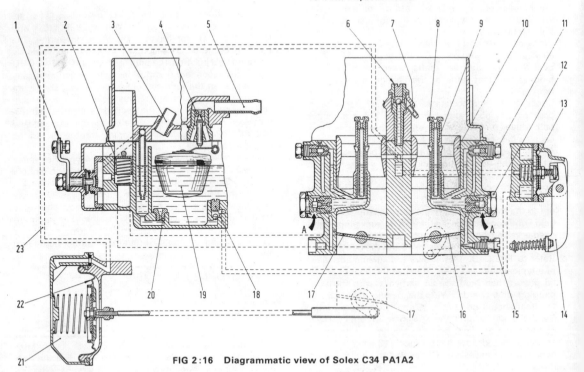

FIG 2:16   Diagrammatic view of Solex C34 PA1A2

Key to Fig 2:16   1 Choke control lever   2 Choke piston   3 Bowl ventilation air inlet   4 Needle housing   Fuel inlet   6 Accelerator pump valve   7 Accelerator pump discharge   8 Air corrector jet   9 Emulsion tube   10 Primary venturi   11 Idling jet   12 Main jet   13 Accelerator pump diaphragm   14 Accelerator pump control lever   15 Idle adjusting screw   16 Primary throat throttle valve   17 Secondary throat throttle valve   18 Accelerator pump drain plug   19 Float   20 Starting jet   21 Vacuum chamber   22 Diaphragm   23 Vacuum passage   **A** Fuel inlet

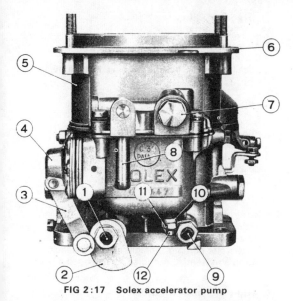

FIG 2:17 Solex accelerator pump

Key to Fig 2:17 1 Primary throat throttle spindle
2 Accelerator pump relay lever 3 Accelerator pump control
lever 4 Accelerator pump cover 5 Body side cover
6 Air cleaner mounting flange 7 Filter inspection cover
8 Fuel delivery line connector 9 Secondary throat throttle
spindle 10 Secondary throat throttle stop lever 11 Throttle
setting screw nut 12 Throttle setting screw

All other servicing arrangements are similar to those
described for the Weber carburetters, except for the
float level adjustment. The Solex float is adjusted by
carefully bending the arm until the top of the float is
6 inch (15 mm) from the face of the float chamber when
the needle is fully home in its seat. The main external
features are shown in **FIG 2:19** and the starting device
and linkage in **FIG 2:20**.

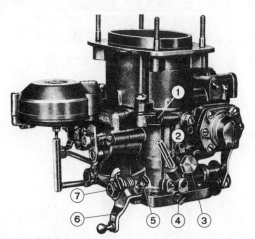

FIG 2:19 Solex control adjustments

Key to Fig 2:19 1 Idling jet 2 Vacuum advance line
connector 3 Main jet 4 Idling mixture volume control
screw 5 Idling throttle stop screw 6 Primary throat throttle
control lever 7 Primary throat throttle spindle

FIG 2:18 Solex accelerator pump dismantled

Key to Fig 2:18 1 Pump 2 Drain plug 3 Starting jet

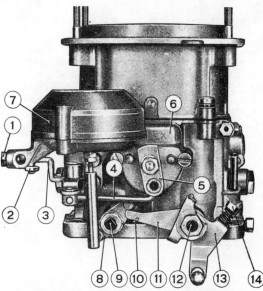

FIG 2:20 Solex starting device and linkage

Key to Fig 2:20 1 Cable sheath retaining screw 2 Choke
control cable retaining nut and screw 3-4-5-6 Choke
control linkage and cover 7 Vacuum device 8 Secondary
throat throttle control lever 9 Secondary throat throttle
spindle 10-11 Secondary throat throttle return spring and
relay lever 12 Primary throat throttle spindle 13 Primary
throat throttle control lever 14 Primary throttle stop screw
at idle

2:4 Setting the idling adjustments

All the carburetters are set for engine idling speed by the same method. Run the engine to operating temperature then adjust the throttle stop screw to the best steady speed obtainable. Adjust the mixture control screw until the engine runs at its fastest without altering the throttle stop screw. Readjust the throttle stop screw to bring the speed down again and then finally readjust the mixture control screw. A good general guide to engine idling speed is to have the engine running steadily with the ignition warning light just about to be extinguished.

The adjusting screws for the Weber 2836 carburetters are shown as items 7 and 8, **FIG 2:7**, for the Weber 34 DCHD as items 4 and 5, **FIG 2:14** and for the Solex C34 PA1A2 as items 4 and 5, **FIG 2:19**.

2:5 Fault diagnosis

(a) Engine will not start from cold

1 Choke valve stuck
2 Blocked starting jet

(b) Engine will not start from hot

1 Incorrect idling adjustment
2 Engine overheated causing fuel to vaporize in float chamber
3 Choke held in due to seized choke piston

(c) Irregular idling

1 Air leaks at inlet manifold or carburetter
2 Air leaks at throttle spindles
3 Blocked pilot jet
4 Sticking throttle linkage keeping throttle away from stop

(d) Flooding

1 Needle valve not seating
2 Punctured float
3 Incorrect float level
4 Pump delivery pressure too high
5 Leaking seal on gauze strainer plug

(e) Poor acceleration or top speed

1 Incorrect fuel level
2 Main jet or jets blocked
3 Accelerator pump ball not seating
4 Accelerator pump diaphragm or piston damaged
5 Throttle movement restricted by damaged linkage

(f) High fuel consumption

1 Excessive use of choke
2 Flooding
3 Choke wrongly adjusted

CHAPTER 3

THE IGNITION SYSTEM

3:1 Description

The cars covered by this manual are fitted with a distributor which incorporates three methods of varying the ignition timing. Two are automatic and one is set by the operator.

The control set by the operator is known as the octane selector, and is clearly shown as item 8, FIG 3:1. Rotation of the toothed wheel one full turn in either direction from its mid-point will advance or retard the ignition by 5 deg. of crankshaft rotation from the static firing point. This control is used to adjust the ignition point to suit varying grades of fuel.

The automatic controls are operated by vacuum and centrifugal force. The vacuum control consists of a diaphragm in a housing (see item 7, FIG 3:1) which is connected at one side to the carburetter primary throttle bore and at the other, by means of a link, to the moving plate carrying the contact breaker. At small throttle openings the vacuum in the carburetter bore causes the diaphragm to move thus advancing the contact breaker against the direction of rotation of the cam thereby advancing the ignition. This device ensures that at low speed, light load conditions, the ignition will be advanced before the speed rises sufficiently for the centrifugal device to take over and also at high speed, light load, extra advance is given.

The centrifugal timing control comes into operation as engine speed rises and the two weights (see item 9, FIG 3:1) move outwards. This movement is transmitted through links to the cam turning it ahead of its direction of rotation and thus advancing the ignition.

3:2 Routine maintenance

Remove the distributor cap and examine the inside surface for any sign of 'tracking'. This will show as a fine pencil line running between the HT terminals and the edge of the cap or between adjacent terminals. If this is present the cap must be renewed since HT current is leaking along these paths. Clean the brass contacts in the cap, being careful not to scratch the surface of the cap.

Examine all the HT leads for perishing or cracking. Renew with genuine FIAT leads if necessary. A good way to check on HT leakage is to run the engine in the dark and watch the leads for signs of blue sparks jumping to adjacent metal parts.

Remove the two screws (see 1, FIG 3:2), lift off the rotor and examine the centrifugal advance mechanism. If dry or corroded, apply the very minimum amount of general purpose grease to all moving parts. Move the cover over the lubricator (see item 6, FIG 3:2), and apply a few drops of FIAT VE oil. Grip the mounting plate

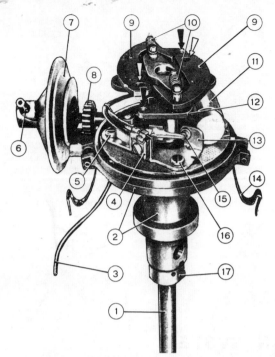

FIG 3:1   Distributor assembled

Key to Fig 3:1   1 Shaft   2 Distributor frame   3 Cable to coil primary winding   4 Terminal bridge fastener   5 Stationary contact bracket screw   6 Vacuum advance port   7 Vacuum advance housing   8 Static advance adjuster roller and ring   9 Automatic advance weights   10 Weight springs   11 Condenser and clamp   12 Cam lobe   13 Stationary contact bracket   14 Cap spring   15 Contact points   16 Bracket retaining and point adjusting screw   17 Oil slinger   White arrows point to rotor location dowel seats on weights; black arrows point to rotor screw seats

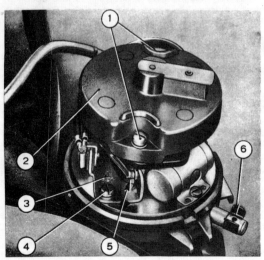

FIG 3:2   Contact breaker and rotor

Key to Fig 3:2   1 Rotor holding screw   2 Rotor   3 Breaker contact plate   4 Contact plate adjusting screw   5 Breaker contact points   6 Lubrication fitting

to which the centrifugal weights are attached and attempt to move the whole shaft sideways. If any significant movement is present renew the distributor rather than the shaft and frame alone.

3:3 Adjusting the contact breaker points gap

With the distributor cap removed, turn the engine over until the moving blade of the contact set is away from the fixed point and the rocker heel is on the high point of one of the cams. Refer to **FIG 3:2** and slacken the two screws 4 (only one shown), holding the fixed contact to the base plate. Insert a screwdriver in the slot just to the right of the screw 4 in **FIG 3:2** and move the fixed contact plate until a gap of .016 inch to .019 inch (.42 to .48 mm), measured with a feeler gauge exists between the contacts. Tighten the two screws 4, and check to see that the gap has not altered.

3:4 Cleaning the contact points

If the contact points are dirty or pitted they must be cleaned with a fine carborundum stone or a special abrasive contact file. Never use emerycloth or glasspaper. Always wipe the points clean with a cloth moistened in petrol after using the stone or file. To assist in cleaning, the contact breaker can be removed from the distributor. Check that the moving point is not sluggish, if it is, clean the pivot pin with a strip of fine emerycloth, wipe clean and apply one small spot of oil.

3:5 Timing the ignition

The method of removing the distributor from the engine was described in **Chapter 1**. To replace the distributor and time the ignition proceed as follows:
1 Rotate the crankshaft until No. 1 cylinder (nearest the radiator) is on its compression stroke. If the rocker cover is removed this condition will apply when the inlet valve has just closed. Otherwise remove the sparking plug and hold the thumb over the hole until air pressure can be felt.

FIG 3:3   Ignition timing marks

2 Refer to **FIG 3:3.** Set the mark on the centrifugal oil filter $\frac{5}{8}$ inch (16 mm) before the mark on the timing case for the 115.000, 116.000 and 116C.000 engines and $\frac{1}{2}$ inch (13 mm) for the 115C.000 engine.

3 Remove the distributor cap and set the rotor blade to point to the contact for No. 1 cylinder. (The cylinder numbers are marked on the cap).

4 See that the contact breaker gap has been correctly set then turn the distributor shaft so that the points are just about to separate. Set the octane selector to its mid-point. Check that the vacuum advance unit points away from the engine.

5 Slide the shaft into the engine, meshing it with the camshaft skew gear splines without moving its position relative to the distributor if possible. Lightly fit the clamp and bolt.

6 Connect the low-tension lead to one contact of a 12-volt bulb and take another lead from the other contact to the distributor low-tension terminal. Switch on the ignition and rotate the distributor body slightly until the bulb is extinguished. This shows that the points have just opened. Tighten the clamp bolt, remove the bulb and connect the low-tension lead to the distributor. Replace the distributor cap.

7 Final adjustments can be made with the octane selector when the car is road tested.

3:6 The sparking plugs

Inspect, clean and adjust sparking plugs regularly. The inspection of the deposits on the electrodes is particularly useful because the type and colour of the deposit gives a clue to conditions inside the combustion chamber, and is therefore most helpful when tuning.

Remove the sparking plugs by loosening them a couple of turns and then blowing away loose dirt from the plug recesses with compressed air or a tyre pump. Store them in the order of removal.

Examine the gaskets. If they are about half their original thickness they may be used again.

Examine the firing end of the plugs to note the type of deposit. Normally, it should be powdery, and range from brown to greyish tan in colour. There will also be slight wear of the electrodes, and the general effect is one which comes from mixed periods of high-speed and low-speed driving. Cleaning and resetting the gap is all that will be required. If the deposits are white or yellowish they indicate long periods of constant-speed driving or much low-speed driving. Again, the treatment is straightforward.

Black, wet deposits are caused by oil entering the combustion chamber past worn pistons, rings or down valve stems. Sparking plugs of a type which run hotter may help to alleviate the problem, but the cure is an engine overhaul.

Dry, black, fluffy deposits are usually the result of running with a rich mixture. Incomplete combustion may also be a cause and this might be traced to defective ignition or excessive idling.

Overheated sparking plugs have a white, blistered look about the centre electrode and the side electrode may be badly eroded. This may be caused by poor cooling, wrong ignition, or sustained high speeds with heavy loads.

Have the sparking plugs cleaned on an abrasive-blasting machine and tested under pressure after attention to the electrodes. File these until they are clean, bright and parallel. Set the electrode gap to .024 inch (.6 mm).

Do not try to bend the centre electrode.

Before replacing the plugs clean the threads with a wire brush. Do not use a wire brush on the electrodes. If it is found that the plugs cannot be screwed in by hand, run a tap down the threads in the cylinder head. Failing a tap, use an old sparking plug with cross-cuts down the threads.

3:7 Fault diagnosis

(a) Engine will not fire

1 Battery discharged
2 Capacitor shorted or insulation broken down
3 Distributor cap cracked, wet or tracking
4 Distributor cap central brush worn or broken
5 Low-tension circuit failure
6 Dirty contact points or incorrect gap
7 Fouled plugs
8 Wrongly connected plug leads
9 Timing incorrect
10 Faulty coil

(b) Engine misfires

1 Check 3, 4, 6 and 9 at (a)
2 Weak contact breaker spring
3 HT leads cracked or perished
4 Sparking plug or plugs loose
5 Sparking plug insulator cracked
6 Sparking plug gap incorrect
7 Intermittent failure in low-tension circuit

CHAPTER 4

THE COOLING SYSTEM

4:1 Description
4:2 Routine maintenance
4:3 The water pump

4:4 The thermostat
4:5 Fault diagnosis

4:1 Description

The engine cooling system operates on the impeller assisted thermo-syphon principle. A centrifugal impeller is attached to the rear of the fan pulley shaft and this draws water from the radiator, circulates it through the engine cylinder block and thence to the cylinder head. The water is heated by the engine and rises to the outlet elbow at the front of the engine. This elbow contains a thermostatic valve which remains closed until the engine reaches a proper operating temperature. While the valve is closed, water is returned to the pump to be recirculated through the engine. When the valve opens water flows through the hose to the top of the radiator where it is cooled and sinks down through the tubes to be drawn into the pump and again circulated through the engine. Most of the air needed to cool the radiator is provided by the forward movement of the vehicle but this air flow is supplemented by the fan, particularly when the vehicle is stationary or moving slowly. Some of the heated water is led from the cylinder head to the inlet manifold jacket to warm the incoming fuel mixture.

4:2 Routine maintenance

Regularly check the drive belt tension. Reference to **FIG 4:1** will show clearly the method to adopt if adjustment is needed. The belt should be capable of between $\frac{13}{32}$ inch and $\frac{19}{32}$ inch movement (1 to 1.5 cm) when pressed by hand in the direction of the arrow. If this movement is not present, slacken the bolt 6 then the two bolts 2 and move the generator either towards or away from the engine as necessary until the right amount of slack is achieved. Tighten bolt 6 then the two bolts 2. Never overtighten the belt as this will quickly wear out the generator front bearing or the pump bearing. Conversely too slack a belt will slip thereby causing a low generator charge, poor pump circulation and premature failure of the belt through heating and therefore glazing of its bearing surfaces.

If the engine overheats and the mixture strength and ignition timing are correct it may be that the radiator is partly blocked. Warm the engine up to operating temperature making sure that the thermostat has opened and that water is reaching the radiator. Switch off and feel the radiator surface. One part much cooler than adjacent areas indicates a blockage. Never carry out this check with the engine running due to the danger of injury from the fan blades. If the radiator does not appear to be blocked it may be general scaling of the water passages due to hard water. A blown cylinder head gasket will also give symptoms of overheating and water loss. To check on this, start up and run up to operating temperature, remove the radiator cap carefully and watch the water surface with the engine running.

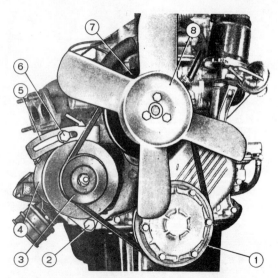

FIG 4:1   Adjustment points for driving belt

Key to Fig 4:1   1 Fan and generator drive driven pulley
2 Lower generator mounting screw   3 Generator pulley
4 Generator   5 Generator clamping and adjusting arm
6 Upper generator mounting screw   7 Fan pulley   8 Fan

If bubbles appear and a film of oil covers the surface, the gasket has failed.

To flush the radiator properly, drain off the coolant and remove the radiator as described in Chapter 1. Make up an adapter to enable a mains pressure water hose to be fitted to the lower radiator hose stub. Turn on the water and allow it to flow through the radiator. Occasionally lift the radiator and shake it to remove loose particles of scale; turn it upside down and let the water flow through for a few minutes in this position. While the radiator is off the vehicle blow through the core to remove leaves and other debris. Do not poke sharp instruments into the core.

If the trouble persists when the radiator is refitted, a chemical cleaner and descaler can be tried but be very sure that the maker certifies that it is suitable for use with aluminium and follow the instructions meticulously.

In cold weather a solution of anti-freeze and water must be used. Before adding this, flush the system by opening the drain cocks and running a hose into the radiator filler orifice. Follow the makers instructions regarding the proportions of anti-freeze to be added to the water. The table below gives the ratios of FIAT anti-freeze and water solutions for varying degrees of frost protection.

4:3 The water pump

FIG 4:2 shows the pump in section. To service the pump proceed as follows:

1 Drain the coolant and release the tension on the drive belt. Slip the belt off the fan pulley.
2 Remove the hoses attached to the pump, then unbolt the pump from the cylinder block. It is now just possible to manoeuvre the pump complete with fan past the radiator cowl and up out of the engine compartment.
3 Clean all traces of rubber from the hose stubs and examine the hoses. If cracked they must be renewed.
4 Unbolt and remove the fan from the pulley boss then remove the pulley.
5 With the pump on the bench, remove the three countersunk screws holding the rear coverplate and remove the plate and gasket (see items 3 and 2, **FIG 4:3**).
6 With a heavy puller tool pull the fan boss from the shaft. Do not apply pressure to any part other than the flange of the boss and the end of the shaft.
7 Unscrew the bearing locating screw 4 (see **FIG 4:2**).
8 The shaft, bearing, seal and impeller should now push out to the rear of the pump. Very little force should be needed. If the bearing does stick apply pressure to the bearing sleeve using a piece of tube slipped over the shaft. Note that the bearing and shaft are supplied as an assembly and cannot be dismantled. The seal is a press fit in the pump body.
9 Refer to **FIG 4:4**. Make up an extractor to fit across the impeller such that two screws can be tightened into the impeller while the third (centre) screw bears on the end of the shaft and pushes the shaft out of the impeller.

Examine the shaft and bearing. Any noticeable play means renewal. If the bearing is noisy or feels rough when rotated this also means renewal. The seal should be renewed as a matter of course.

To rebuild the pump, carry out the following operations:

1 Press a new seal into the body.
2 Push the shaft and bearing assembly into the body with the longer end to the rear through the seal. The bearing is prepacked with FIAT Jota 3 grease when new. If a shaft is being fitted which has seen previous service, force more grease in through the locating hole but do not overdo this.
3 See that the hole in the bearing is lined up with the locating screw hole then fit the screw. Indent the metal round the screw so that it cannot loosen. A centre punch applied to the body at each end of the screwdriver slot in the screw will drive sufficient metal over to lock the screw.

	ANTI-FREEZE			WATER			FREEZING POINT	
% in volume	Liters	Imp. Pints	U.S. Pints	Liters	Imp. Pints	U.S. Pints	°F	°C
20	1.35	2.37	2.85	5.35	9.41	11.31	17.6	—8
30	2.00	3.52	4.22	4.70	8.26	9.94	5	—15
40	2.70	4.75	5.70	4.00	7.03	8.46	—13	—25

4 Press the impeller onto the shaft until it is between .02 inch to .04 inch (.5 to 1 mm) from the inside face of the pump chamber (see **FIG 4 : 4**).

5 Refer to **FIG 4 : 5** and by the use of a straightedge with a feeler gauge see that there is between .008 inch and .010 inch (.20 to .25mm) clearance between the rear face of the impeller and the pump body face.

6 Support the shaft at its impeller end and press the pulley boss onto the front of the shaft until the parts are flush.

7 Fit a new gasket to the rear of the pump and then install the coverplate tightening the three counter-sunk screws evenly.

Replace the pump on the engine by reversing the dismantling process. Refit the hoses and refill with coolant.

4 : 4 The thermostat

To remove the thermostat, first drain the coolant down to below the level of the cylinder head. If an anti-freeze solution is being used, retain this in a clean container. Loosen the top hose clamp and remove the hose from the thermostat cover. **FIG 4 : 6** shows the thermostat mounted below the cover. Remove the three nuts and spring washers from the cover, lift it off and then lift out the thermostat. Clean away all traces of the old gasket from between the mating faces.

To test the thermostat, support it by a piece of wire from a rod placed across the top of a container of clean water. Do not let it rest on the bottom of the container or touch the sides. It must be surrounded by the water. Raise the water temperature by any suitable means such as a gas ring or electric hot plate, checking all the time with a thermometer which will safely read 100°C. When the temperature of the water reaches 180°F to 183°F

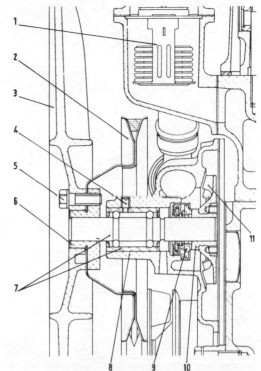

FIG 4 : 2   Sectioned view of water pump

Key to Fig 4 : 2   1 Thermostat   2 Water pump and fan drive pulley   3 Fan   4 Bearing stop screw   5 Fan mounting screws   6 Pulley hub   7 Bearing and shaft assembly   8 Pump body   9 Seal   10 Impeller bushing   11 Impeller

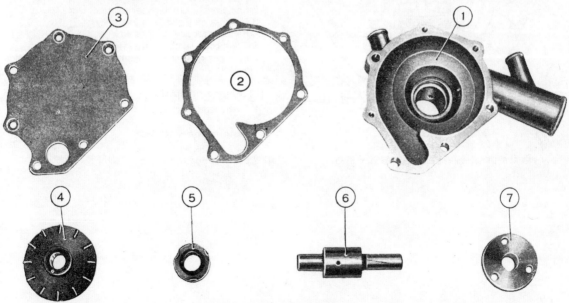

FIG 4 : 3   Water pump components

Key to Fig 4 : 3   1 Body   2 Gasket   3 Cover   4 Impeller   5 Seal   6 Shaft and bearing assembly   7 Fan pulley boss

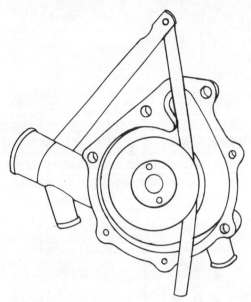

FIG 4:4   Checking impeller to body clearance

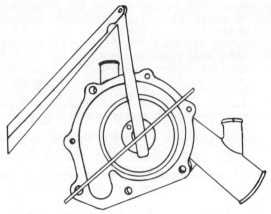

FIG 4:5   Checking impeller to flange clearance

(82°C to 84°C) the bellows of the thermostat should begin to open the valve. At 203°F (95°C) the valve must be wide open. If readings other than these are given, the thermostat must be renewed. It cannot be adjusted in any way. Sometimes a thermostat will fail wide open, if so the trouble will be obvious as soon as it is removed from the engine. Any signs of the valve being open when cold must also involve renewal.

To replace the thermostat reverse the dismantling process, using a new gasket under the thermostat cover. (Water elbow).

4:5 Fault diagnosis

(a) Engine overheats

1 Slipping belt
2 Radiator choked externally with debris
3 Radiator partly blocked internally
4 Radiator pressure cap failed
5 Thermostat stuck in the closed position
6 Incorrect fuel mixture, ignition setting or mechanical defects

(b) Engine runs cold

1 Thermostat stuck in the open position

(c) Engine loses coolant

1 Blown cylinder head gasket
2 Leaks at pump, hoses or radiator core

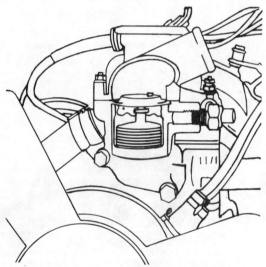

FIG 4:6   Thermostat mounted in water elbow

CHAPTER 5

THE CLUTCH

5:1 Description

The clutch is of the single dry plate type operated by a hydraulic system. The friction plate has cushion springs in the hub to reduce shock caused by harsh engagement. The hydraulic system consists of a conventional master cylinder connected to a slave cylinder by a fluid line. The slave cylinder contains a piston which operates the clutch release fork through a pushrod. A view of the complete operating mechanism is shown at FIG 5:1.

5:2 Maintenance

No maintenance is necessary or possible for the clutch unit itself. All periodic attention must be directed towards the operating system. Regularly remove the hydraulic fluid reservoir cap and inspect the fluid level. The reservoir feeds the brake system as well as the clutch so that should the fluid level need constant replenishment, first check the clutch master cylinder, pipeline and slave cylinder for leaks then check the brake components.

Always use FIAT blue label fluid for topping up the reservoir.

The clutch pedal height and free travel must be checked to correspond with the dimensions given in

FIG 5:1. If the clutch release bearing is kept in contact with the clutch levers due to incorrect adjustment, both the clutch driven plate and the release bearing will quickly wear out. Proceed to set the mechanism as follows:

1 Slacken the locknut 15 (see FIG 5:1), and screw the buffer stop 14 in or out until the pedal is at a convenient height for the driver but still has $5\frac{23}{32}$ inch (145 mm) of movement without fouling the bulkhead. Tighten the locknut.

2 Unhook the spring 11 which is connected between the slave cylinder and the clutch release lever.

3 Slacken locknut 8 and adjust nut 9 until there is $1\frac{37}{64}$ inch (40 mm) free travel of the pedal before resistance is felt. Tighten the locknut. Feel the clutch release lever and move it back and forth to check that free play does exist before the lever contacts the release bearing. Replace the spring.

5:3 Servicing the hydraulic system

Removing the master cylinder:

Although the clutch and brake hydraulic systems are fed from one reservoir, removal of the clutch master cylinder will not affect the brake system since the clutch

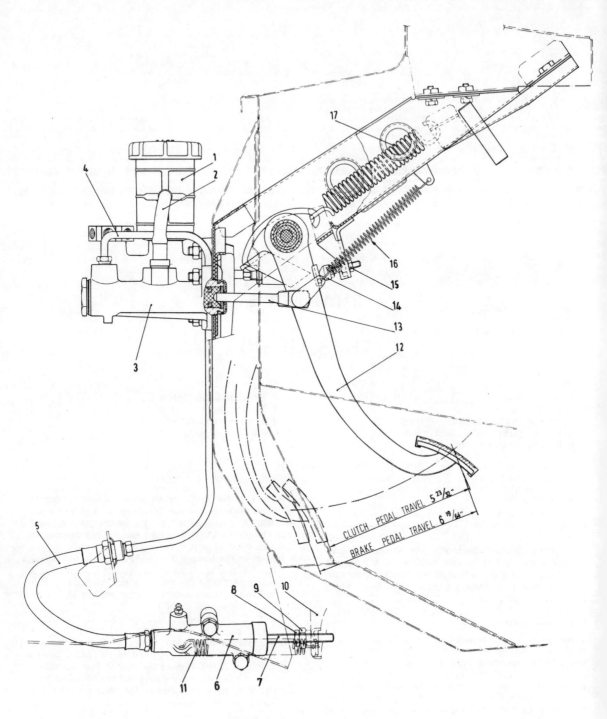

FIG 5 : 1   Clutch operating system

Key to Fig 5 : 1   1 Special FIAT blue label fluid reservoir   2 Reservoir-to-master cylinder line   3 Hydraulic clutch control master cylinder   4 Fluid pipe   5 Fluid hose to slave cylinder   6 Hydraulic clutch control slave cylinder   7 Pushrod   8-9 Clutch pedal free travel adjusting nut and locknut   10 Clutch release yoke lever   11 Yoke lever return spring   12 Clutch pedal   13 Master cylinder piston pushrod   14 Pedal travel stop buffer   15 Buffer positioning nut   16 Clutch pedal return spring   17 Hydraulic clutch control spring

fluid is taken from a point in the reservoir higher than that which feeds the brakes. To remove the master cylinder proceed as follows:

1 Fit a flexible tube to the bleed nipple on the slave cylinder and put the other end of the tube in a suitable jar or container.

2 Loosen the bleed nipple and operate the clutch pedal until all fluid is exhausted from the clutch system.

3 Remove the hose clamp on the reservoir to master cylinder hose at the master cylinder.

4 Unscrew the union nut holding the outlet pipe to the master cylinder then undo the nuts holding the master cylinder to the bulkhead. There is no need to remove the pushrod from the pedal. Lift the master cylinder off the studs.

Overhauling the master cylinder:

Absolute cleanliness is essential when working on hydraulic components. See that a good bench covered with clean newspaper is available and that no mineral oil, paraffin or petrol is near enough to accidentally come into contact with any of the hydraulic components. Strip off a sheet of newspaper whenever it becomes soiled. Use clean, lint-free rag and FIAT blue label fluid for cleaning and during reassembly. It is permissible to use denatured alcohol (methylated spirit) for cleaning provided it is allowed to evaporate thoroughly afterwards.

Before commencing work, obtain an overhaul kit which will contain all new rubber seals. **Never refit old seals under any circumstances.**

FIG 5:2 shows the master cylinder in section and **FIG 5:3** shows the components in order of assembly.

First clean as much dirt from the external surfaces of the unit as possible, then proceed to dismantle it as follows:

1 Refer to **FIG 5:3** and remove the rubber boot 12; with a pair of circlip pliers release the circlip 11.

2 Components 10, 9, 8, 7 and 6 will now come out of the cylinder bore.

3 Remove end plug 1 and seal 2.

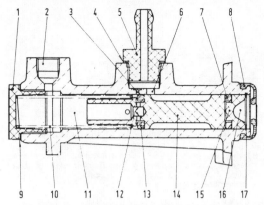

FIG 5:2   Sectioned view of master cylinder

Key to Fig 5:2   1 Cylinder lock and spring seat plug   2 Fluid outlet hose pipe connection seat   3 Transfer port   4 Connection gasket   5 Fluid reservoir hose connection   6 Fluid inlet port   7 Seal ring   8 Rubber boot   9 Gasket   10 Piston and valve carrier return spring   11 Fluid compression chamber   12 Fluid passage holes on valve carrier   13 Floating rubber valve   14 Floating valve carrier   15 Piston   16 Pushrod seat   17 Circlip

Carefully examine the cylinder bore and the piston surfaces. These should have a mirror finish. Any scores or scratches, blemishes or pits mean that these parts must be renewed. Thoroughly clean the body and the components to be reassembled then refit the end plug 1 with a new seal 2 and tighten soundly. Lubricate the cylinder bore with FIAT blue label fluid and replace spring 6. Slip the rubber valve 7 into the groove in the carrier 8, lubricate with fluid and fit into the bore. Lubricate the seal 9 with fluid, fit to the piston 10 and fit these into the bore. Make sure that all the components are well lubricated with fluid then refit the circlip 11. Replace the boot 12. Throughout all these operations remember that any contact with mineral oil, petrol,

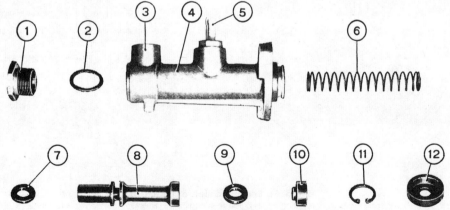

FIG 5:3   Clutch master cylinder components

Key to Fig 5:3   1 Cylinder lock and spring seat plug   2 Seal ring   3 Fluid outlet hose pipe connection seat   4 Cylinder body   5 Fluid reservoir hose connection   6 Piston and valve carrier return spring   7 Floating rubber valve   8 Floating rubber valve carrier   9 Seal ring   10 Piston   11 Circlip   12 Rubber boot

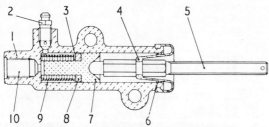

FIG 5:4 Sectioned view of slave cylinder

Key to Fig 5:4 1 Cylinder body   2 Air bleed screw
3 Backing washer   4 Push rod and cylinder head
5 Threaded pushrod operating clutch release yoke lever
6 Circlip 7 Piston 8 Seal ring 9 Spring 10 Fluid inlet
hose connection seat

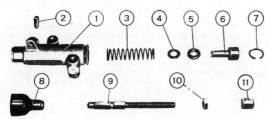

FIG 5:5 Slave cylinder components

Key to Fig 5:5   1 Cylinder body   2 Bleed nipple
3 Spring   4 Backing washer   5 Seal ring   6 Piston
7 Circlip   8 Rubber boot   9 Threaded pushrod operating
the yoke lever   10-11- Clutch pedal free travel adjusting
nut and locknut

paraffin or diesel oil will ruin the seals and the contamination will spread through the whole of the hydraulic systems.

Refit the master cylinder to the vehicle by reversing the removal process, top up the reservoir, and bleed the system as described in the next Section of this Chapter.

Removing the slave cylinder

FIG 5:4 shows the slave cylinder in section and **FIG 5:5** shows the components in order of assembly.

To remove the slave cylinder, fit the flexible tube to the bleed nipple as described when removing the master cylinder, then slacken the bleed nipple. Depress the clutch pedal and wedge it down. This will prevent fluid loss. Remove the tube. Refer to **FIG 5:1** and just slacken the flexible hose connection at the slave cylinder. **Do not move it more than a quarter turn.** Unhook the spring between the release lever and the slave cylinder then remove the splitpin from the end of the slave cylinder pushrod. Undo the two bolts holding the cylinder to the clutch housing then, holding the flexible hose stationary rotate the cylinder until it is free of the hose.

Overhauling the slave cylinder:

The remarks concerning cleanliness and the dangers of mineral oil contamination made when describing the master cylinder apply equally to the slave cylinder.

Dismantle the cylinder by first pulling out the pushrod 9 and rubber boot 8 (see **FIG 5:5**). Release the circlip 7 and components 6, 5, 4 and 3 will emerge from the bore of the cylinder.

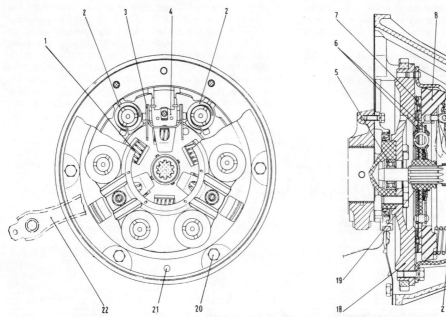

FIG 5:6 Sectioned view of clutch

Key to Fig 5:6   1 Driven plate cushion ring spring   2 Pressure springs   3 Release lever spring retainers   4 Release levers
5 Clutch shaft pilot bearing   6 Driven plate flange   7 Driven plate with linings   8 Pressure plate   9 Fulcrum   10 Release
lever pin   11 Eyebolt nut   12 Eyebolt   13 Release bearing   14 Clutch or direct drive shaft   15 Slip sleeve   16 Bellhousing
17 Clutch cover   18 Flywheel   19 Driven plate hub   20 Clutch cover-to-flywheel screws   21 Clutch cover dowel pins
22 Release yoke lever
*2 mm=.0787 inch value to be obtained through release yoke lever pushrod setting

FIG 5:7   Cutaway view of clutch

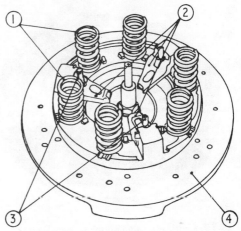

FIG 5:8   Pressure plate and springs

Key to Fig 5:8   1 Pressure springs   2 Release levers
3 Eyebolts   4 Setting plate

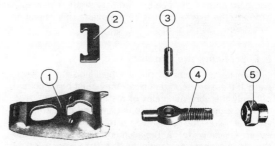

FIG 5:9   Release lever components

Key to Fig 5:9   1 Release lever   2 Fulcrum   3 Pin
4 Eyebolt   5 Eyebolt nut

Examine the piston 6 and cylinder bore 2 exactly as described for the master cylinder. If all is well, rebuild the unit using all new seals from the overhaul kit well lubricated with FIAT blue label fluid. Reassembly is a reversal of the dismantling process.

Refit the cylinder to the vehicle by reversing the removal operations. Be careful not to twist the hydraulic hose when tightening it onto the cylinder and always fit a new splitpin in the pushrod. Top up the reservoir, release the clutch pedal and bleed the system as described in the next Section.

5:4 Bleeding the hydraulic system

See that the reservoir is filled with FIAT blue label fluid and keep it topped up throughout the following operation.

Fit a flexible tube to the bleed nipple on the slave cylinder with its other end immersed in clean fluid in a glass jar. Slacken the bleed nipple half a turn. Depress the clutch pedal quickly and allow it to return slowly.

Continue this pumping action until no more air bubbles appear at the end of the tube in the jar. Depress the pedal, hold it down and then tighten the bleed nipple. Remove the flexible tube and then the jar. Discard the fluid which has been pumped through the system. No great force should be used when tightening the bleed nipple; it is easy to strip these small threads.

5:5 Removing the clutch

The gearbox must first be removed as described in **Chapter 1** if work is to be carried out with the engine in the vehicle. **FIG 5:6** shows a sectioned view of the clutch complete with release mechanism and **FIG 5:7** gives a cutaway view of the clutch itself.

To remove the clutch, first make a small mark such as a centre punch dot on both the flywheel and the clutch cover. This will help to replace the cover if the same one is used again, although due to the dowels the cover can only fit in two positions. Release the six bolts holding the cover to the flywheel by working round them

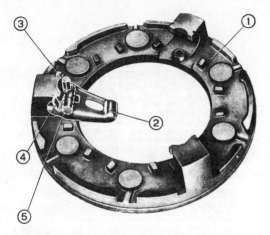

FIG 5:10   Installing clutch release levers

Key to Fig 5:10   1 Pressure plate   2 Release lever
3 Eyebolt   4 Fulcrum   5 Release lever pin

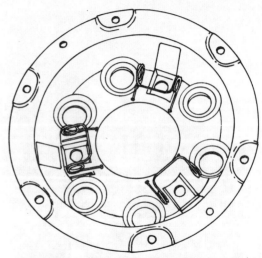

FIG 5:11   Cover and release lever retainers

evenly so that the spring pressure is equally released. Lift off the cover and remove the friction plate. If the bearing in the centre of the crankshaft which carries the outboard end of the gearbox primary shaft is damaged or worn, the flywheel must be removed. This operation was described in **Chapter 1.**

5:6 Servicing the clutch

Examine the faces of the flywheel and the pressure plate. If these are scored or burnt they must be machined, but only the very minimum of metal must be removed.

If the clutch pressure plate is damaged or the release levers are worn the wisest plan is to exchange the whole cover assembly for a replacement at a FIAT dealer. Should the operator decide to dismantle and reset the assembly, a surface plate or the flywheel removed from the engine and laid horizontally on a bench will be essential equipment.

Proceed to service the cover assembly as follows:
1 Clamp the cover to the surface plate or bolt it to the flywheel (see previous sentence).
2 Unscrew the three nuts holding the release levers.
3 With a centre punch, mark one of the projecting lugs of the pressure plate and the slot in the cover through which it protrudes.
4 Unscrew the clamps or bolts holding the cover slowly and evenly until all the pressure is released from the coil springs. Lift off the cover. **FIG 5:8.** shows how the pressure plate and springs will appear.
5 Remove the springs and release lever components. **FIG 5:9** shows the release lever components in detail.

Examine and clean all the cover components and check the coil spring free length. If any are less than 2.3 inch (58.4 mm) replace all the springs as a set. See that the release levers, fulcrums, eyebolts and pins are not worn then rebuild the cover as follows:
1 Apply a light coat of FIAT KG15 grease to the sides of the lugs on the pressure plate which protrude through the cover, the contact faces of the fulcrums,

the lever pins, the faces of the clutch cover where the eyebolt nuts seat and the plain parts of the eyebolt shanks.
2 Position the pressure plate on the surface plate or flywheel then put the three release levers, lever pins, eyebolts and fulcrums in place as shown in **FIG 5:10.**
3 Stand the six coil springs in their seats so that the pressure plate now looks like **FIG 5:8.**
4 Fit the release lever retainers to the cover (see **FIG 5:11**), then put the cover over the pressure plate to the marks made when dismantling. See that each coil spring is properly seated in the cover and the eyebolts are through the cover holes.
5 Tighten the clamps or bolts until the cover is held hard down against the surface plate or flywheel then screw the eyebolt nuts onto the eyebolts roughly to the position from which they were removed. Make sure the release lever assemblies are properly seated. Release the cover from the clamps or bolts.

The release lever height must now be properly set and in the absence of the FIAT jig proceed from first principles as follows:
1 Make up three distance pieces .339 inch to .340 inch thick (8.60 to 8.65 mm). These can be turned and parted from approximately $\frac{7}{8}$ inch bar, brass will do, or made from flat steel off cuts surface ground to size.
2 Put the three distance pieces on the surface plate or flywheel 120 deg. from each other and so positioned that the pressure plate will seat on them. They do in fact represent the clutch friction plate but **do not attempt to take a short cut and use a new friction plate since the accuracy is not high enough.**
3 Bolt or clamp the cover assembly to the surface plate or flywheel with the pressure plate seated on the distance pieces.
4 Set a scribing block pointer to 1.764 inch + or − .020 inch (44.8 + or − .5 mm) from its base then adjust each eyebolt nut until the tip of the related release lever just contacts the pointer. The three release levers must lie in a plane within .004 inch

(.1 mm) of each other. With a centre punch stake each eyebolt nut into the slot in the eyebolt so that it cannot unscrew. Remove the cover from the bolts or clamps.

The friction plate should be examined and discarded if any springs are broken, the linings are in any way contaminated or glazed or the thickness is reduced to near the rivet heads. It is good practice to replace the plate at each major engine overhaul especially if the engine is out of the vehicle.

5:7 Replacing the clutch

The friction plate must be centralized on the flywheel. Ideally an old gearbox primary shaft should be used, but if this is not available a satisfactory substitute can be made by turning a piece of hardwood to fit in the friction plate bore with a reduced diameter to fit the bearing in the end of the crankshaft. Position the friction plate on the centralizing tool with **the longer side of its hub away from the engine**. Replace the cover to the marks made when dismantling and tighten the six bolts evenly. Remove the centralizing tool.

5:8 The release bearing

If this bearing is loose or noisy it can be easily replaced. Slip the release lever which protrudes through the bellhousing off its stud and pull the release bearing and sleeve from the gearbox primary shaft. The bearing can be pressed off the sleeve and a new one pressed on. The bearing is prepacked with lubricant and will need no attention. Replace the bearing and sleeve on the shaft, slipping the release lever into place as it goes home. Put a very light smear of FIAT KG15 grease on the faces of the release lever which contact the bearing.

5:9 Fault diagnosis

(a) Noise when pedal is depressed

1 Release bearing dry or worn
2 Release lever and bearing faces worn or seized
3 Release levers striking clutch cover
4 Broken pedal springs
5 Broken release lever spring

(b) Dragging clutch

1 Excessive pedal clearance
2 Bent friction plate
3 Damaged friction linings
4 Friction plate hub tight on splines
5 Oil or grease on friction linings
6 Gearbox primary shaft bearing seized in crankshaft
7 Air in hydraulic system or lack of fluid

(c) Clutch grabs

1 Oil or grease on friction lining
2 Loose friction plate linings
3 Pressure plate running out of true
4 Incorrect release lever adjustment
5 Worn friction plate linings

(d) Clutch slips

1 Worn friction plate linings
2 Oil or grease on friction linings
3 Broken pressure springs in clutch
4 Incorrect pedal adjustment, no free travel
5 Slave cylinder piston partly seized

CHAPTER 6

THE GEARBOX

6 : 1 Description

The gearbox is a robust unit with all transmission shafts mounted on ball or roller bearings. Gear selection is by a steering column lever connected by links to two operating spindles at right angles to each other at the rear of the box. The vertical spindle controls the movement of the selector shafts while the horizontal spindle selects which one of the three selector shafts shall be moved. Synchromesh is fitted to all four forward speeds. A sectional view of the gearbox is given at **FIG 6 : 1**.

6 : 2 Maintenance

This is confined to maintaining the oil level by adding SAE.90.EP oil through the combined filler and level plug at the righthand side of the casing. The capacity of the gearbox is just over 2 Imperial pints (1.345 litres).

6 : 3 Servicing the gearbox

The gearbox must be removed from the vehicle as described in **Chapter 1**. Support on blocks and remove the oil drain plug. At this stage clean off as much external dirt as possible, put clean paper on the bench and proceed to dismantle the unit in the following sequence:

1 Remove the oil filler plug.
2 Remove the two nuts and spring washers holding the mounting bracket to the rear of the gearbox extension. Lift the bracket away.
3 Remove the ten nuts holding the sump and remove the sump and gasket.
4 Remove the clutch release lever and release bearing complete with sleeve.
5 From inside the bellhousing remove the seven mounting nuts and spring washers. Carefully slide the bellhousing away from the gearbox. The gearbox primary shaft bearing casing, oil seal and spring washer are now free.
6 Refer to **FIG 6 : 2** and remove the set bolt holding selector fork 5 to the selector shaft. This is to allow the fork to be moved so as to engage two gears at once in order to lock the shafts.
7 Refer to **FIG 6 : 3** and remove the circlip from the flexible joint.
8 With a heavy puller, withdraw the flexible joint locating ring as shown in **FIG 6 : 4**.

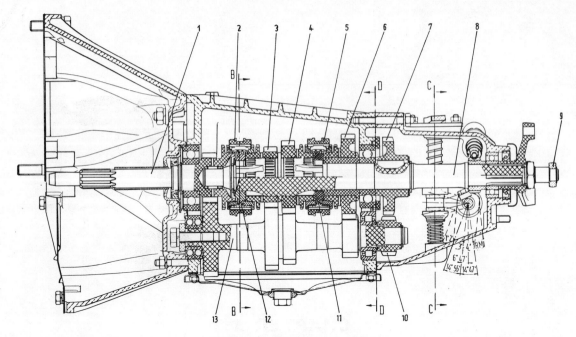

FIG 6:1   Sectional view of gearbox

Key to Fig 6:1   1 Clutch shaft with constant mesh and high speed gear   2 Third and high speed synchromesh sleeve   3 Third speed gear   4 Second speed gear   5 Low and second speed synchromesh sleeve   6 Low speed gear   7 Reverse speed gear on mainshaft   8 Mainshaft   9 Flexible joint location ring   10 Reverse speed gear on countershaft   11 Low and second speed synchromesh sleeve hub   12 Third and high speed synchromesh sleeve hub   13 Countershaft with low, second, third and constant mesh gears

FIG 6:2   View of gearbox interior

Key to Fig 6:2   1 Low speed drive gear   2 Low and second selector fork   3 Second speed drive gear   4 Third speed drive gear   5 Third and high selector fork   6 Constant mesh driven gear   7 Low speed driven gear   8 Low and second synchromesh sleeve   9 Second speed driven gear   10 Third speed driven gear   11 Third and high synchromesh sleeve   12 Constant mesh drive gear

FIG 6:3   Removing flexible joint circlip

Key to Fig 6:3   1 Circlip   2 Location ring   3 Dust shield

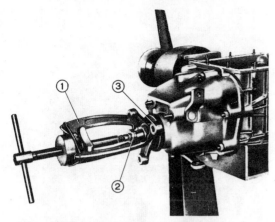

FIG 6 : 4   Removing the location ring

Key to Fig 6 : 4   1 Puller   2 Location ring   3 Yoke

9 Slide the third/top selector fork along the shaft and lock two gears together (see operation 6). Undo the centre nut and remove the yoke flange (see **FIG 6 : 4**, item 3).

10 Undo the nut and remove the speedometer drive housing.

11 Refer to **FIG 6 : 5** and remove the nuts holding the plate retaining the detent springs and balls. Remove the springs but do not mix them up. The reverse spring **1** is heavier than the other two. Tip the box sideways and remove the balls.

12 Remove the six nuts and washers which hold the rear extension to the gearbox. Slide it away complete with gasket and the gear selector and operating shafts. Slide the main shaft ballbearing and speedometer drive gear from the shaft.

13 Slide the reverse selector shaft, fork and idler gear from their positions and lift away.

14 Remove the circlip holding the reverse drive gear to the end of the layshaft, the circlip holding the reverse driven gear to the mainshaft and remove both gears. Remove the Woodruff key from the mainshaft.

15 Lock two gears together and undo the bolt in the front end of the layshaft. Up end the box and bump it gently to free the layshaft bearings front and rear, from the gearbox. Tilt the layshaft and lift it out.

16 Slide the top/third gear selector shaft out and lift out the selector fork. Undo the bolt holding the first/second gear selector shaft to its fork and remove the shaft and fork. The interlock rollers will be freed as the first/second gear selector shaft is removed.

17 Refer to **FIG 6 : 6** and remove the mainshaft intermediate bearing.

18 Remove the gearbox primary shaft from the front of the box complete with bearing and top gear synchromesh assembly (see **FIG 6 : 7**). Twenty-three needle rollers and their thrust rings will almost certainly fall from between the front and rear halves of the main shaft when the front half (primary shaft) is released. Collect and count these to make sure none are lost.

19 Remove the rear half of the mainshaft and the gearbox is now empty.

FIG 6 : 5   Detent spring and balls

Key to Fig 6 : 5   1 Reverse detent   2 3rd/top detent
3 1st/2nd detent

20 Dismantle the mainshaft as follows:
From the rear of the shaft slide off the first gear and bush, first gear synchromesh ring, first and second gear hub with sliding sleeve (complete with blocks and springs) the second gear synchromesh ring and the second gear. From the front of the shaft release the circlip (see **FIG 6 : 8**), then slide off the spring washer, third/top gear hub with the sliding sleeve (complete with blocks and springs), the third gear synchromesh ring and the third gear.

21 Remove the circlip from the primary shaft and slide off the spring washer and ballbearing.

FIG 6 : 6   Removing mainshaft intermediate bearing

FIG 6:7 Removing the primary shaft

FIG 6:9 Selector mechanism

Key to Fig 6:9   1 Gear selector spindle and lever
2 Reverse idler gearshaft rear bore   3 Reverse gear stiffening
spring casing   4 Reverse gear stiffening spring   5 Internal
gear selector lever   6 Gear operating cam   7 Low and
second gear stiffening spring   8 Gear operating spindle
9 Extension oil seal   10 Lever rubber bushing   11 Gear
operating lever

22 To dismantle the selector mechanism from the
   extension case refer to **FIG 6:9**. Remove the two nuts
   and spring washers holding the operating spindle 8
   and lever 11 to the case. Slide the spindle 8 out
   thereby releasing the springs and sliding sleeve.
   Remove the bolt which holds the selector lever 5
   to the spindle 1 and remove the spindle and lever.

Examine all the gearbox components after they have
been thoroughly washed in paraffin and dried off. Look
for the following defects and rectify or renew as necessary.

(a) Cracks and burrs on the castings.
(b) Damaged oil seals (it is best to replace all these as a
    matter of course).
(c) Mainshaft must not be bent. Check by rotating
    between centres. Any run-out greater than .001 inch
    (.025 mm) means renewal.
(d) Splines must not be worn, chipped or indented.
(e) Gears must not show any signs of heavy pressure,
    chipping, flaking or cracks.
(f) All shaft bearing surfaces must be unmarked and
    unworn.
(g) All ball or roller races must be without slack and must
    turn freely without roughness. Examine the tracks and
    balls or rollers closely for any discolouration, flaking
    or pitting. Discard at once if any such signs are found.
(h) If the shafts are temporarily assembled with the gears
    in the box there must be no backlash between gears
    exceeding .004 inch (.10 mm). All gears must have less

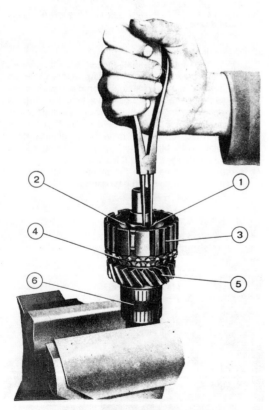

FIG 6:8 Removing top gear circlip

Key to Fig 6:8   1 Circlip   2 Spring washer   3 3rd/top
gear sliding sleeve   4 Synchromesh ring   5 3rd driven gear
6 Mainshaft

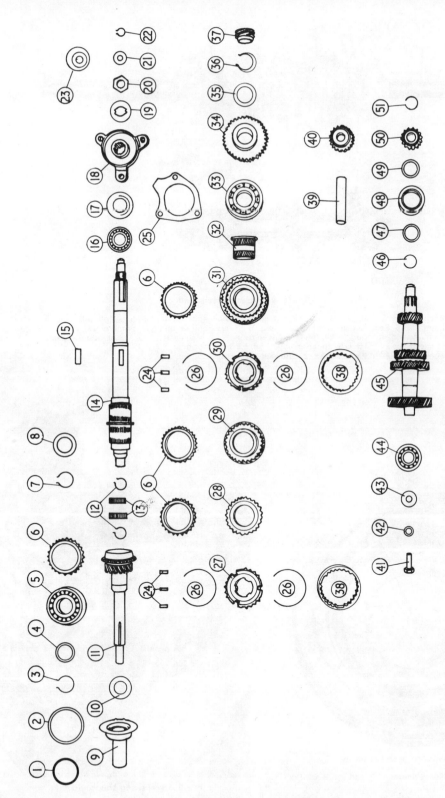

FIG 6:10 Rotating components of gearbox

Key to Fig 6:10 1 Clutch shaft bearing casing oil seal 2 Spring washer 3 Bearing circlip 4 Spring washer 5 Clutch shaft ballbearing 6 Synchromesh rings 7 Mainshaft gear cluster circlip 8 Spring washer 9 Clutch shaft bearing casing 10 Casing inner seal 11 Clutch shaft 12 Clutch shaft-to-mainshaft needle bearing thrust rings 13 Needles 14 Mainshaft 15 Key 16 Mainshaft rear ballbearing 17 Transmission extension seal 18 Flexible joint yoke flange 19 Flat lockwasher 20 Flexible joint yoke flange nut 21 Flexible joint location ring 22 Circlip 23 Flexible joint dust shield 24 Synchromesh sleeve shifting blocks 25 Mainshaft intermediate ballbearing flange 26 Shifting block springs 27 Third and high synchromesh sleeve hub 28 Third speed driven gear 29 Second speed driven gear 30 Low and second synchromesh sleeve hub 31 Low speed driven gear 32 Low speed gear bushing 33 Mainshaft intermediate ballbearing 34 Reverse speed driven gear 35 Spring washer 36 Reverse driven gear circlip 37 Speedo drive gear 38 Synchromesh sleeves 39 Reverse idler gearshaft 40 Reverse idler gear 41 Countershaft front ballbearing screw 42 Spring washer 43 Plain washer 44 Countershaft front double-race bearing 45 Countershaft with low, second and third gear cluster 46 Thrust ring 47 Countershaft rear roller bearing cone 48 Roller bearing cup 49 Spring washer 50 Reverse drive gear 51 Circlip

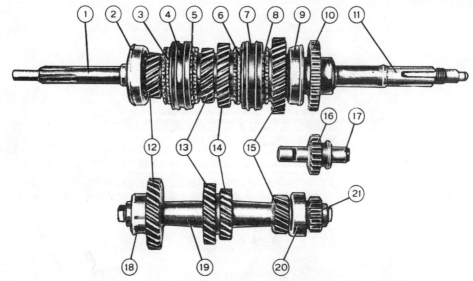

FIG 6:11   Shafts and gears assembled

Key to Fig 6:11   1 Clutch shaft   2 Ballbearing   3 High gear synchromesh ring   4 Third and high gear synchromesh sleeve   5 Third gear synchromesh ring   6 Second gear synchromesh ring   7 Low and second gear synchromesh ring   8 Low gear synchromesh ring   9 Intermediate ballbearing   10 Reverse driven gear   11 Mainshaft   12 Constant mesh gears   13 Third speed gears   14 Second speed gears   15 Low speed gears   16 Reverse idler gear   17 Reverse idler gearshaft   18 Front ballbearing   19 Countershaft   20 Rear roller bearing   21 Reverse drive gear

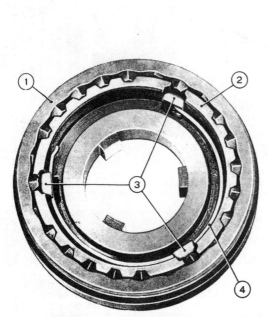

FIG 6:12   Synchromesh assembly

Key to Fig 6:12   1 Sliding sleeve   2 Hub   3 Blocks   4 Spring

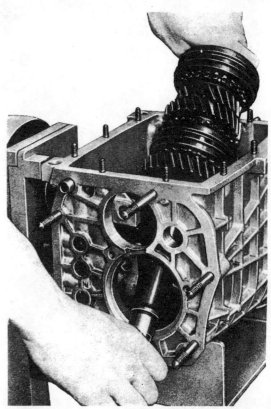

FIG 6:13   Fitting the mainshaft

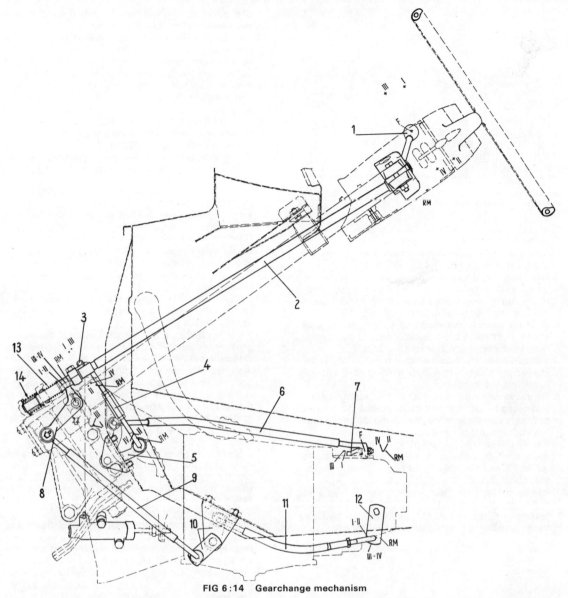

FIG 6:14 Gearchange mechanism

Key to Fig 6:14   1 Gearchange lever   2 Gearchange rod   3 Gearchange rod lever   4 Front operating rod, with adjuster   5 Relay operating lever   6 Rear operating rod, fixed   7 Operating lever and spindle at transmission extension   8 Selector lever at steering housing   9 Relay rod, selector, fixed   10 Relay lever, selector   11 Relay rod, selector, adjustable   12 Selector lever and spindle, at transmission extension   13 Selector lever return spring   14 Reverse gear stiffening spring   F = Neutral   RM = Reverse speed

than .006 inch (.15 mm) clearance between their bores and the shafts.

(j) Check the synchromesh components for damage or wear, particularly scoring of the sliding faces. See that there is no excessive clearance between the selector forks and the grooves in the sliding sleeves. To rebuild the gearbox proceed as follows:

1 Obtain all new gaskets and locking washers; fit new oil seals to the mainshaft housings. Smear a little clean gear oil on all parts as they are fitted together.

Refer to **FIGS 6:10** and **6:11** for guidance as work proceeds. These illustrations clearly show the assembly sequence.

2 Take the rear half of the mainshaft and slide the third speed gear 13 (see **FIG 6:11**) on the front end and up to the flange on the shaft, 11.

3 Now slide the synchromesh ring 5 (see **FIG 6:11**), up to the third speed gear.

4 Assemble the third/top synchromesh hub and sliding sleeve as shown in **FIG 6:12**, then slide this assembly

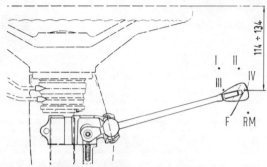

FIG 6:15 Correct neutral position of gearchange lever

Key to Fig 6:15 $114 \div 134 = 4\frac{1}{2}$ inch to $5\frac{9}{32}$ inch
F = Neutral   R.M. = Reverse

onto the shaft. (Do not have the ends of the springs 4, in the same block 3). Fit the spring washer to the shaft then the circlip to hold the whole assembly to the shaft. These are items 8 and 7 of **FIG 6:10**.

5 Now slide the second speed gear 14 (see **FIG 6:11**) on from the rear of the shaft followed by the synchromesh ring 6, synchromesh assembly 7, first speed synchromesh ring 8 and the first speed gear 15.

6 Hold the gears to the shaft and fit it to the case as shown in **FIG 6:13**. Fit the intermediate ballbearing over the shaft and seat it into the box bore.

7 Fit the reverse idler gearshaft then the shaft and bearing lockplate as shown in **FIG 6:6**. Stake the screw heads into the lockplate.

8 Fit the ballbearing 2 (see **FIG 6:11**), spring washer and circlip to the front half of the mainshaft. A piece of tube is a convenient tool for driving the circlip over the shaft and into the groove.

9 Put the thrust ring 12 (see **FIG 6:10**) into the bore of the mainshaft followed by the twenty-three needle rollers 13, and the other thrust ring 12. Hold them in place with grease.

10 Hold the top gear synchromesh ring 3 (see **FIG 6:11**), on the front of the top/third synchromesh assembly 4 (see **FIG 6:11**), and carefully feed the front mainshaft (primary shaft) into the gearbox and

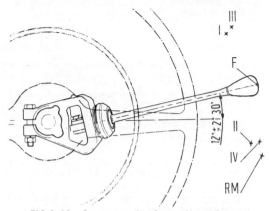

FIG 6:16 Correct angle of gearchange lever

Key to Fig 6:16   F = Neutral   R.M. = Reverse

over the end of the rear half of the shaft. **Watch that no needle rollers are dislodged.**

11 Hold the first/second selector fork in the groove of the synchromesh assembly and fit the first/second speed selector shaft. Slide the interlock roller into place and bolt the fork to the shaft. Turn up the tabwasher.

12 Repeat operation 11 for the top/third selector fork and shaft but do not bolt the fork to the shaft at this stage.

13 Fit the layshaft and its bearings. Engage two gears to lock the shafts then tighten the bolt at the front of the layshaft to 68 lb ft (9.5 kg m).

14 Fit the Woodruff key at the rear of the mainshaft and then slide the reverse driven gear over it. Fit the circlip.

15 Repeat operation 14 with the reverse drive gear on the rear of the layshaft.

16 Fit the reverse selector shaft interlock roller and bolt the reverse gear selector fork to the selector shaft. Hold the reverse gear idler gear into the fork and slide the whole assembly into the rear of the gearbox with the idler gear on its shaft.

17 Slide the speedometer drive gear and the rear ballbearing onto the mainshaft.

18 Refit the selector mechanism to the extension case by reversing the dismantling process. Fit new oil seals to the spindles.

19 Move the third/top selector shaft as far to the rear as possible without disengaging the fork. Now slide the extension case onto the rear of the gearbox engaging the selector mechanism with the selector forks. The shaft moved to the rear will come forward as the mechanism engages. Secure the extension case to the gearbox by tightening the six nuts to 22 lb ft (3.0 kg m).

20 Fit the speedometer drive housing and tighten the nut.

21 Engage two gears together. Slide the flexible joint yoke onto the rear of the mainshaft, fit the plain washer and the nut. Tighten the nut to 58 lb ft (8.0 kg m). Slide the flexible joint dust shield 23 (see **FIG 6:10**) onto the shaft followed by the location ring 21, and then fit the circlip 22.

22 Return to the front of the gearbox and fit the oil seal to the mainshaft bearing casing followed by the seal ring. Fit the casing to the bellhousing and slide the spring washer onto the mainshaft.

23 Fit the bellhousing to the gearbox, tightening the six large nuts to 40 lb ft (5.5 kg m). Use a new gasket. The seventh small nut is tightened to 21 lb ft (3.0 kg m).

24 Now bolt the third/top selector fork to its shaft and lock with the tabwasher. Fit the detent balls and springs (remember that the reverse spring is the heavier) and bolt up the coverplate. Check the engagement of the gears.

25 Fit the sump cover with a new gasket and tighten the ten nuts evenly to 7 lb ft (1.0 kg m). Replace the drain plug. Refit the rear mounting crossmember tightening the nuts to 24 lb ft (3.3 kg m). Install the clutch release lever and bearing in the bellhousing.

26 Turn the box right way up and refill with SAE.90.EP oil. Replace the filler/level plug.

Refit the gearbox to the vehicle as described in **Chapter 1**.

6:4 Servicing the gearchange mechanism

First check the mechanical condition of the linkage. Renew any worn bushes and pivot pins. If the springs 13 and 14 (see **FIG 6:14**), are weak this will adversely affect gear engagement, so these must be renewed if any doubt exists. Properly lubricate any sliding surface appearing to be dry or tight.

To adjust the linkage proceed as follows:

1 The gearchange lever when in neutral must be in the position shown in **FIG 6:15,** i.e. the top of the lever must be between $4\frac{1}{2}$ inch and $5\frac{5}{32}$ inch (114 and 134 mm) from a line drawn across the top face of the steering wheel.

2 The gearchange lever must also be set so that it makes an angle of 12 deg. $\pm$ 2 deg. 30' from the horizontal as shown in **FIG 6:16** when it is in neutral. To adjust this angle, rotate sleeve 4 (see **FIG 6:14**), afterwards tightening the locknuts.

3 The operation of the individual selector rods cannot be changed and will not require adjustment but the selection of any one of the three rods may be adjusted. To do this adjust the length of rod 11 (see **FIG 6:14**).

4 To check the correct movement, disconnect the rod 11 (see **FIG 6:14**) and move the lever 12, to each position for engaging a selector rod. Check the gear-lever angles by temporarily engaging the rod and compare the angles with those shown for the gear-lever in **FIG 6:16**. An assistant will be needed for this.

Instructions for removing the gearchange mechanism are given in **Chapter 9, Steering gear.**

6:5 Fault diagnosis

(a) Noisy transmission

1 Excessive gear backlash
2 Worn bearings
3 Bent mainshaft
4 Chipped or fractured gear teeth
5 Lack of oil

(b) Difficult gearchange

1 Bush or pin seized in linkage
2 Bent control rod
3 Incorrect adjustment of gearchange mechanism
4 Selector shaft binding
5 Synchromesh failed, broken springs or worn rings
6 Wrong grade of oil
7 Clutch not freeing

(c) Gears disengage inadvertently

1 Hand lever not being moved to correct position
2 Gearchange mechanism out of adjustment
3 Worn detent balls or broken springs
4 Selector shaft interlock rollers worn or wrongly assembled
5 Worn synchromesh rings

CHAPTER 7

PROPELLER SHAFT, REAR AXLE, REAR SUSPENSION

7:1 Description

From the gearbox the drive is taken via a divided propeller shaft to a semi-floating hypoid axle. Rear suspension is by leaf springs and telescopic dampers. The propeller shaft is of interest in that it has a flexible joint between its forward flange and the sliding joint and is supported part way along its length on a flexibly mounted plummer (or pillow) block with a roller bearing. From here it has two universal joints to connect it between the front shaft and the axle input flange. This construction ensures a particularly vibration free and long-lasting shaft. **FIGS 7:1** and **7:2** show details of the assembly.

7:2 Removing the propeller shaft assembly

Refer to **FIG 7:1**. Undo the nuts 33 and 49, push the bolts from the flanges and lower the shaft from the vehicle after noting which way round it was fitted. Now remove the bolts 9 from the sliding joint yoke then release the two bolts 30 from below the centre bearing (plummer block). The front shaft will now lift away complete with the bearing.

If the sliding joint is to be dismantled, remove the cap 21 and spring out the circlip 18 and seal 17. The shafts must be marked to mate with the sliding joint sleeve on reassembly before it is pulled apart.

To release the shaft from the bearing 24, undo the large nut 35 and pull the flange 32 off the shaft. The shaft will now pull forwards out of the bearing.

Note that mating marks should have been etched on all flanges and yokes during manufacture, check before dismantling.

7:3 Servicing the propeller shaft

Inspect all components for wear or distortion; particularly note the following points:
Sliding joint: The backlash on the splines must not exceed .012 inch (.3mm). See that the grease nipple on the sleeve is clean and the drill way clear. If the seal or circlip in the cap are damaged, renew them otherwise the shaft will not retain its lubricant.
The flexible joint: Refer to **FIG 7:3**. If the rubber pads are swollen or dry, loose and cracked, renew the joint. The centre bush can be renewed without renewing the

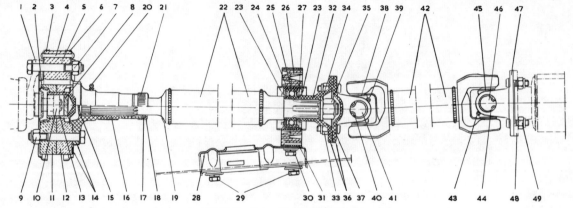

FIG 7:1   Propeller shaft assembly

Key to Fig 7:1   1 Mainshaft yoke flange   2 Dust shield   3 Flexible joint cover   4 Rivet   5 Drive dog   6 Cover
7 Self-locking nut, flexible joint-to-transmission screw   8 Lubricating wick   9 Self-locking nut, flexible joint-to-propeller shaft
screw   10 Flexible joint location ring   11 Front driven plate   12 Rear driven plate   13 Location bushing   14 Assembly marks
15 Plug   16 Slip sleeve   17 Seal   18 Snap ring   19 Assembly mark   20 Lubrication fitting   21 Casing   22 Front propeller
shaft   23 Bearing shields   24 Ballbearing   25 Bearing carrier   26 Rubber pad   27 Bearing snap ring   28 Propeller shaft
cross rail   29 Cross rail-to-body shell screws   30 Pillow block-to-cross-rail screws   31 Pillow block   32 Front shaft flange
sleeve   33 Universal joint flange yoke-to-front shaft sleeve flange screw nuts   34 Plain washer   35 Flange nut   36 Assembly
marks   37 Universal joint flange yoke   38 Universal joint spider   39 Lubrication fitting   40 Circlip   41 Needle bearing
42 Rear propeller shaft   43 Lubrication fitting   44 Circlip   45 Universal joint spider   46 Needle bearing   47 Universal joint
flange yoke   48 Drive pinion companion flange   49 Universal joint-to-drive pinion companion flange screw nut

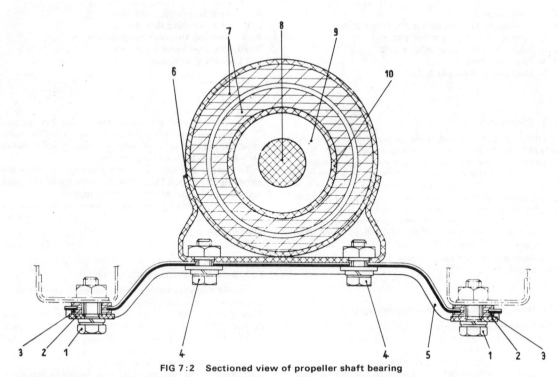

FIG 7:2   Sectioned view of propeller shaft bearing

Key to Fig 7:2   1 Cross rail-to-body screws   2 Plain washer   3 Insulators   4 Pillow block-to-cross rail screws   5 Propeller
shaft cross rail   6 Base   7 Rubber pad   8 Propeller shaft end   9 Ballbearing   10 Bearing carrier

complete joint. Examine the bore of the bush for wear which can occur if the mounting bolts have ever been allowed to run in a loose condition. To renew the bush, remove the circlips, push out the bush and fit the new one with new circlips. If the bush has worn it is likely that the location collar on the gearbox mainshaft is also worn. Renew this by referring to **Chapter 6** for instructions.

The centre bearing: If the ballrace shows any sign of slackness or roughness, renew it immediately. Support the metal housing into which the bearing is pressed then either pull the bearing out with a puller or press it out with a small press. Do not attempt to drift it out. If the rubber mounting is perished it will be necessary to renew the casing and mounting together as a unit. When assembling the shaft to the bearing do not forget the bearing shields. Reference to **FIG 7:1** will show how these are fitted.

The universal joints: Provided that these have not been so neglected that the bores are worn oval, it is possible to obtain a reconditioning kit which will restore the joint to new standard. The need for an overhaul is present when the movement between any one of the four spider journals and its bearing exceeds .006 inch (.156 mm). The kit will contain a new spider, needle rollers, caps, seals and circlips. **FIG 7:4** shows a joint dismantled to its component parts.

Before stripping a joint mark the yoke on the shaft and the flange so that they can be reassembled in the same angular relationship.

Proceed as follows:

1 Wipe off as much grease and dirt as possible then with a small pair of pliers remove the four circlips.
2 Hold the shaft firmly in the lefthand and tap on the back of the shaft yoke just behind the spider bearing with a soft-faced hammer. The bearing cup will gradually jar up out of the yoke. Turn the yoke over

FIG 7:3 The flexible joint

as the cup comes out and catch the needle rollers. The spider can now be driven down against the other bearing then lifted free. Drive this bearing out with a drift then support the flange yoke on a piece of tube and drive the spider downwards until the third bearing cup is removed. Lift the spider from the flange yoke, turn the yoke over and drive out the last bearing cup.

To rebuild the joint, make sure all parts are clean then assemble as follows:

1 Place the new cork seals on the spider journals.
2 Grease each bearing cup and insert the needle rollers.

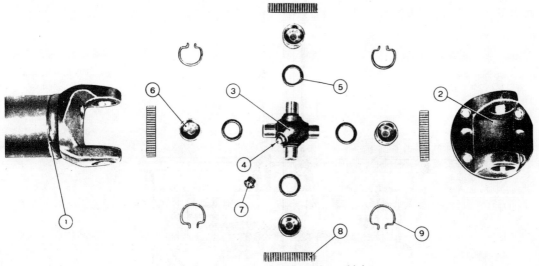

FIG 7:4 Components of a universal joint

Key to Fig 7:4 1 Shaft   2 Flange yoke   3 Spider   4 Grease nipple   5 Seal   6 Bearing cup   7 Overflow valve
8 Needle rollers   9 Circlip

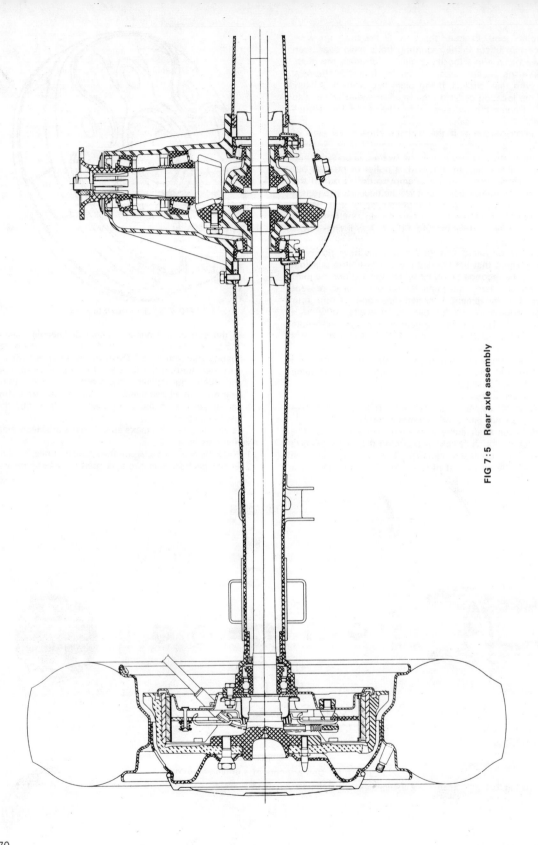

FIG 7:5   Rear axle assembly

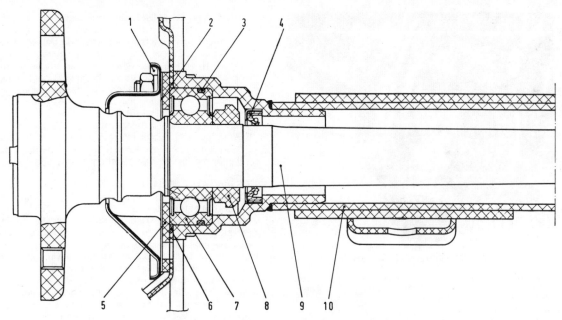

FIG 7:6   Rear axle shaft and bearing assembly

Key to Fig 7:6   1 Oil shield   2 Gasket   3 Bearing seal   4 Inner oil seal   5 Bearing retainer plate   6 Brake backplate
7 Bearing   8 Bearing retaining collar   9 Shaft   10 Axle case

3 Refer to **FIG 7:4.** Hold the spider 3 in the yoke of the flange yoke 2 with the overflow valve 7 facing towards the flange yoke 2. Enter a bearing cup 6 into one of the yoke bores over the spider journal until the rollers are safely held in place. Repeat for the other side. Press both cups into the yoke until the new circlips can be fitted. Now tap the back of each side of the yoke to make the cups seat back hard against the circlips.

4 Fit the propeller shaft 1 over the spider making sure that the marks made when dismantling are in proper alignment.

5 Fit the bearing cups in the same way as the cups were fitted to the flange yoke. Make sure that they seat back against the circlip.

6 Pump FIAT Jota 1 grease into the spider until it exudes from the overflow valve.

7:4 Replacing the propeller shaft

1 Bolt the flexible joint to the gearbox mainshaft with the bolt heads next to the gearbox.

2 Fit the front shaft to the centre bearing and tighten the large nut to 145 lb ft (20.0 kg m).

3 Manoeuvre the front shaft up into place and connect the sliding joint spider to the flexible joint, fitting the bolts so that the nuts are next to the gearbox. If the bolt and nut positioning is correct, the nuts of all six bolts will be against the flexible joint case. Tighten the bolts to 38 lb ft (5.2 kg m).

4 Fit the bolts holding the centre bearing but do not tighten.

5 Fit the rear shaft and tighten the nuts securely. The nuts should be nearest to the centre bearing at the front and nearest to the axle at the rear of the shaft.

6 Tighten the centre bearing bolts to 18 lb ft (2.6 kg m).

7 Check that all the shaft and flange marks are in alignment then apply the grease gun to the sliding joint and fill with FIAT Jota 1 grease.

7:5 The rear axle

It is not an economic proposition for a private owner to overhaul the differential unit or to fit new bearings to the halfshafts. In the case of the differential, 16 special tools, gauges and jigs are needed apart from any new components which will have to be purchased. If any trouble shows up in the differential it can be removed from the axle and an exchange unit obtained. The half-shaft bearings are held onto the halfshaft by a collar which must be pressed onto the shaft with a force of 11,000 lb (5000 kg) after heating the collar to 300°C. This is most definitely a job for a FIAT agent.

To remove the differential it is not necessary to remove the whole axle unit. First drain the oil from the differential case then jack up the rear of the vehicle and support safely on axle stands.

Continue as follows:

1 Remove the rear road wheels. It may be necessary to apply the handbrake to enable the wheel studs to be removed but make sure the brake is right off when the wheels are clear of the vehicle.

2 Undo the screws which hold the brake drum to the axle shaft flange then reinsert them in the threaded

FIG 7:7   Extracting axle shaft

Key to Fig 7:7   1 Puller   2 Brake backplate   3 Axle case
4 Axle shaft flange   5 Puller mounting plate   6 Screws
securing puller to shaft flange

holes in the drum. By tightening these screws the
drum will now be forced off the axle shaft flange.

3 Apply a box spanner through the large holes in the
axle shaft flange and undo the nuts from the bolts
which hold the brake backplate to the end of the axle
casing. There is no need to disturb the brake shoes or
mechanism.

4 Reference to **FIG 7:6** will show that the axle shaft
is now held by the fit of the bearing in the axle case

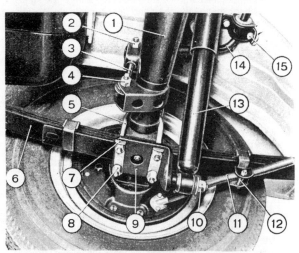

FIG 7:8   Rear axle attachment points

Key to Fig 7:8   1 Rear axle housing   2 Link-to-anti-roll
bar nut   3 Link   4 Link-to-axle housing nut   5 U-bolt
6 Semi-elliptic spring   7 Lockplates   8 U-bolt saddle
plate nuts   9 Saddle plate, rear axle-to-semi-elliptic spring
U-bolt and lower damper mounting   10 Damper lower
mounting self-locking nut   11 Handbrake control cable
12 Handbrake control cable clamp   13 Hydraulic
damper   14 Anti-roll bar   15 Anti-roll bar rubber cushion-
to-underbody screw

alone. A proper puller is almost essential here and the
correct application of it is shown in **FIG 7:7**. In
emergency, replace the road wheel on the axle shaft
flange but leave all the studs approximately $\frac{9}{16}$ inch
slack. Now jerk the wheel outwards against the
studs as hard as possible. The shock loading will
usually release the bearing but it may indent the
tracks. A new bearing should always be fitted if this
method of removal has to be adopted.

5 Repeat operation 4 for the opposite side axle shaft.

6 With the axle shafts released from the differential
gears, undo the propeller shaft at the differential input
flange and lay the shaft carefully over to one side out
of the way.

7 Support the differential carrier and undo the eight
nuts holding it to the axle casing. It can now be
lifted out of the casing.

To replace the differential, reverse the dismantling
process being careful to install a new gasket between
the differential carrier and the axle casing. Tighten the
eight nuts to 16 lb ft (2.2 kg m). Connect the propeller
shaft to the input flange. Push the axle shafts into the
axle casing, turning them so that they engage with the
splines in the differential gears. Fit the bearing plate and
oil shield over the four bolts which hold the brake backplate to the axle casing then tighten the nuts evenly to
pull the bearing and shaft right home against the seat
in the casing. Finally tighten the four bolts to 21 lb ft
(2.9 kg m). Replace the brake drums and road wheels
tightening the road wheel nuts finally when the vehicle
is lowered to the ground. Refill the axle with the correct
grade of oil.

The axle shafts:

It will be necessary to work on an axle shaft for any one
of three reasons, (a) failure of the oil seal, (b) failure of
the bearing or (c) a broken shaft.

(a) If oil continually leaks from the brake drum, first
check that the axle is not overfilled and that the
breather is clear. This will be found near the top of
the axle casing above the differential. Assuming that
these points are in order, remove the axle shaft from
the casing as described for the removal of the differential. The oil seal can now be carefully prised out of
the axle casing and a new one drifted in. Make sure
it seats squarely and smear the outside with a non-
hardening jointing cement before fitting. **FIG 7:6**
clearly shows which way round the seal is fitted.
Smear a coat of axle oil on the shaft where the seal
lips run so that they are lubricated immediately the
shaft revolves. Before replacing the shaft make sure
that the surface of the shaft in contact with the seal
is smooth and polished. Any roughness here will
quickly destroy the seal. Refit the shaft as described
previously.

(b) Should the bearing have failed, remove the shaft and
take to a FIAT agent for fitting a new bearing and collar.
See the remarks at the beginning of this Section
concerning the special procedure to be adopted to fit
the bearing. When replacing the axle shaft in the
casing make sure a new seal ring 3 (see **FIG 7:6**)
is fitted.

(c) A broken axle shaft will need to be tackled in a way
dependent on the point of fracture. Usually a shaft

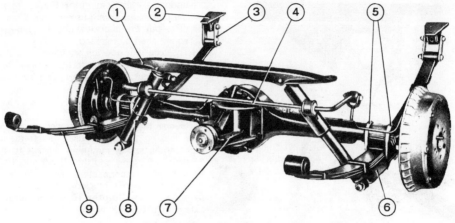

FIG 7:9   Rear axle and suspension

Key to Fig 7:9   1 Crossmember, upper damper mounting   2 Semi-elliptic spring-to-underbody rear mounting bracket   3 Shackle
4 Anti-roll bar   5 Rear axle-to-spring U-bolts   6 U-bolt and lower damper mounting saddle plate   7 Rear axle   8 Damper
9 Semi-elliptic spring

will break flush with the end of the splines in the differential. In this case remove the shafts and lift out the differential, so that the broken piece of shaft can be pushed out of the side gear. If the shaft breaks near the bearing a special service tool must be used to grip the shaft and pull it free.

7:6   Removing the axle

To remove the axle as a complete unit proceed as follows:

1 Remove the brake fluid reservoir cap and plug the outlet port at the bottom of the reservoir with a clean piece of hard wood. Cover the reservoir so that dirt cannot enter.

2 Slacken the rear wheel studs then jack up the rear of the vehicle and support on substantial wooden blocks under a solid part of the body forward of the leaf spring mountings.

4 Drain the oil from the differential and remove the brake drums.

5 Disconnect the flexible hydraulic brake hose taking care not to twist it then plug both the hose and the pipe from which it has been released.

6 Disconnect the handbrake cable ends from the levers on the brake shoes then from behind the brake backplate release the two screws holding the outer cable to the backplate.

7 Refer to **FIG 7:8** and release the clamps 12. The brake cables are now free.

8 Disconnect the propeller shaft from the differential input flange.

9 Remove the nuts 4 (see **FIG 7:8**) and pull the anti-roll bar links 3 out of the brackets.

10 Remove the damper nut 10 and pull the damper forwards away from the spring saddle plate 9.

11 Place two jacks or suitable packing under the axle to take its weight. Release the lockplates 7 and nuts 8. (Release these nuts evenly). Pull the saddle 9 away from the U-bolts then lift the U-bolts off the axle.

12 At the rear of each leaf spring, a shackle holds the spring to the body bracket. It is usually easiest to

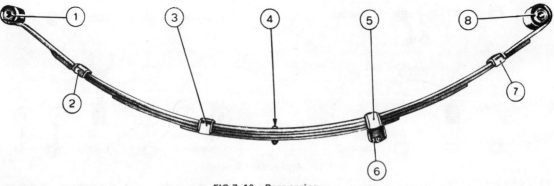

FIG 7:10   Rear spring

Key to Fig 7:10   1 Rear bush   2, 3, 5 and 7 Clips   4 Bolt   6 Cable clamp   8 Front bush

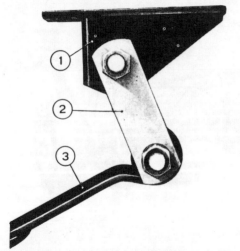

FIG 7:11   Rear mounting bracket

Key to Fig 7:11   1 Bracket   2 Shackle   3 Spring

undo the nuts holding the bracket to the body and then lower the spring to the ground rather than try to drive out the shackle bolts. Only the rear of each spring need be released.

13 The axle will now be standing on jacks or packing free of all connection to the vehicle. With the aid of an assistant, lower the axle and lift it rearwards and away from the vehicle.

7:7 Replacing the rear axle

Reverse the dismantling procedure, making sure that new locking plates are used under the U-bolt nuts. Tighten the spring mounting bracket to body nuts to 11 lb ft (1.5 kg m) and the U-bolt nuts to 23 lb ft (3.1 kg m). After reconnecting the hydraulic brake pipe, remove the wooden blocking plug and bleed the brakes as described in **Chapter 10.** Do not forget to refill the axle with SAE.90.EP oil.

7:8 The rear suspension

If both rear springs are to be renewed, proceed to remove the axle as described in **Section 7:6** then finally remove the bolts holding the front ends of the

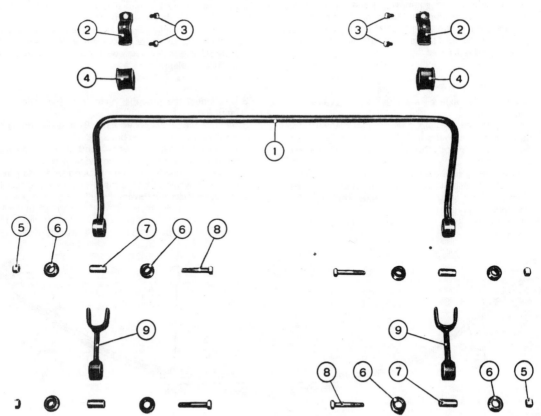

FIG 7:12   Anti-roll bar assembly

Key to Fig 7:12   1 Anti-roll bar   2 Anti-roll bar-to-underbody clamps   3 Clamp screws   4 Rubber cushions   5 Anti-roll bar-to-link and axle housing self-locking nuts   6 Rubber bushings   7 Spacer   8 Mounting screws   9 Anti-roll bar-to-axle housing links

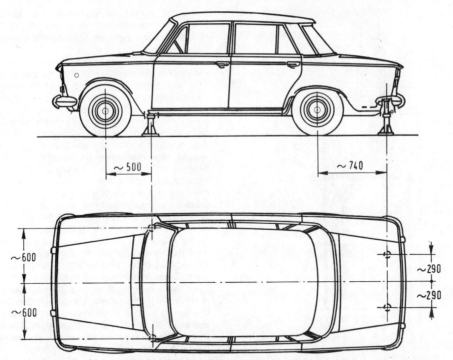

FIG 7:13   Checking suspension height

Key to Fig 7:13 $500=19\frac{11}{16}$ $600=23\frac{5}{8}$ $740=29\frac{1}{8}$ $290=11\frac{11}{32}$

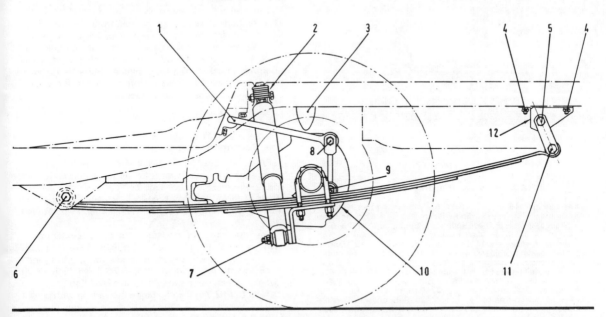

FIG 7:14   Setting diagram for rear suspension

Key to Fig 7:14   1 Anti-roll bar   2 Crossmember, upper damper mounting   3 Rear axle rubber bumpers   4 Rear damper mounting bracket-to-underbody nuts   5 Shackle-to-mounting bracket pin   6 Semi-elliptic spring-to-underbody front mounting pin   7 Lower damper self-locking nut   8 Anti-roll bar link-to-bar screw   9 Anti-roll bar link-to-rear axle screw   10 Rear axle   11 Semi-elliptic spring-to-shackle pin   12 Semi-elliptic spring-to-underbody mounting bracket

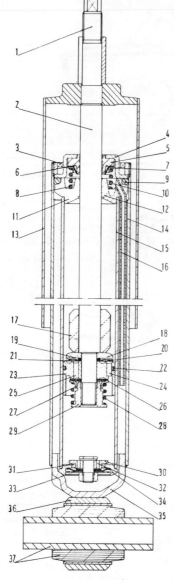

FIG 7:15   View of hydraulic damper

Key to Fig 7:15   1 Body mounting threaded end
2 Stem   3 Upper cylinder locknut   4 Packing case
5 Stem packing   6 Blade spring   7 Spring cup   8 Packing
spring   9 Lower cylinder packing   10 Vapour pocket
bleeding chamber   11 Stem guide bushing   12 Vapour
pocket bleeding capillary hole   13 Dust shield   14 Outer
cylinder and reservoir   15 Inner cylinder   16 Vapour
pocket draining tube   17 Rubber buffer   18 Inlet valve
lift check disc   19 Valve lift adjusting washer   20 Valve
star spring   21 Inlet valve   22 Piston ring   23 Piston
24 Inlet valve piston holes   25 Rebound valve piston
holes   26 Rebound valve   27 Spring guide case
28 Rebound valve spring   29 Piston plug   30 Transfer
valve   31 Transfer valve annular space   32 Compression
valve ports   33 Gradual action compression valve
34 Transfer and compression valve carrier plug   35 Lower
plug   36 Lower attaching eye to control arm   37 Rubber
bushing

springs to the vehicle. Whenever both springs and their associated components are removed, it is a good plan to identify each part with the side of the vehicle to which it belongs.

When removing only one spring there is no need to disconnect the propeller shaft or the brake hydraulic line. The handbrake cable clamp must be released but the cable need not be disconnected from the brake drum.

Jack up and safely support the rear of the vehicle with both road wheels clear of the ground. Remove the wheel from the side where the spring is to be replaced. Put a jack under the axle at each side to just take the axle weight. Now disconnect the damper, U-bolts, rear spring bracket and front spring mounting bolt. The spring will now be free of the vehicle and can be taken away for cleaning and service. Replace it by reversing the removal procedure noting that the large spring eye fits at the forward side of the axle (see **FIG 7:10**).

The spring may be dismantled by prising the clips 2, 3, 5 and 7 apart and then undoing bolt 4. If any of the intermediate leaves are broken the whole spring must be renewed as only the main leaf is supplied as a replacement. Clean and wire brush the leaves for this inspection. Keep them in order of removal although wrong assembly is unlikely. If the rubber bonded bushes have worn at the spring ends or in the mounting bracket these can be pressed out and new ones pressed in. A heavy vice will perform this operation satisfactorily. If a press is used the load should not exceed 1100 lb (500 kg).

Renew the rubber pads of the leaf clips if they are damaged and when the spring is being assembled pack the recess at the leaf ends with FIAT CA.1 G grease.

Refer to **FIG 7:11** for correct assembly of the rear mounting bracket.

The anti-roll bar assembly is shown at **FIG 7:12**. The method of removing the bar from the vehicle is straightforward and will be easily apparent upon inspection. When the bar is released, clean it carefully and inspect for cracks or other damage. Renew if at all doubtful. Check all the links, pins and bushes for wear and renew where necessary. Refit the bar to the vehicle by reversing the dismantling process.

7:9 Setting the rear suspension

When the suspension has been dismantled and reassembled, the vehicle must be set to its normal loaded condition before any bolts are tightened which have the effect of locking rubber bushes in a particular position. If this is not done, the bushes will fail after a very limited life.

See that the tyre pressures are as specified in the owner's handbook (front 21 lb/sq inch (1.5 kg/sq cm), Saloon and Station wagon. Rear, Saloon 25 lb/sq inch (1.75 kg/sq cm), Station wagon 28 lb/sq inch (2.00 kg/sq cm) then stand the vehicle on a level floor.

Refer to **FIG 7:13** and arrange the vehicle with height gauges placed where shown. The front gauges must be set to $9\frac{3}{16}$ inch (233 mm) and the rear to $14\frac{31}{64}$ inch (368 mm). Now load the vehicle until the underframe just touches the top of the gauges. These gauges may be improvised and the help of several assistants enlisted to sit in the car until the loading is right.

Refer to **FIG 7:4** and tighten the following bolts:
Item 6, front spring eyebolts—68 lb ft (9.5 kg m).
Items 5 and 11, rear spring shackle bolts—68 lb ft (9.5 kg m).
Item 7, lower damper mounting nuts—tight enough to compress bush.
Item 8, anti-roll bar link—tight enough to just compress bushes.
Item 9, link to axle—as item 8.

Check that all other bolts and nuts are properly tightened, unload the car and remove the gauges.

7:10 The hydraulic dampers

A sectional view of a damper is given at **FIG 7:15**. To test a damper. remove it from the vehicle by releasing the bolt at the top and the nut holding the lower mounting to the spring saddle then clamp it vertically in a vice, holding it by the lower mounting boss.

Grip the lower diameter and move the halves back and forth, to and fro. There should be a greatly increased resistance when attempting to extend the damper. If there is little or no resistance the damper should be exchanged for a replacement. Unless the vehicle has done a very low mileage it is wise to always renew dampers in pairs.

The private owner is advised not to attempt to overhaul these dampers since any inaccuracy in setting can dangerously affect the handling of the vehicle. The FIAT agent has special equipment on which dampers are tested to see that they conform to the manufacturer's damping diagrams.

7:11 Fault diagnosis

(a) Noisy propeller shaft

1 Wrongly assembled, marks not in alignment
2 Bent shaft
3 Loose mounting bolts
4 Worn flexible joint bushes
5 Worn sliding joint
6 Damaged or worn centre bearing
7 Worn centre bearing rubber bonding
8 Worn or dry universal joints

(b) Rear axle noisy, general

1 Brake backing plate bolts loose
2 Axle shaft bearing worn
3 Lack of oil
4 Bent axle shaft
5 Damaged axle shaft splines
6 Damaged differential bearings
7 Broken leaf spring or loose spring
8 Faulty damper

(c) Axle noisy on drive

1 Damaged differential bearings
2 Crownwheel and pinion too far in mesh
3 Axle shaft bearing damaged
4 Lack of oil

(d) Axle noisy on overrun

1 Crownwheel and pinion too far out of mesh
2 Excessive play in pinion bearings
3 Pinion bearing spacer collapsed

(e) Axle noisy at all times

1 Worn bearings
2 Insufficient crownwheel and pinion backlash

(f) Axle noisy when turning corners

1 Bevel gears too tight on shaft
2 Bevel gear face uneven
3 Side gears seized in differential case

(g) Noisy rear suspension

1 Unbalanced wheels
2 Badly adjusted brakes
3 Broken spring
4 Worn bushes in springs or anti-roll bar
5 Damaged damper cover fouling lower body
6 Damper fluid leaking
7 Damper valves stuck

CHAPTER 8

FRONT SUSPENSION AND HUBS

8:1 Description

The front suspension consists of an upper wishbone and lower link controlled by coil springs and hydraulic dampers. An anti-roll bar is mounted between the right and lefthand units. The suspension is particularly well designed to resist longitudinal movement incorporating as it does a strut between the lower swinging link and the chassis. The whole suspension assembly is mounted on a crossmember bolted to the body structure. This crossmember can be renewed in case of damage. It also carries the engine forward mountings. The kingpins are ball joints which are integral with the swinging links. **FIG 8:1** shows a sectional view of the lefthand assembly.

The hubs are mounted on taper roller bearings and carry the discs for the disc brakes.

8:2 Routine maintenance

There are six greasing points in all, three at each side. Two are shown in **FIG 8:1,** one at the top ball joint and one at the bottom joint on which the stub axle swivels. These must be regularly greased since the housings are an integral part of the swinging links and wear at this point will mean renewal of the whole link. The other grease nipples are situated one at each side of the vehicle on the ball joint which attaches the reaction strut to the body and the remaining two on the ball joints of the other stub axle swivel. Use FIAT Jota 1 grease for all these six grease nipples and pump in enough to fill the housings but do not overdo the greasing such that grease is exuded over all adjacent parts. All the rest of the suspension is mounted on rubber bushes for which no maintenance is required. It is advisable to jack up the vehicle and inspect the suspension components at regular intervals, looking carefully at the rubber bushes for any signs of failure. Check the tightness of all nuts and bolts at the same time. The hydraulic dampers are not adjustable and require no servicing or maintenance. In the event of failure they must be renewed.

8:3 The front hubs

To remove a hub proceed as follows:
1 Loosen the wheel studs then jack up and safely support the front of the vehicle. Remove the road wheel.
2 The brake caliper must be removed and this means that the hydraulic circuit must be disconnected. Unfortunately the caliper cannot be released and held up out of the way temporarily since it is connected by

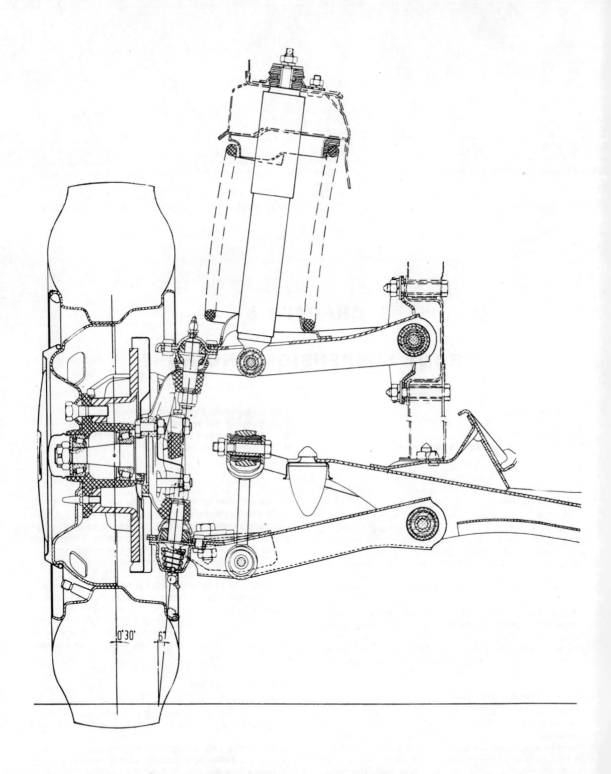

0°30'   6'

FIG 8:1   Sectional view of front suspension

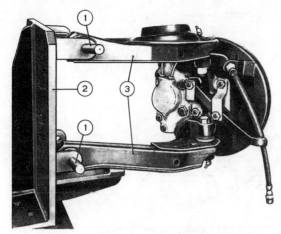

FIG 8 : 2   Hydraulic brake pipe mounting

Key to Fig 8 : 2   1 Bearing pins   2 Fixture   3 Suspension arms

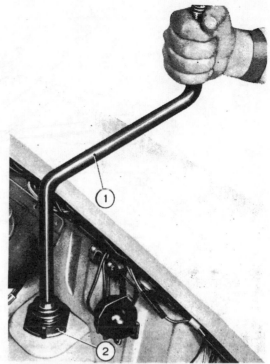

FIG 8 : 3   Spring compressor, top view

Key to Fig 8 : 3   1 Handle   2 Flange of tool fitted to spring seat

a rigid steel pipe to the hose mounting on the back-plate (see **FIG 8 : 2**). Either place a hose clamp across the hose and tighten it to block the hose or plug the hydraulic reservoir as described in **Chapter 7**. Now disconnect the steel pipe either at the hose connection or the caliper. Plug the pipe and the caliper orifice to prevent dirt entering. Remove the brake pads as described in **Chapter 10**.

3 Knock back the locking tags and remove the two bolts holding the caliper to the mounting plate, then lift the caliper away. Store in a clean place.

4 Pull the hub cap from the centre of the hub then extract and discard the splitpin. Undo the axle nut and remove it and the tag washer. The hub should now pull off the stub axle. If not, it will be necessary to make up a puller from a flat strip of steel or better still, channel section, through which three bolts can be passed, two to tighten up in the threaded holes in the hub flange while the centre one presses on the end of the axle and pulls the hub clear. The inner race will almost certainly stay on the stub axle and a puller will be needed to remove this.

5 Undo the screws holding the brake disc to the hub and remove the disc.

Thoroughly wash all the parts in paraffin and dry off. Examine the races for cracks, pitting, flaking or dis-colouration. See that the rollers are not chipped or pitted. If either of the race inner elements has been rotating on the axle so as to show signs of wear, the axle must be renewed. Pay particular attention to the surface of the axle on which the oil seal runs. Any roughness which cannot be entirely removed by the use of very fine emery-cloth will mean renewal of the axle since the seal will quickly fail.

If there are signs that the seal has been allowing grease to escape, first see that it is not just due to an overfilled hub. Any doubt here and the seal should be renewed. Prise out the old one but before fitting the new seal make sure that the outer element of the inner race does not need renewing. If it does, it can either be pulled out or drifted

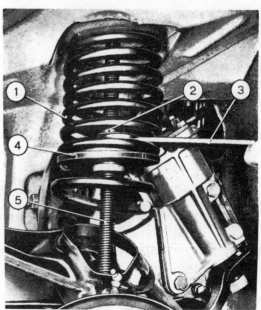

FIG 8 : 4   Spring compressor, lower view

Key to Fig 8 : 4   1 Spring holding runner   2 Locking runner   3 Spanner   4 Lower flange   5 Centre threaded mandrel

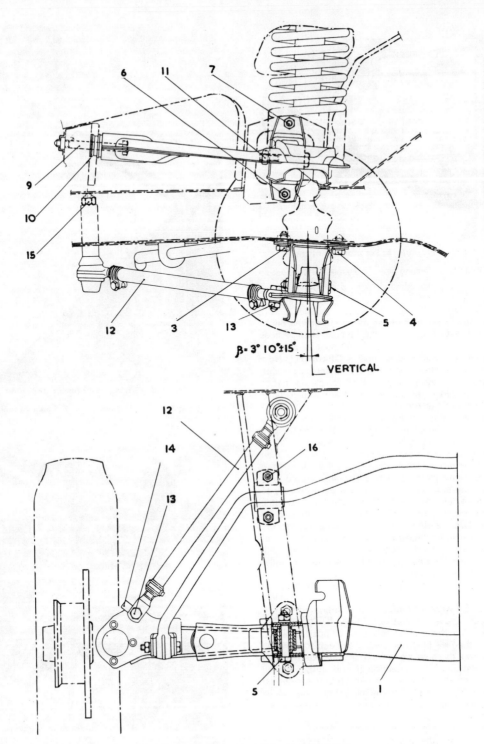

$\beta = 3° 10' \pm 15'$

VERTICAL

FIG 8 : 5   Reaction strut fitted to lower link

Key to Fig 8:5   1 Crossmember   3-4 Crossmember bolts   5 Lower arm bolt   6-7 Upper arm bracket nuts   9 Upper arm front mounting bolt   10 Castor shims   11 Upper arm mounting bolt   12 Reaction strut   13 Strut yoke bolt   14 Yoke shims   15 Reaction strut ball joint nut   16 Anti-roll bar mounting bolts

out from the outer end of the hub. Press the new race in squarely against its seating. Do not try and drift a new race element in. Smear the outside diameter of the seal with a little non-hardening jointing cement and press this into the hub with the lips facing inwards. The outer element of the outer race can be renewed in the same way as that of the inner race.

To rebuild a hub, reverse the dismantling process, making sure that new locking washers and a new splitpin are fitted. The brakes will have to be bled as described in **Chapter 10**. Tighten the caliper mounting bolts to 72 lb ft (10.0 kg m) and bend over the new lockplates. To obtain the correct wheel bearing preload, tighten the axle nut to 22 lb ft (3.0 kg m) slacken back $\frac{1}{6}$ of a turn and insert the splitpin. Open the ends to prevent it from working out. Spin the hub to seat the bearings. The recess in the hub between the bearings should be packed with FIAT MR grease but do not overfill. See that a smear of grease was put on the seal bearing surface before the hub was assembled so that the seal does not run dry at first. Put a little of the same grease in the hub cap and tap it back into the hub. Replace the road wheel and lower the vehicle to the ground. Finally tighten the road wheel studs.

8:4 Removing the front suspension

Before attempting to dismantle the front suspension be sure that the tool shown in **FIGS 8:3** and **8:4** (Fiat No. A74112) can be obtained or an equivalent made up. This tool has to hold and compress the spring while work is carried out below it. **The amount of stored energy in the spring is very high and should it be accidentally released, the most serious injury to the operator could be caused. Under no circumstances can any make-shift apparatus or methods be tolerated when dealing with dangerous items such as this.**

The following instructions refer to dismantling either side of the vehicle suspension.

1 Jack up and safely support the front of the vehicle then remove the front road wheels.
2 Open the bonnet and remove the damper top fixings. Grip the squared end of the damper rod and remove the nut and spring washer. Take off the plain washer and the upper circlip. Remove the nuts and washers holding the mounting plate to the body and lift the mounting plate and rubber buffers away. Remove the lower circlip. Now undo the bolt holding the lower end of the damper to the suspension top link (wishbone). Lift the damper straight up through the spring and out from the centre of the upper spring seating in the engine compartment.
3 Insert the spring compressing tool through the hole left by removal of the damper and thread the lower flange through the last but one coil of the spring. Lock it in place then rotate the screwed rod and compress the spring so that it is well clear of the suspension top link. **FIGS 8:3** and **8:4** show the method.
4 Remove the brake and hub assembly as described in the previous section.
5 Refer to **FIG 8:1** and undo the bolt which holds the anti-roll bar to the suspension lower arm. Do not lose any of the spring washers or the spacer.

6 Remove the splitpin, undo the nut and release the ball joint from the track rod end to the steering arm. If a special ball joint puller is not available jar the tapers free by holding a heavy hammer against one side of the steering arm and tapping the other side with a lighter hammer.
7 Remove the locknut, washer and bolt holding the reaction strut to the suspension lower arm (see **FIG 8:5**). Shims may be fitted between the clevis end and the suspension arm. Retain these for reassembly. There is no need to take the reaction strut right off the vehicle unless the forward mounting ball joint is unserviceable. If it is, undo the nut and pull the shank of the joint out of the vehicle body.
8 Refer to **FIG 8:6** and remove the nuts 6 and 7, but do not pull the bracket away at this stage. Undo the bolt 9 and carefully pull it back from the suspension top link. When the bolt is removed the shims 10 will be free. Be particularly careful to keep these together, identified with the position from which they were removed. Now ease the bracket from the studs and save and identify the shims 8. This insistence on the need to be able to replace the shims exactly in their correct order is due to the fact that they control the camber and caster angles.
9 Release the bolt 5 (see **FIG 8:6**), when the upper and lower arms and the stub axle assembly will be released from the vehicle. Unwind the spring compressor and remove the coil spring.
10 The suspension arms can be detached from the stub axle by removing the ball joint nuts and pressing the ball joints out of the stub axle forging. A view of the suspension arms and stub axle before dismantling is given at **FIG 8:7**.

With all the components dismantled the private owner can renew any worn parts but should not under any circumstances attempt to repair any part damaged or distorted by an accident. Renew any thing which is even slightly doubtful or have the suspect part checked by a FIAT agent on the proper jigs. Failure to do this could lead to bad handling of the vehicle, rapid tyre wear or suspension failure. Remember that since the caster and camber angles can be adjusted and that this adjustment must be checked on special equipment, only a FIAT agent can finally set up the suspension to the makers limits. However, the renewal of worn parts such as bushes or ball joints is unlikely to alter the suspension angles.

Refer to **FIG 8:8**. If the ball joint is worn or the rubber bushes show signs of swelling, seizure or distortion, the whole arm must be renewed.

Refer to **FIG 8:9**. If the ball joint is worn the arm must be renewed but if only the rubber bush 1 is suspect this can be renewed without renewing the complete arm. Press the worn bush out using a suitable piece of steel tube to press against the outer sleeve and press in the new bush by the same method.

Examine the reaction struts for slackness of the ball joint and damage to the clamps, clamp bolts or screwed ends of the strut. Look carefully for stripped threads on the clamp bolts.

The anti-roll bar is shown dismantled at **FIG 8:10** which also shows all the bushes and mounting bolts. The parts most likely to wear are the rubber bushes 3 and 10. If the bar seems distorted grip it at its mid-point in a

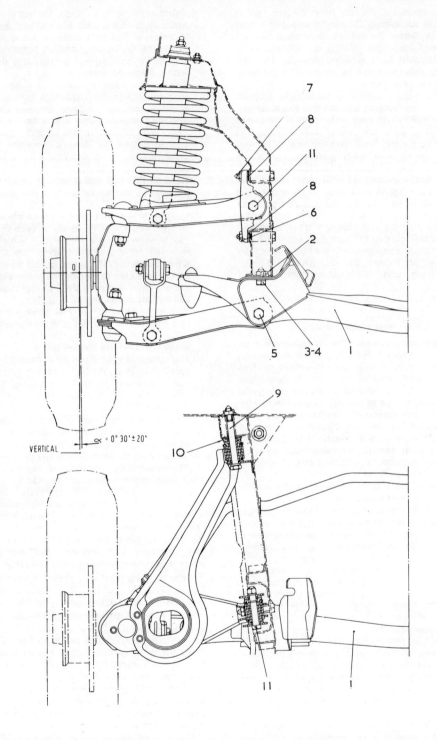

VERTICAL $\alpha = 0°30' \pm 20'$

FIG 8:6   Front suspension adjustment diagram

Key to Fig 8:6   1 Crossmember   2 Dowel   3-4 Crossmember bolts   5 Lower arm bolt   6-7 Upper arm bracket nuts
8 Camber shims   9 Upper arm front mounting bolt   10 Caster shims   11 Upper arm mounting bolt

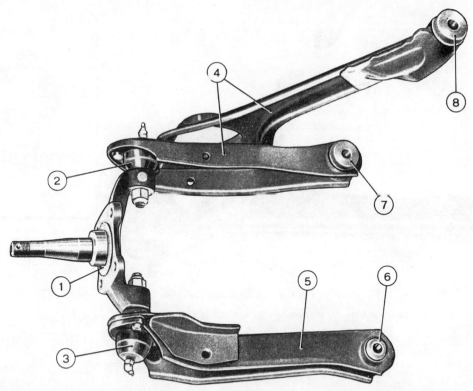

FIG 8:7   Suspension arms and stub axle assembly

Key to Fig 8:7   1 Stub axle   2 Upper ball joint   3 Lower ball joint   4 Upper arm   5 Lower arm   6 Rubber bush
7-8 Rubber bushes

vice with the ends upright as shown in **FIG 8:10**. The ideal method of checking is to pass a mandrel through the two eyes but if no suitable steel bar is available, a very good check can be made by passing a length of strong cord or piano wire through from one side to the other and stretching it taut. The cord should not be attached to the bar but to some convenient wall or similar on each side. Line it up with the side of the bore of one eye and inspect the other eye. Slight out of straightness is permissible up to .06 inch (1.5 mm) and the manufacturers allow for small inaccuracies to be removed by straightening with the bar cold. If the vehicle has been in an accident it is safer to renew the bar if any doubt exists. Note that if new rubber bushes 10 are fitted, the inner groove in the bush should be packed with grease.

Check the free height of the coil spring. This should be approximately 16.34 inch (415 mm). If it is much less than this it has begun to fail and must be renewed. Look carefully for any small cracks in the spring, these usually show as hair-lines running the length of the wire.

Refer to **FIG 8:11**. This shows the crossmember which carries the engine forward mountings and the suspension lower arms. If it has been damaged in a collision it is probable that the body shell itself has suffered distortion and a FIAT agent will have to check the body on the proper jigs. If, however, only the mounting holes are

worn, the crossmember can be renewed easily. Jack up the engine to take its weight off the bearers then unbolt them and also remove the bolts holding the crossmember to the body shell. Lower it from below the vehicle and bolt a new one in place making sure that the dowels 3, are properly located. If the rubber buffers 2, are damaged or missing these can be easily renewed by pressing new ones in. Replace and tighten the engine bearer bolts and remove the jack. The crossmember to body shell bolts must be tightened to 69 lb ft (9.5 kg m) and the engine bearer bolts to 25 lb ft (3.5 kg m).

8:5 Rebuilding the front suspension

1 Commence by assembling the upper and lower suspension arms to the stub axle as illustrated in **FIG 8:7.** Tighten the ball joint nuts to 65 lb ft (9.0 kg m).

2 Fit the brake caliper mounting plate, the disc shield gasket, the disc shield and the steering arm. Fit the four bolts, two long and two short, with new locking plates as shown in **FIG 8:12**. Tighten them to 43 lb ft (6.0 kg m).

3 Fit the bracket to the upper suspension arm but do not tighten the bolt 11 (see **FIG 8:6**) at this stage.

4 Fit the reaction strut and tighten the ball joint nut to 43 lb ft (6.0 kg m).

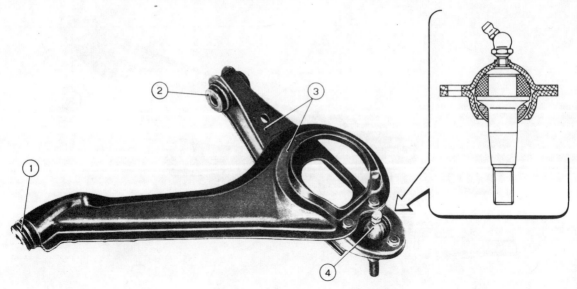

FIG 8:8 Upper suspension arm

Key to Fig 8:8   1-2 Rubber bushes   3 Upper arm   4 Ball joint

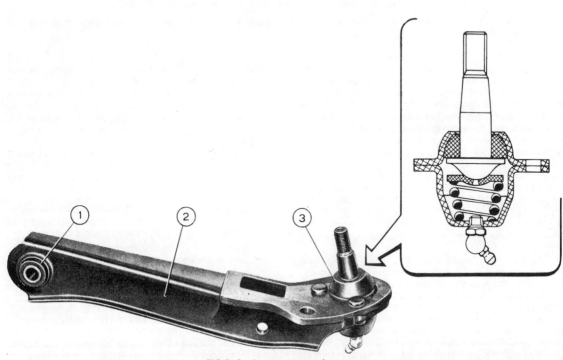

FIG 8:9 Lower suspension arm

Key to Fig 8:9   1 Rubber bush   2 Arm   3 Ball joint

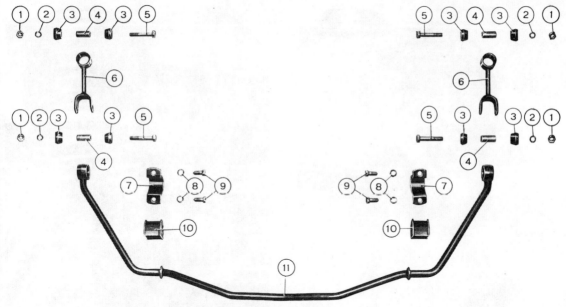

FIG 8:10   Anti-roll bar

Key to Fig 8:10   1 Nuts   2 Spring washers   3 Rubber bushes   4 Spacers   5 Bolts   6 Links   7 Mounting brackets   8 Spring washers   9 Mounting bolts   10 Mounting rubbers   11 Anti-roll bar

5 Fit the anti-roll bar but do not tighten the mounting brackets 7 (see **FIG 8:10**) at this stage.

6 Position the coil spring up under the wing against its seating and fit the compressor tool (FIAT No. A74112). Compress the spring.

7 Fit the suspension lower arm to the crossmember but do not tighten the nut hard at this stage.

8 Fit the upper suspension arm to the vehicle body using the same amount of shims at each point as were removed. **FIG 8:13** shows the shims being fitted to the front mounting point. Do not tighten the bracket nuts 6 and 7 (see **FIG 8:6**), or the bolts 9 and 11 at this stage.

9 Connect the anti-roll bar to the lower suspension arm. The nuts holding the bar to the link and the link to the suspension arm can be tightened hard home.

10 Fit the track rod end ball joint to the steering lever and tighten the nut to 22 lb ft (3.0 kg m). Fit a new splitpin.

11 Fit the reaction strut to the lower suspension arm using the shims removed when dismantling. Do not tighten the nut at this stage. If the strut length has been altered or new parts fitted, the caster angle will have to be reset. This will mean setting the length of the strut and will need the proper gauges as used by a FIAT agent. **Section 8:6** gives an explanation of the methods used to set the suspension angles.

12 Gradually release the coil spring compressor until the spring sits firmly on the seat at the top face of the upper suspension arm. Remove the compressor.

13 Fit the lower rubber bush to the top of the damper, extend the damper as far as possible and lower it down from inside the engine compartment through the coil spring. Fit the bolt through the damper lower mounting and the upper suspension arm. Tighten the nut right home.

14 Place a jack below the lower suspension arm with a piece of wood packing between it and the arm to

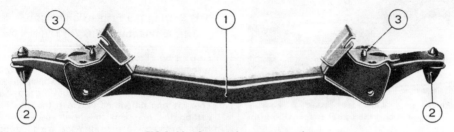

FIG 8:11   Suspension crossmember

Key to Fig 8:11   1 Crossmember   2 Rubber buffers   3 Dowels

FIAT 1300/1500

87

FIG 8:12 Fitting the brake shield and steering arm

Key to Fig 8:12 1 Locknuts 2 Steering arm
3 Suspension arms

FIG 8:14 Fitting shims behind the suspension arm bracket

Key to Fig 8:14 1 Spring 2 Spring compressor 3 Shim
4 Bracket

FIG 8:13 Fitting shims to the upper suspension arm

Key to Fig 8:13 1 Shims 2 Lockplate 3 Spring
washer 4 Bolt 5 Upper arm 6 Spring 7 Spring
compressor

avoid damaging the arm. Operate the jack and raise the suspension against the coil spring until the damper projects through the hole in the upper spring seat. Fit the damper mounting plate and tighten the retaining nuts. Put the upper rubber bush on the damper spindle, then the plain washer, the spring washer and the nut. Grip the squared end of the spindle and tighten the nut. Remove the jack.

15 Refit the hub, brake disc and caliper, and connect the hydraulic pipe as described in **Section 8:3**. Bleed the brakes as described in **Chapter 10**.

16 Refit the road wheels and lower the vehicle to the ground. Finally tighten the road wheels studs.

The suspension must be finally tightened up with the car in the normally loaded condition. **Section 8:6** describes the method.

8:6 Setting the suspension height

Refer to **Chapter 7, FIG 7:13**. This shows the height gauges in position for checking and setting the rear suspension. Proceed as described in **Chapter 7** by placing the car on a level floor with all tyres correctly inflated and with the gauges in the positions shown.

Load the car until it just touches the top of each gauge. There is one difference between the gauge heights for setting the rear and the front suspensions. For both front and rear suspensions the front gauges must be set to $9\frac{3}{16}$ inch (233 mm) but for setting the front suspension the rear gauges must be set to $12\frac{13}{16}$ inch (325 mm). See that the road wheels are in the straight-ahead position.

Now tighten the bolts left loose during assembly as follows:

(a) Lower suspension arm to crossmember bolt to 65 lb ft (9.0 kg m).

(b) The nuts securing the upper suspension arm bracket to the body shell to 39 lb ft (5.4 kg m).

(c) The upper suspension arm to bracket bolt to 43 lb ft (6.0 kg m).

(d) The upper suspension arm front bolt to 43 lb ft (6.0 kg m).

(e) Tighten the anti-roll bar mounting bracket bolts hard home.

Check the reaction strut length as follows:

Remove the nut and bolt connecting the strut to the lower suspension arm. Allow the suspension to settle to its natural position then try to reconnect the strut. Adjust the length of the strut by rotating the sleeve until the bolt will pass through the strut yoke and the lower suspension arm without any forcing. Clamp the strut sleeve with the clamp bolts at each end. If the yoke is slack on the suspension arm fit shims until all play is removed. Finally tighten the nut to 72 lb ft (10.0 kg m).

8:7 Checking the suspension geometry

This is a job for a FIAT agent equipped with the special gauges and fixtures. If the vehicle has been involved in a collision which has damaged any part of the front suspension it is an essential operation. If any parts have been replaced due to normal wear it is still desirable to carry out the operations to ensure that the vehicle handles in accordance with the high standards set by the manufacturer.

The angles are as follows:

Castor .. .. .. 3 deg. 10′ ± 15′
Camber .. .. .. 0 deg. 30′ ± 20′

To set the castor angle, shims are added to or taken away from the front mounting point of the upper suspension arm (see item 10, **FIG 8:6**), coupled with a corresponding adjustment of the reaction strut length (see **FIG 8:5**).

The camber angle is altered by adding to or removing shims 8 (see **FIG 8:6**) from behind the upper suspension bracket. **FIG 8:13** shows the fitting of shims to the upper suspension arm and **FIG 8:14** the shims behind the suspension arm bracket.

The camber angle is increased by adding shims and decreased by removing them. Adding shims to the suspension arm will increase the castor angle and vice versa.

8:8 Fault diagnosis

(a) Wheel bounce

1 Unevenly worn tyre
2 Unequal tyre pressures
3 Incorrect tyre pressure
4 Unbalanced wheel
5 Weak coil spring
6 Damper inoperative
7 Damaged wheel rim

(b) Excessive tyre wear

1 Incorrect camber
2 Incorrect tyre pressures
3 Fast cornering
4 Loose wheel bearing
5 Wheel wobble
6 Partly seized suspension arm

(c) Vehicle pulls to one side

1 Unequal tyre pressures
2 Incorrect suspension geometry
3 Bent stub axle or steering arm
4 Damper inoperative
5 Weak coil spring

(d) Noisy suspension

1 Lack of lubrication
2 Damper failed
3 Anti-roll bar loose
4 Suspension bushes worn
5 Ball joints slack
6 Reaction strut broken or loose
7 Worn wheel bearings

(e) Wheel wobble

1 Uneven tyre pressures
2 Worn or slack wheel bearings
3 Damper failed
4 Worn suspension joints
5 Incorrect suspension geometry

CHAPTER 9

THE STEERING GEAR

9:1 Description

The steering gear is of the worm and roller type with a gear ratio of 16.4 to 1. It requires three full turns of the steering wheel to turn from lock to lock. From the steering box a drop arm is connected to an intermediate track rod which passes under the car and is supported at the further end by an idler arm. Near each end of the intermediate rod a short adjustable track rod transfers the movement to a steering lever on each stub axle.

9:2 Routine maintenance and adjustment

The oil evel in the steering box must be inspected regularly and fresh SAE.90.EP oil added when necessary. To check the oil level, remove the plug from the top of the steering box. This plug can be seen in FIG 9:1 just in front of the adjusting screw and locknut (see items 1 and 2). If the level falls by the equivalent of a teaspoonful in a year the box is leaking enough for an overhaul to be needed. A worn roller shaft, shaft bearings or seal will probably be the cause of the leakage unless the end plate has become loose. With the front of the car raised so that both road wheels are clear of the ground, set the wheels straight-ahead and then turn the steering wheel from full lock to full lock. See that the same amount of movement of the steering wheel is required from straight-ahead to each full lock. If this is not so, check all the linkage for damage and distortion. It may be that an incorrect assembly has been made at some time but the cause must be found and remedied.

Make sure that the car is safely supported, then check each ball joint for movement. Owing to the spring seat incorporated in each joint it is just possible to compress the joint slightly with a short bar between the back of the joint and an adjacent part of the vehicle. **Do not apply heavy pressure or the spring seat can be damaged.** If no movement in an axial direction can be felt with **very light hand pressure** the joint is in good condition. Pump in FIAT Jota 1 grease until a small quantity exudes from the rubber boot. Do not overfill. Wipe away all surplus after using the grease gun. See that all nuts on the ball joints, steering box and idler arm bracket are tight and that splitpins are in place in the ball joint nuts. See FIG 9:2 for a view of a typical ball joint.

The ball joints and the idler arm are not adjustable but the steering box can be adjusted to remove all backlash from the worm and roller. With the road wheels

FIG 9:1 Steering box installed on vehicle

Key to Fig 9:1
1 Adjusting screw   2 Locknut
3 Steering box   4 Mounting bolts   5-6 Lockstops
7 Drop arm

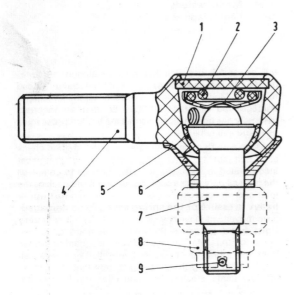

FIG 9:2 Sectioned view of ball joint

Key to Fig 9:2   1 Cover   2 Spring   3 Spring seat
4 Threaded shank   5 Socket   6 Boot   7 Ball stud
8 Nut   9 Splitpin

supported clear of the ground set the steering straight-ahead. Refer to **FIG 9:1** and slacken locknut 2. With a screwdriver, screw the adjusting screw 1 down until all backlash is taken up. Rock the steering wheel slightly and watch that the drop arm moves immediately. The amount of backlash can be felt at the wheel rim if the rim is held lightly with the finger tips while rocking it backwards and forwards a few degrees. Tighten the locknut and again check for backlash. Turn the steering from lock to lock to make sure that there is no tight spot or binding at any point. Lower the car to the ground

9:3 Removing the steering box

Reference to **Chapter 6, FIG 6:14,** will show the assembly of the gearchange mechanism to the steering column and **FIG 9:3** shows the steering column fitted with either the standard ignition switch or the anti-theft locking switch.

Remove the steering gear as follows:

1 Disconnect both battery leads and the horn lead. Jack up and safely support the front of the vehicle so that the road wheel nearest to the steering box can be removed. This will give room to work on the box.
2 Release the screws holding the centre trim to the steering wheel then undo the centre nut and pull the wheel from the steering shaft (see **FIG 9:4**).
3 Undo the ignition switch ring nut then remove the five screws holding the upper and lower halves of the steering column covers (see items 7 and 13 in **FIG 9:3**).
4 Disconnect the direction indicator and lighting switch leads.
5 Loosen the gearlever support to steering column nut and bolt.
6 Release the lockplate and remove the gearchange rod to gearlever bolt, slide the direction indicator, light switch assembly, the gearchange lever and the support from the column.
7 Undo the bolts and remove the steering column to facia mounting bracket.
8 Working from the engine side of the bulkhead, release the clamp holding the steering column outer tube then slide the tube up into the vehicle and off the steering shaft.
9 Remove the splitpin and disconnect the gearchange operating rod from the operating rod lever, remove the operating lever to gearchange rod bolt.
10 Disconnect the reversing lamp leads.
11 Remove the pivot splitpin from the steering housing and slide off the plain washer, the spring and the gear selector lever.
12 Remove the circlip from the end of the gearchange rod then carefully pull the rod back and into the vehicle. An assistant is needed to hold the components which will be released from the end of the rod as it is removed. These components in order of removal are, the outer cup, reverse gear spring, inner cup, pivot, selector lever return spring, shoulder washer and selector lever. **FIG 6:14** shows these items clearly.
13 Undo the nut and remove the ball joint from the drop arm.
14 Remove the reversing lamp switch by undoing both mounting screws.

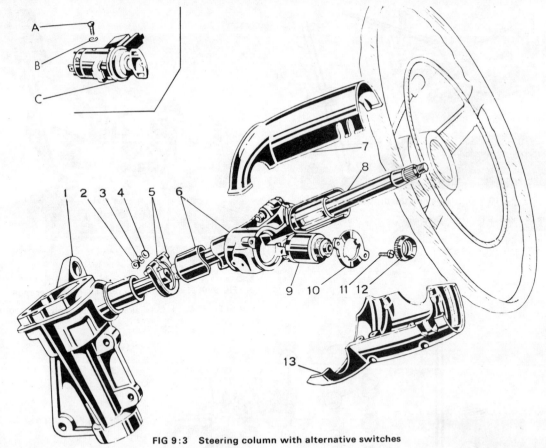

FIG 9:3 Steering column with alternative switches

Key to Fig 9:3 1 Steering box 2 Clamp nut 3 Spring washer 4 Plain washer 5 Clamp 6 Column 7 Cover 8 Wormshaft 9 Ignition switch (early type) 10 Locking plate 11 Screw 12 Nut 13 Cover **A** Mounting screw **B** Spring washer **C** Ignition switch (late type with anti-theft lock)

15 Unscrew the three bolts and self-locking nuts which hold the steering box to the body shell. The steering box will now come away by lowering it and pulling downwards and towards the front of the vehicle.

9:4 Servicing the steering gearbox

Some of the illustrations in this Section show the steering box attached to a special jig. This is a service tool which permits the movement of the box from one attitude to another to be made quickly as well as holding the box securely and safely. An ordinary vice can be used instead but be careful where the pressure of the jaws is applied.

Dismantle the steering gear in the following sequence:

1 Remove the filler plug, turn the box upside down and allow all the oil to drain out. Do not save this oil.

2 Remove the drop arm locknut and spring washer then attach a heavy puller to the drop arm and pull it from the roller shaft. There is no need to mark the position of the drop arm and shaft since a double spaced spline on each component ensures that they can only assemble one way, **FIG 9:5** shows the drop arm being pulled from the shaft.

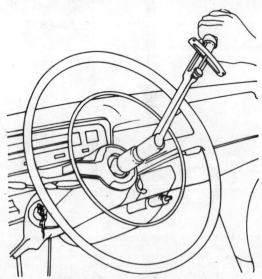

FIG 9:4 Removing the steering wheel

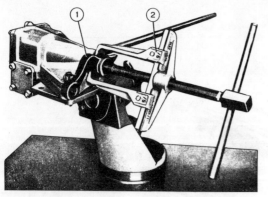

FIG 9:5   Removing the drop arm

Key to Fig 9:5   1 Drop arm   2 Puller (Part No. A40005/1/5)

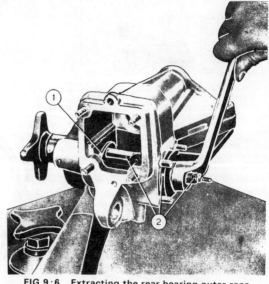

FIG 9:6   Extracting the rear bearing outer race

Key to Fig 9:6   1 Outer race   2 Puller (Part No. A47004)

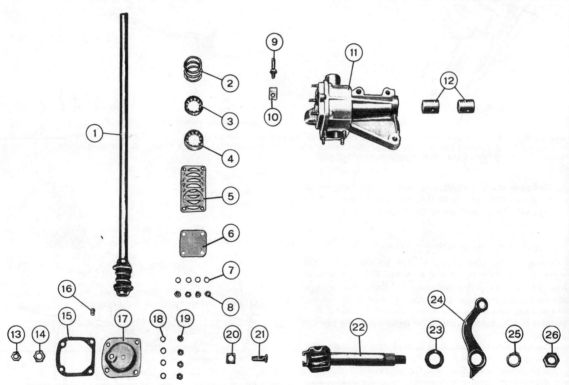

FIG 9:7   Steering box components

Key to Fig 9:7   1 Steering column and worm assembly   2 Worm rear bearing shims   3 Worm rear roller bearing   4 Worm front roller bearing   5 Worm front roller bearing shims   6 Worm thrust cover   7 Spring washers   8 Cover nuts   9 Gear selector lever pivot   10 Pivot lockplate   11 Steering housing   12 Roller shaft bushings in steering housing   13 Roller shaft adjusting screw nut   14 Lockplate   15 Steering housing cover gasket   16 Steering housing plug   17 Steering housing cover   18 Spring washers   19 Cover mounting nuts   20 Adjusting screw lockplate   21 Roller shaft adjusting screw   22 Roller shaft assembly   23 Roller shaft oil seal   24 Drop arm   25 Spring washer   26 Drop arm nut

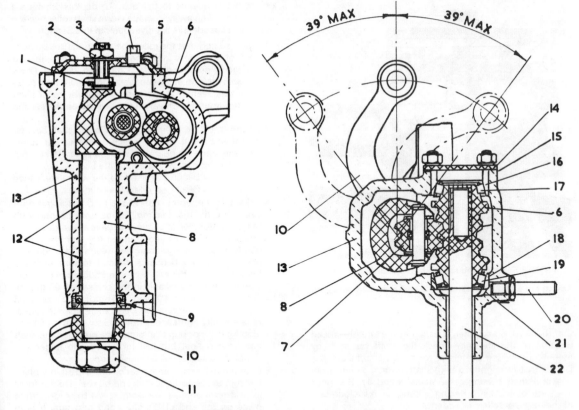

FIG 9:8   Sectional view of steering box

Key to Fig 9:8   1 Roller shaft adjusting screw shim   2 Adjusting screw nut   3 Roller shaft adjusting screw   4 Steering housing plug   5 Steering housing cover   6 Worm   7 Worm roller   8 Roller shaft   9 Roller shaft gasket   10 Drop arm   11 Drop arm-to-roller shaft nut   12 Roller shaft steering housing bushings   13 Steering gear housing   14 Worm thrust cover   15 Front roller bearing shims   16 Front roller bearing cup   17 Front roller bearing cone   18 Rear roller bearing cup   19 Rear roller bearing cone   20 Gear selector lever mounting pivot   21 Rear bearing shims   22 Drop arm

3 Hold the steering box by its mounting flange with the filler plug aperture uppermost. Release the adjusting screw locking plate and then loosen the locknut. Unscrew the locknut completely from the adjusting screw.

4 Undo the four nuts from the cover and just free it from the main box. Now screw the adjusting screw inwards and the cover will come away leaving the roller shaft in place. Alternatively the cover can be lifted straight off with the roller shaft attached to the adjusting screw. Be careful not to strain the screw if this latter method is adopted.

5 With the roller shaft removed, undo the four nuts holding the cover over the lower end of the steering worm shaft, remove the cover complete with the adjusting shims which will be found behind it. Keep these shims together with the cover.

6 Tap gently on the steering wheel end of the worm shaft until the worm with the two taper roller bearing races can be extracted from the box.

7 If the outer element of the rear roller bearing is to be renewed, a special puller, FIAT No. A47004 must be

used as shown in **FIG 9:6**. When the outer element is removed, the shims which are fitted behind it can be extracted from the seating. Keep these shims together.

8 Drive out the oil seal from the lower end of the roller shaft bush housing. If the roller shaft bushes are worn new ones can be fitted but they must be reamed in position to 1.1298 inch to 1.1307 inch (28.698 to 28.720 mm). The criterion here is a clearance between the shaft and bushes of between .0003 inch and .002 inch (.008 and .051 mm). If the clearance exceeds .004 inch (.10 mm) the bushes must be renewed. The FIAT reamer, Part No. A90336, is essential.

Refer to **FIG 9:7**. This shows all the components of the steering box. Thoroughly clean everything and inspect for wear and damage.

The worm shaft (see item 1). Any indentations, seizure marks, scores or pitting of the worm must involve rejection. Heavy wear marks come under the heading of indentations. A good shaft will just exhibit a bearing mark right at the centre of the length of the worm showing

FIG 9:9 Fitting the roller shaft adjusting screw

Key to Fig 9:9 1 Locknut 2 Lockplate 3 Adjusting screw 4 Cover studs 5 Roller shaft

that the roller is accurately meshed in the straight-ahead position of the steering. Check the shaft for truth by mounting between centres or rolling on a surface plate. Do not try to straighten a bent shaft, it must be renewed.

Worm shaft bearings (see items 3 and 4). Renew if any sign of cracking, flaking, pitting or discolouration of the tracks or rollers is evident.

Main casting (see item 11). Check for cracks and if any are found, renew the box. Remove any burrs found at mating faces.

Roller shaft bushes (see item 12). See paragraph 8 under the dismantling instructions.

Oil seal (see item 23). If the bushes are being renewed, this item will be renewed as a matter of course. Otherwise, unless severe oil leakage has occurred, this seal will outlast the life of the vehicle since there is very little movement between the shaft and the sealing surfaces.

Drop arm (see item 24). Examine for damage or cracks. (A method of crack detecting is described in the 'Hints on maintenance and overhaul section' at the end of this manual).

Roller shaft (see item 22). With a micrometer, measure the shaft diameter. The dimension must be between 1.1287 inch to 1.1295 inch (28.669 to 28.690 mm) and the bearing surfaces must be bright and unscratched. See that he roller has no end float; is not tight on its bearing pin but has no measurable slack. Check that the roller faces which mesh with the worm are bright and undamaged.

9:5 Rebuilding the steering gearbox

Refer to **FIG 9:8** Notice particularly how the roller meshes with the worm in the straight-ahead position. The roller shaft bearing pin lies parallel to the worm shaft and the roller is right at the centre of the length of the worm. This condition is obtained by moving the position of the worm relative to the box. To do this, shims are added to or taken away from the worm shaft roller bearing seatings. Exact details are given later in this Section.

1 It is assumed that the roller shaft bearings are serviceable or that new ones have been pressed in and reamed as described earlier. Coat the outside of a new oil seal with non-hardening jointing cement then press it into its seating at the outer end of the roller shaft bearing housing. Smear a little gear oil on the sealing lips.

2 Fit the adjusting shims to the rear worm shaft bearing seat then drive the bearing race outer element home. Use the same number of shims that were taken out even if new bearings are being fitted.

3 Fit the roller bearing cages onto the worm shaft then smear a little clean gear oil on their surfaces.

4 Assemble the worm shaft to the box, pushing it right back onto the rear bearing. Fit the front bearing with the same number of shims that were taken out when the box was dismantled. Tighten the four cover nuts gently and evenly, rotating the worm shaft continually. If the shaft becomes difficult to turn with the fingers, remove the end cover and add an extra shim. These shims are available in thicknesses of .0039 inch and .0059 inch (.10 and .15 mm). The specified torque required to turn the worm shaft when the cover nuts are fully tightened is from .09 to .47 lb ft (.013 to .065 kg m). For practical purposes, provided the shaft has no end float but just turns between finger and thumb pressure, it will be satisfactory.

5 Coat the roller shaft with gear oil and slide it into place through the bearing bushes and oil seal. Do not force in or drop it against the worm. Hold the drop arm in place on the end of the shaft and turn until it is in the straight-ahead position shown in **FIG 9:8**. If it appears that the roller is meshing with the worm as illustrated continue the assembly. Remove the drop arm.

6 Fit the adjusting screw and shim to the roller shaft, place a new gasket on the face of the box, then fit the top cover. Screw the adjusting screw through the cover until the cover seats against the gasket then continue turning the adjusting screw enough to ensure that the roller shaft is well clear of the worm shaft. Tighten the cover nuts. **FIG 9:9** shows this operation in progress.

7 Fit the drop arm to the roller shaft but do not tighten at this stage. Hold the box as shown in **FIG 9:8** and set the drop arm to straight-ahead. Now screw the adjusting screw down until all backlash between the roller shaft and the worm has been taken up. Do not force the screw beyond this point. Fit a new locking tag washer then the locknut. Tighten the locknut and check that the adjustment has not altered. If correct bend up the locking washer.

8 Now turn the worm shaft from lock to lock and see that the drop arm moves an equal amount each side of straight-ahead. It should move through an angle of 39 deg. each way. Check that up to approximately 30 deg. each way, no backlash appears. If the drop arm moves through a greater angle one way than the other, then the worm is not properly central in the box and the roller shaft is not meshing with the centre of the worm. The box must be dismantled and the worm

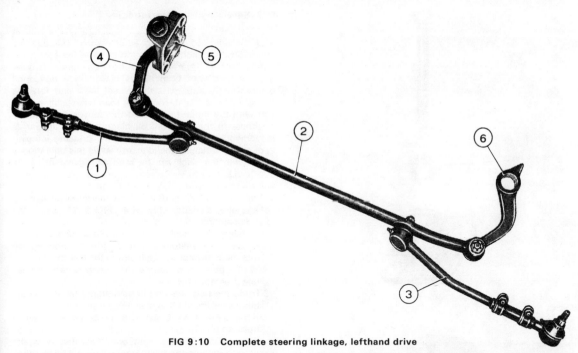

FIG 9:10   Complete steering linkage, lefthand drive

Key to Fig 9:10   1 Righthand track rod   2 Intermediate track rod   3 Lefthand track rod   4 Idler arm   5 Idler bracket
6 Drop arm

position altered by either removing shims from behind the rear bearing and adding to those at the front bearing (to allow the drop arm to move more to the right) or vice versa. Keep the same thickness of shims over all so that the bearing preload is not disturbed. Rebuild the box and again check the movement.

When the worm and roller shaft setting is correct the drop arm must be finally fitted. Tighten the nut to between 145 and 174 lb ft (20 to 24 kg m). Grip the drop arm in the vice while doing this so that the load is not transmitted through the roller and worm. Be careful not to damage the drop arm, particularly at the eye where the ball joint will fit.

10 Fill the box with SAE.90.EP oil and replace the filler plug.

9:6   Replacing the steering gearbox

The vehicle must be jacked up and safely supported at the front. The road wheel nearest to the steering box must be removed.

Proceed as follows:

1 From below the vehicle, insert the steering shaft up through the bulkhead and hold the box against its seating on the body shell. Have an assistant slide the column outer sleeve down and over the shaft until it locates on the box with the dowel in the slot. Fit and tighten the clamp (see item 5, **FIG 9:3**).

2 Secure the steering box to the body shell with the three bolts and self-locking nuts. Tighten these to 22 lb ft (3.0 kg m).

3 Refit the reversing lamp switch and tighten the two screws hard onto the serrated washers.

4 Slide the gearchange rod down from inside the vehicle then, working from the engine side of the bulkhead, fit the operating lever and tighten the bolt, the shouldered washer, the gear selector return spring and the rod pivot. Slide the end of the rod through the bearing on the steering box.

5 Fit the inner cup, reverse spring and the outer cup to the gearchange rod and lock all these in place with the circlip. See that the circlip seats properly in the groove in the rod.

6 Install the spring, plain washer and selector lever on the pivot attached to the steering box and fit a new splitpin to the lever.

7 Connect the upper end of the gear operating adjustable rod to the lever and secure it with a plain washer and a new splitpin.

8 Connect the reversing lamp leads to the switch and fit the rubber boot.

9 From inside the vehicle, slide the gearchange lever and support assembly over the steering column and the gearchange rod. Secure the lever to the rod by means of the bolt, nut, spring washer and locking washer. Bend the locking washer over the bolt head.

10 Tighten the gearlever support bolt to lock the support to the column.

11 Fit the steering column support bracket, complete with the upper and lower packing pieces, to the body shell and tighten the two bolts. At this stage check that the steering shaft still rotates freely. If not, release the steering box bolts and the support bracket bolts to

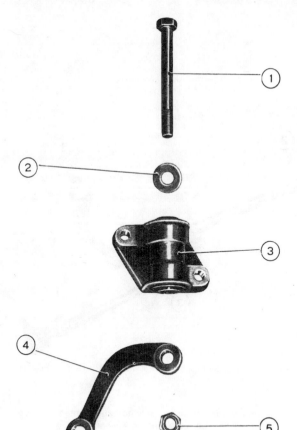

FIG 9:11   Idler dismantled

Key to Fig 9:11   1 Idler pivot bolt   2 Plain washer
3 Bracket   4 Idler arm   5 Self-locking nut

9:7 Servicing the steering idler

If slackness develops in the idler assembly, the bracket must be renewed since no adjustment is possible. To check on the condition of the idler, raise the front road wheel furthest from the idler from the ground. Now grip the tyre with both hands placed in a horizontal plane and try and twist the wheel back and forth as though moving the steering. The road wheel still in contact with the ground will resist this movement and any slackness in the idler will be magnified and appear as movement of the wheel to which the pressure is being applied. By watching the idler arm while this operation is proceeding the slack can be seen as movement of the arm in addition to movement of the wheel. This check will also show up any defective ball joints.

Reference to **FIG 9:10** will show the complete steering linkage and idler assembly while **FIG 9:11** shows the idler dismantled.

To remove the steering idler proceed as follows:

1 Remove the splitpin and undo the nut holding the intermediate track rod ball joint to the idler arm.
2 With a puller or by jarring the tapers, release the ball joint from the idler arm.
3 Undo the two nuts and bolts holding the idler to the body shell then lift the idler away from the vehicle.
4 Refer to **FIG 9:11**. Undo nut 5 and dismantle the arm 4 from the bolt 1.

Examine the bracket, bolt and arm. Renew where necessary. Rebuild the idler by reversing the dismantling process. Tighten the nut 5 (see **FIG 9:11**), to 54 lb ft (7.5 kg m) and the two bolts holding the bracket to the vehicle to 36 lb ft (5.0 kg m). Refit the ball joint and tighten the nut to 22 lb ft (3.0 kg m). Fit a new splitpin.

9:8 Adjusting the track

The private owner is recommended to have the track checked and adjusted by a FIAT agent at regular intervals. To set the toe-in correctly demands the use of proper optical equipment which it would be uneconomic for anyone other than a service garage to acquire. However in an emergency and to enable the vehicle to be driven to a FIAT agent the following procedure can be adopted.

1 Set the vehicle on a level floor with the front road wheels set straight-ahead. Load it to its normal carrying capacity. Push it backwards and forwards until absolutely certain that it is moving in a straight line.
2 Make a chalk mark on the side of a front tyre at hub height and in front of the hub.
3 Measure the inside distance between the front wheels, preferably at the rims, at hub height and in front of the hub. Record the measurement.
4 Push the vehicle backwards half a turn of the wheels. The chalk mark will now be at hub height again but this time behind the hub.
5 Measure the inside distance again from the same spot on the rims but this time it will be behind the hub. The measurement should now have increased by .118 inch + or — .04 inch (3 + or — 1 mm). This is the correct amount of toe-in. If the dimensions quoted have not been met then the length of the track rod must be adjusted. It must be increased to increase the toe-in and vice versa.

allow the assembly to adopt an unstressed condition then retighten the bolts.

12 Install the direction indicator switch and lighting switch assembly, mating the dowel with the groove on the steering column. Connect the electrical leads.
13 Replace the steering column covers and tighten the five screws.
14 Set the road wheels straight-ahead, then fit the steering wheel to the splines on the steering shaft. Have the steering wheel spoke horizontal. Tighten the nut holding the wheel to 36 lb ft (5.0 kg m).
15 Reconnect the horn and fit the steering wheel trim plate. Tighten the two screws.
16 See that the intermediate track rod ball joint tapers are clean and dry and then fit it to the drop arm. Tighten the nut to 22 lb ft (3.0 kg m) and fit a new splitpin.
17 Refit the road wheel and lower the vehicle to the ground.

Slacken the clamps, two at each side, on the track rods (see items 1 and 3, in **FIG 9:10**), and rotate the screwed sleeves as necessary. Turn each sleeve by the same amount so that the steering remains centralized. Tighten the clamps and recheck the measurements. When the operation is completed see that the split in the sleeves and the clamp bolts are on the same side. These must coincide otherwise the clamps may not grip the sleeves sufficiently.

9:9 Modifications

Commencing at serial number 25764, the steering column, steering box, worm shaft and column covers have been modified to accept an anti-theft steering lock. This is shown inset in **FIG 9:3**. These parts are not interchangeable with earlier ones and if it is desired to fit the anti-theft lock then the whole steering assembly must be changed.

9:10 Fault diagnosis

(a) Inconsistent steering

1 Incorrect front wheel alignment
2 Incorrect front hub bearing adjustment
3 Unbalanced wheels
4 Worn ball joints
5 Worn idler assembly
6 Worn suspension
7 Backlash in steering box

(b) Wheel shimmy

1 Check 1 to 7 at (a)
2 Incorrect adjustment of worm and roller in steering box

(c) Vehicle pulls to one side

1 Check defects listed in Chapter 8
2 Incorrect front wheel alignment

(d) Vehicle wanders

1 Check 1 to 7 at (a)
2 Incorrect tyre pressures
3 Check defects listed in Chapter 8

CHAPTER 10

THE BRAKING SYSTEM

10:1 Description

A general view of the braking system is shown at **FIG 10:1**. Disc front brakes with drum type rear brakes are standard. Operation of the system is by foot pedal controlling the hydraulic circuit and a centrally mounted lever controlling the cable operated parking brake.

The discs and calipers at the front are of cast iron and three pistons are fitted to each caliper. The rear drums are of aluminium with a cast iron insert for the braking surface. These rear brakes each have one cylinder in which two pistons operate and are thus single leading shoe type. The parking or handbrake operates a lever in each rear drum which is pivoted on one shoe and by means of a reaction strut applies equal pressure to both shoes.

An electrical switch is fitted to the bracket carrying the brake pedal. This closes as soon as the pedal is depressed, thereby causing the stoplights to glow.

The hydraulic system master cylinder is mounted on the engine bulkhead and is fed from a reservoir common to the clutch master cylinder. A failure of the clutch system which allowed fluid to be lost would not affect the brake system since the feed to the clutch cylinder is taken from a point in the reservoir higher than that which feeds the brakes.

10:2 Routine maintenance and brake adjustment

It is essential that a regular inspection is made of the fluid level in the hydraulic reservoir. If the level is low it must be topped up but at the same time a close examination of all the hydraulic system must be carried out to find the cause of the fluid loss. A very gradual and slight lowering of the level may be expected due to brake shoe and pad wear. It is worth noting that this system has some inbuilt safety due to the one reservoir supplying the clutch and the brake. If the fluid level drops so low that the clutch supply port is uncovered, the clutch will probably fail thus forcing the driver to seek the cause. Since the brake supply is taken from a lower point, some fluid would remain after the clutch failed. Obviously a burst brake hose, fractured hydraulic pipe or other source of rapid loss cannot be catered for by this arrangement, therefore the value of regular inspection and checking of all brake components is clear. **FIAT blue label brake**

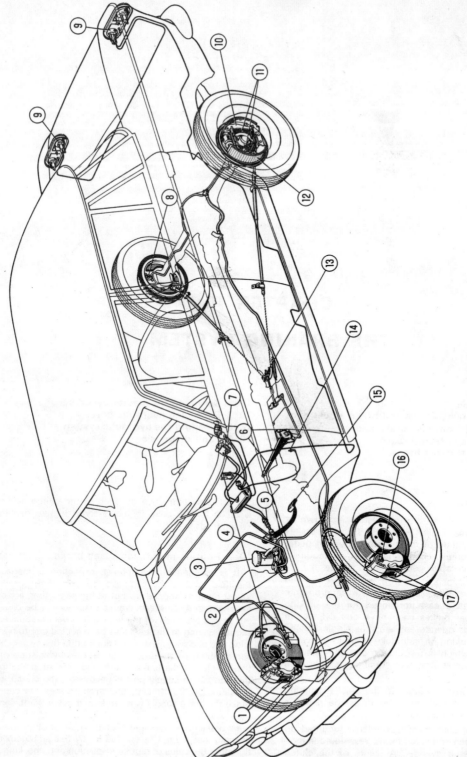

FIG 10:1   Brake system layout

Key to Fig 10:1   1 Front disc brake   2 Master cylinder   3 Brake fluid reservoir   4 Line to clutch master cylinder   5 Stoplight pressure-operated switch   6 Handbrake ratchet lever   7 Handbrake ON signal indicator   8 Rear brake circuit bleed connection   9 Stoplights   10 Rear brake shoe operating lever, actuated by lever (6)   11 Rear brake shoe-to-drum clearance adjusting cams   12 Rear brake shoes   13 Handbrake lever stroke adjuster   14 Handbrake ON signal indicator jam switch   15 Service brake pedal   16 Front brake circuit bleed connection   17 Front brake shoe friction pad carrier plates

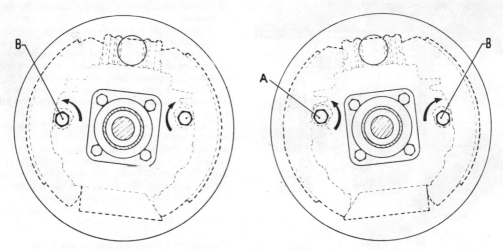

FIG 10:2   Brake adjustment diagram

Key to Fig 10:2   **A** Leading shoe adjuster   **B** Trailing shoe adjuster—Large arrows show direction of rotation

fluid is the only one recommended by the makers for use in this system and it would be unwise to depart from this since all types of fluid may not be compatible.

No adjustment is necessary or possible for the front disc brake pads but the rear drum brake shoes are adjusted as follows:

1 Jack up and safely support the rear of the vehicle so that both rear road wheels are clear of the ground and are free to rotate. Remove the road wheels.

2 Chock the front wheels then release the handbrake.

3 Depress the footbrake pedal hard and hold down. This will apply the shoes to the drum. Refer to **FIG**

10:2 and turn the hexagon adjusters in the direction of the arrows until the cams contact the shoes. Greatly increased resistance will be felt at this point.

4 Release the foot brake pedal then turn each adjuster back until .004 inch to .006 inch (.10 to .15 mm) clearance exists between the shoe and the drum. This clearance is checked by inserting a feeler gauge through the slots machined in the drum.

5 Depress the pedal two or three times then check the clearance again. Readjust if necessary then refit the road wheels and lower the vehicle to the ground.

If the handbrake requires adjustment proceed with this before lowering the vehicle.

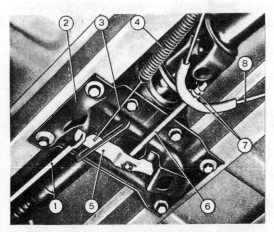

FIG 10:3   Handbrake adjustment, early vehicles

Key to Fig 10:3   1 Link   2 Support plate   3 Spring hook
4 Return spring   5 Intermediate link   6 Screwed rod
7 Adjusting nuts   8 Cable to rear wheels

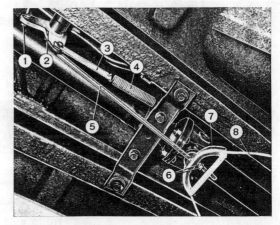

FIG 10:4   Handbrake adjustment, later vehicles

Key to Fig 10:4   1 Link   2 Relay lever   3 Spring link
4 Spring   5 Screwed rod   6 Adjusting nuts   7 Equalizer
8 Cable to rear wheels

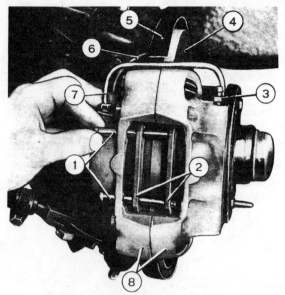

FIG 10:5   Removing disc brake pads

Key to Fig 10:5   1 Retaining pins   2 Friction pad carriers
3 Bleed nipple   4 Disc   5 Shield   6 Hydraulic pipe
7 Connecting pipe   8 Caliper

Refer to **FIG 10:3.**

1 See that the handbrake lever is right off.

2 Tighten nut 7 until the cable is taut and the wheels are locked.

3 If the wheels are in place, unscrew the nut 7, five full turns. If only the brake drums are installed, unscrew the nut four full turns. Lock the locknut. Operate the handbrake several times then check that when it is released both wheels turn freely.

If work is being carried out on a later type vehicle which has a simplified mechanism, refer to **FIG 10:4** and adjust at nut 6.

The operation of adjusting the brakes may show that considerable movement of the adjusters is required. This will mean that the shoes are worn and should be inspected. If the rear shoe lining thickness is reduced to less than .06 inch (1.5 mm) the shoes must be renewed. Always renew all four shoes and use the correct FIAT shoes which have the lining bonded to the shoe.

The front disc pads must be renewed when they wear down to $\frac{5}{32}$ inch (4 mm) thickness.

10:3 Renewing front disc brake pads

All operations which involve handling the friction surfaces must be conducted with clean hands This applies to the rear brake linings as well.

1 Jack up and safely support the front of the vehicle, apply the handbrake, then remove both road wheels.

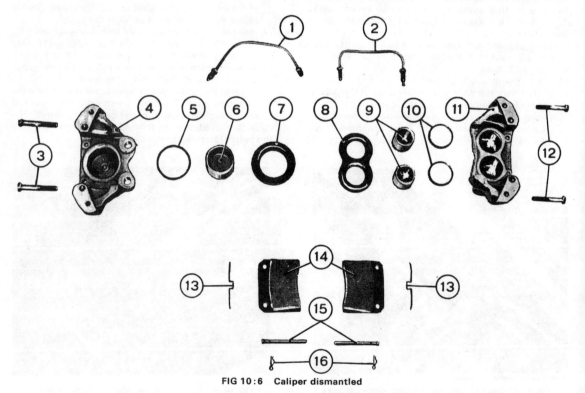

FIG 10:6   Caliper dismantled

Key to Fig 10:6   1 Caliper fluid hose pipe   2 Pipe interconnecting caliper halves   3 Bolts retaining caliper halves   4 Inboard caliper half   5 Seal   6 Inside power piston   7 Inside piston dust cover   8 Outside piston dust cover   9 Outside power pistons
10 Seals   11 Outboard caliper half   12 Bolts retaining caliper halves   13 Friction pad carrier plate spring fasteners   14 Pad and carrier plate assemblies   15 Plate retaining pins   16 Plate pin cotter pins

2 Release the spring which will be found clipped across the top of each pad with its ends under the caliper aperture.

3 Pull out the splitpins from the pad retaining pins then extract the pad retaining pins. **FIG 10:5** shows this operation clearly.

4 The friction pads can now be lifted out. Wipe away all dirt and dust from the caliper with a dry rag. Do not use any solvent or petrol as this will destroy the seals. Only FIAT LDC detergent in warm water should ever be used as a liquid cleaner. See that the piston dust covers are undamaged and that no signs of fluid leakage are present. Gently push the pistons back into their bores.

5 Insert the new pads making sure that the piston dust covers are not trapped or pulled away from the piston face.

6 Refit the pad retaining pins and insert a new splitpin in each. Replace the springs clipped to the pads. Depress the foot pedal to bring the pads into position.

7 Replace the road wheels and lower the car to the ground.

10:4 Servicing the front brakes

If the pistons have seized or fluid is leaking past the seals then the calipers must be overhauled. Heavy scoring of the brake disc will be another reason for dismantling the brake.

Prepare the vehicle as described for renewing the brake pads.

1 Remove the brake pads then open the bonnet, take the cap from the hydraulic reservoir and plug the outlet port at the bottom with a pointed hard wood plug. This will minimise fluid loss when the caliper is removed.

2 Undo the union nuts and remove the steel pipe which runs across the rear face of the brake shield between the hose and the caliper. (This pipe is clearly shown in **FIG 8:2, Chapter 8**). Plug the hose end and the orifice in the caliper.

3 Bend back the tags of the locking plate and remove the bolts holding the caliper to the stub axle. Lift the caliper away from the vehicle.

4 Thoroughly wash the caliper in FIAT LDC detergent and dry off. It is essential that the utmost cleanliness is observed throughout all the following operations. Cover the workbench with clean newspapers and discard each sheet as it becomes soiled. Use nothing but FIAT blue label brake fluid for cleaning hydraulic components and never allow any mineral oil, petrol, paratfin or diesel oil to come near them. The contamination caused by mineral oils, etc. can quickly spread throughout a hydraulic system causing the seals to fail and the brakes to become inoperative. The consequences of any carelessness in this direction can be too serious to contemplate.

5 Reference to **FIG 10:6** will guide further stripping of the caliper. Remove the pipe 2 then grip the caliper in a vice and remove the retaining bolts 3 and 12. The caliper halves 4 and 11 can now be separated.

6 Remove the dust covers 7 and 8 then gently tap each caliper half on a soft wood block until the pistons 6 and 9 emerge. If the pistons are seized try applying

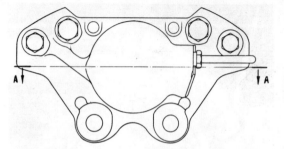

SECTION A-A

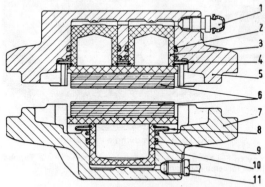

FIG 10:7   Sectioned view of disc brake

Key to Fig 10:7   1 Bleed nipple   2 Piston seal   3 Piston
4 Dust cover   5 Caliper (outer half)   6 Friction pads
7 Caliper (inner half)   8 Dust cover   9 Piston seal
10 Piston   11 Union for connecting pipe

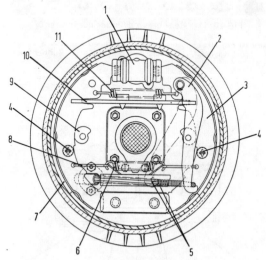

FIG 10:8   Rear brake assembled

Key to Fig 10:8   1 Cylinder   2 Handbrake lever   3 Shoe
4 Steady pin   5 Handbrake cable   6 Return spring
7 Friction lining   8 Spring hook   9 Adjusting cams
10 Strut   11 Return spring

FIG 10:9   Removing a rear drum

Key to Fig 10:9   1 Drum retaining screws   2 Tapped holes for removing drum

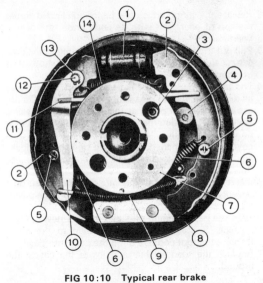

FIG 10:10   Typical rear brake

Key to Fig 10:10   1 Cylinder   2 Shoes   3 Backplate nut
4 Adjusting cams   5 Steady pins   6 Return spring
7 Axle shaft   8 Backplate   9 Handbrake cable
10 Handbrake lever   11 Strut   12 Pivot pin   13 Circlip
14 Return spring

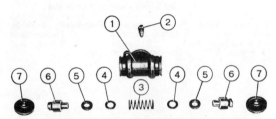

FIG 10:11   Rear brake cylinder components

Key to Fig 10:11   1 Cylinder   2 Bleed nipple   3 Spring
4 Thrust washers   5 Seals   6 Pistons   7 Rubber boots

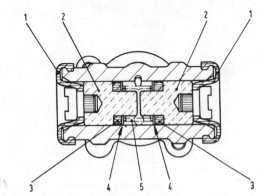

FIG 10:12   Rear brake cylinder assembled

Key to Fig 10:12   1 Rubber boots   2 Pistons   3 Seals
4 Thrust washers   5 Piston springs

a low pressure air jet to the fluid inlet port being careful that the pistons cannot fly out inadvertently. If this fails then the seizure is so bad that the piston and caliper bore surfaces will be damaged beyond use and new components must be obtained. When the pistons are removed, discard the seals 5 and 10.

7 Examine the piston surfaces and the caliper bores for any sign of scoring or damage. If any defect is seen, reject the component immediately. It will be impossible to achieve a good seal if the surfaces are less then perfect.

Assemble the caliper as follows:

1 Obtain an overhaul kit and fit new seals to the pistons. Coat the caliper bores with brake fluid and carefully insert the pistons, pushing them in as far as they will go.

2 Fit new dust seals making sure that one lip seats in the caliper groove and the other in the piston groove.

3 Bolt the halves of the caliper together and tighten the two short bolts to between 20 and 34 lb ft (2.8 to 4.8 kg m). Tighten the longer (inner) bolts to 40 to 55 lb ft (5.5 to 7.6 kg m).

4 Refit the pipe which connects the caliper halves.

5 Before replacing the caliper, the disc should be examined for truth of rotation and surface finish. Set up a dial indicator against the face of the disc as near to the periphery as possible. If the disc runs out more than .006 inch (.15 mm) it must be corrected or renewed. The cause of the runout may be damaged hub bearings, in this case renew the bearings as described in **Chapter 8**. If the disc faces are scored or worn more than .0197 inch (.5 mm) on either side the disc must be renewed. If facilities exist it is permissible to regrind to these limits provided an equal amount of metal is removed from each face.

The disc is removed from the vehicle as described in **Chapter 8**. A correctly assembled hub and disc will measure .833 inch (21.16 mm) from the caliper mounting face on the stub axle to the disc inner face and 1.149 inch (29.2 mm) from the mounting face to the disc outer face.

6 Bolt the caliper to the stub axle with a new locking plate under the bolts. Tighten the two bolts to 72 lb ft (10.0 kg m) and bend up the locking plate.

7 Refit the hydraulic pipe between the hose and the caliper. Remove the hard wood plug from the reservoir.

8 Refit the brake pads and bleed the brakes. **FIG 10:7** shows a correctly assembled brake in section.

9 Replace the road wheels and lower the vehicle to the ground.

10:5 Servicing the rear brakes

FIG 10:8 shows a typical rear brake. To dismantle the rear brakes, proceed as follows:

1 Prepare the vehicle as for brake adjustment and remove the road wheels.

2 Release the handbrake and turn the two hexagon-headed adjusters in the opposite direction to the arrows shown in **FIG 10:2** so that the shoes are quite clear of the drums.

3 To remove the drum, refer to **FIG 10:9**, and unscrew the bolts 1. Screw two bolts into the tapped holes 2 and tighten them evenly until the drum is pushed from the halfshaft flange.

4 Refer to **FIG 10:10**. Unhook the handbrake cable 9 from the lever 10, release the circlip 13, push the pin 12 towards the backplate and lift out lever 10.

5 Unhook the return springs 14 and 6. Early brakes will have two lower springs, later types will have only one.

6 Twist the guide pins 5 until the flattened end will pass through the slot in the spring cups. Remove the cups, springs and pins.

7 The shoes will now lift out. Do not touch the friction surfaces with dirty, oily hands if the same shoes are to be refitted. If it is not intended to dismantle the hydraulic cylinder assembly, put a strong rubber band or wind string round it to prevent the pistons being accidentally released. Remove the strut 11.

8 If the hydraulic cylinder is to be removed, plug the outlet port in the reservoir as described when dealing with the front brakes. Disconnect the hydraulic pipe at the wheel cylinder and plug the end to prevent the ingress of foreign matter. Remove the cylinder mounting bolts and lift the cylinder from the brake backplate.

9 To service the cylinder, clean the external surfaces before dismantling. The directions given in **Section 10:4** regarding cleanliness apply with equal force here. Refer to **FIG 10:11**. Remove the boots 7 then the pistons 6 with their seals 5, washers 4 and spring 3. Examine the pistons and the cylinder bore for scores or discolouration. Discard if these defects or any other damage is found. Release the bleed nipple 2 and see that the drilled ports are clear. Rebuild the cylinder by reversing the dismantling operation. Coat the cylinder bore and the piston seals with FIAT blue label fluid before assembly. **FIG 10:12** shows the cylinder assembled.

10 Refit the cylinder to the backplate and tighten the two bolts to 4 or 5 lb ft (.6 or .7 kg m). Replace the hydraulic

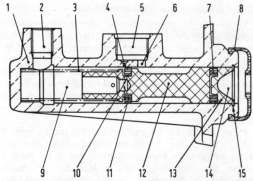

FIG 10:13   Sectioned view of master cylinder
Key to Fig 10:13   1 Body   2 Outlet port   3 Return spring   4 Transfer port   5 Inlet port and reservoir seating   6 Inlet port to piston   7 Piston seal   8 Boot   9 Compression chamber   10 Valve seal ports   11 Valve seal   12 Valve carrier   13 Piston   14 Pushrod seating face   15 Circlip

pipe and tighten the union nut. Temporarily tighten the bleed nipple and remove the plug from the reservoir.

11 Refit the rest of the brake components by reversing the dismantling procedure, being careful not to touch the friction linings with dirty hands.

12 If the brake drum is scored it is permissible to regrind it. The standard inside diameter is 9.8425 inch (250 mm) and this may be increased to not more than 9.874 inch (258 mm).

13 Refit the brake drum and bleed the brakes. Carry out the brake adjustment as described in **Section 10:2**, then fit the road wheels and lower the vehicle to the ground.

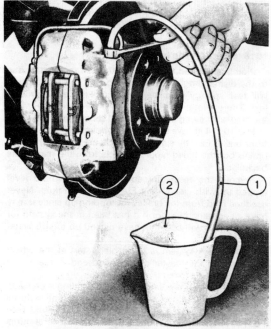

FIG 10:14   Bleeding a front brake
Key to Fig 10:14   1 Tubing   2 Container

10:6 Servicing the master cylinder

To remove the master cylinder, unscrew the reservoir cap and plug the clutch and brake outlet ports to minimise fluid loss. Disconnect the clutch supply hose and the brake outlet T-piece. Remove the two mounting nuts and lift the master cylinder away from the bulkhead. The pushrod from the pedal will free itself from the piston.

To dismantle the master cylinder, work on a clean bench observing the rules of cleanliness detailed earlier in this Chapter.

Refer to **FIG 10:13** and release the rubber boot 8. Remove the circlip 15 and the piston, valve carrier and spring will emerge from the bore. There is no need to remove the reservoir unless a leak has developed between it and the master cylinder. Clean all parts carefully and examine the valve carrier, piston and cylinder for damage. Reject any unsatisfactory components.

Obtain an overhaul kit and fit all the new seals and other parts supplied.

To rebuild the master cylinder, first coat the valve seal and the piston seal with fluid then ease them into place on the valve carrier and piston respectively. Lubricate the bore of the cylinder with fluid and replace the components in the reverse order to dismantling. Fit a new circlip and then the rubber boot.

Refit the master cylinder to the vehicle by reversing the removal procedure. See that the reservoir ports are clean and refill the reservoir with FIAT blue label fluid.

Bleed the brake and clutch hydraulic systems.

10:7 Removing hydraulic hoses

The greatest care must be taken to prevent a hose from twisting when being removed or refitted. Always grip the hexagon on the hose so that it cannot move then undo the steel pipe union nut. Release the hose locknut which holds the hose to the bracket then unscrew the hose from the caliper or rear brake pipe.

10:8 Bleeding the hydraulic system

If air has entered the system either by accident or due to the dismantling of some component, the brake pedal will feel 'spongy' and the proper braking effort will be lost. The operation of bleeding will be necessary when the fluid is renewed at the specified service intervals.

FIG 10:14 shows the operation being carried out on a front brake. Exactly similar methods are used at the rear brakes but the bleed nipple projects from the rear of the backplate.

Remove the reservoir cap and keep the fluid level topped up with clean, new FIAT blue label fluid. Never use fluid bled from the brakes for topping up since it may have air entrained in it or if it has been in the system for some while it will certainly have picked up a high water content.

If the whole system is to be bled, start at the wheel furthest from the master cylinder and end at the wheel nearest to it.

Wipe the bleed nipple and the surrounding area clean then attach a length of plastic or rubber tubing with its lower end submerged in a container of clean fluid (see **FIG 10:14**). Unscrew the bleed nipple several turns then have an assistant depress the brake pedal quickly and return it slowly until no more air bubbles emerge from the tubing into the container. When this stage is reached hold the pedal down at the end of a stroke and tighten the bleed nipple. Release the pedal and remove the tubing. Repeat for the other wheels.

If air bubbles continue to appear no matter how long the operation is continued, it is a clear indication that air is being pulled into the system through a leaking connection or defective seals at a wheel cylinder or the master cylinder.

Do not forget to keep the reservoir topped up throughout the operation.

If the brakes are correctly adjusted and the bleeding has successfully removed all air from the hydraulic system, the pedal will automatically have less than $\frac{1}{2}$ inch of free travel (13 mm). More movement than this indicates a defect which must be found and corrected.

10:9 Fault diagnosis

(a) Spongy pedal operation

1 Air in system
2 Brake hose swollen or soft
3 Worn piston seal in master cylinder
4 Wrong fluid, boiling point too low
5 Reservoir vent hole blocked
6 Floating valve seal failing in master cylinder

(b) Poor brakes

1 Worn linings, pads, discs or drums
2 Contaminated friction pads or linings
3 Badly adjusted rear shoes
4 Master cylinder transfer port blocked
5 Wrong grade of friction material
6 Hose perished and bore restricted
7 Scored drums or discs

(c) Brakes fail to release

1 Broken return spring
2 Check 4 and 6 at (b)
3 Wheel piston seized
4 Wheel piston seal swollen

(d) Brake failure

1 Lack of hydraulic fluid
2 Burst hose or split pipe
3 Master cylinder seals leaking

(e) Unbalanced brakes

1 Fluid leak at one wheel
2 Seized piston at one wheel
3 Mixed grades of friction material
4 Uneven tyre treads
5 Hydraulic pipe or hose restricted
6 Friction pads or linings contaminated

(f) Brake squeal

1 Dust in drums
2 Contaminated friction pads or linings
3 Excessively worn pads or linings
4 Weak return springs
5 Eccentric brake drum
6 Front pad carrier spring broken

CHAPTER 11

THE ELECTRICAL EQUIPMENT

11 : 1 Description

The electrical system is of the **negative** earth type and any transistorized equipment fitted to the car must be arranged to suit this polarity. A radio is the most likely addition, therefore check that it is suitable before connecting it into the circuit.

A 12-volt 48 amp/hr battery is standard and this is charged by a 12-volt DC generator rated at 28 amps continuous loading. The starter motor has a pre-engaged drive operated by a solenoid which also closes the motor supply contacts when the pinion has meshed with the engine ring gear

Four headlamps give extremely good illumination; the two outermost lamps provide dipped beam while all four are switched on for high beam. A very comprehensive set of useful lamps additional to those usually supplied is built into all the vehicles covered by this Manual. These include reversing lamps, glove compartment lamp, boot lamp, engine compartment lamp and a handbrake 'on' warning lamp.

11 : 2 Battery maintenance

Regularly inspect the level of electrolyte in each cell and if necessary add sufficient distilled water to bring the level flush with the bottom of the filler neck. Do not overfill as this will encourage acid spray when the battery is being charged.

Keep the battery dry and clean since moisture will allow current to leak away to the nearest metallic part of the battery support. If corrosion is present, remove the battery and wash all the affected parts with dilute ammonia and water. Dry thoroughly and paint with anti-sulphuric paint.

Check the terminal posts for the characteristic white or yellowish salts which appear when corrosion has gained a hold. Clean thoroughly and coat with petroleum jelly. When removing the cable clamps do not twist or wrench violently on them in case the terminal post is moved and the battery case cracked. Remove the clamp bolt and carefully open the clamp with a screwdriver in the split until the clamp can be lifted off. If the clamp has been neglected and the corrosion has so eaten the metal away that the section is reduced it is wise to replace it. Otherwise this can be a source of high resistance which may impair the starter motor performance.

To determine the state of charge of the battery a hydrometer is essential but certain rules must be observed when using it. Do not allow it to drip after use as the acid will cause damage to most metals. Do not take the readings

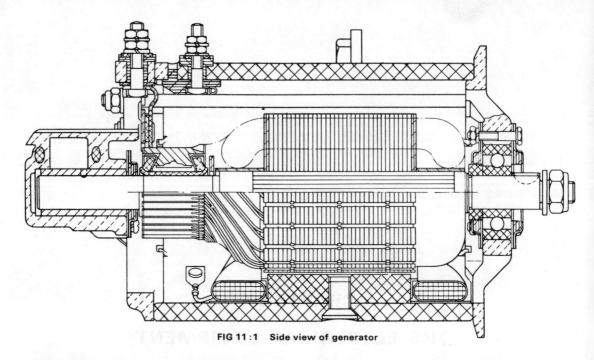

FIG 11 : 1   Side view of generator

immediately after topping up with distilled water, wait at least an hour.

The electrolyte must be at 68°F ± 9°F (20°C ± 5°C); the following table will then apply:

Specific gravity	Battery condition
1.280	Fully charged
1.250	75 per cent charged
1.220	50 per cent charged
1.190	25 per cent charged
1.110	Discharged

If it is ever necessary to make up electrolyte always add the acid to the distilled water, **it is highly dangerous to add water to acid.** Be very careful when handling electrolyte but if an accident should occur and a splash enter the eyes or reach any unprotected skin, wash immediately with large quantities of clean water and seek medical help without delay.

A battery must not be allowed to stand idle and discharged. It is important to give a freshening charge at 3 amps every month or more frequently if tests show this to be needed. Never apply a naked light to the vents of a battery on charge. Highly explosive gases are constantly escaping.

11 : 3 Servicing the generator

This generator must not be operated without the regulator connected to it. The conventional method of testing for output by connecting the two generator terminals together is forbidden. If this is done the generator will act as a simple shunt excited machine and the field current developed will be high enough to damage the field windings.

To check the voltage, insert a voltmeter between terminal 30 on the regulator and the battery lead. A

reading of 12 volts should be given when the engine speed reaches 1400 ± 50 rev/min. If an ammeter is substituted for the voltmeter, 28 amps should pass at 2550 ± 100 rev/min.

If the generator fails to charge, first check the leads between the generator and regulator for continuity. If all is well continue to work through the circuit with the aid of the wiring diagrams in the **Appendix.** Be very careful never to interchange leads 51 and 67 between the generator and regulator. If this happens and the engine is started, the regulator will be ruined due to the contacts welding together. Similarly a failure to earth the regulator base to the vehicle when the generator is running will cause the generator field winding to burn out.

A further warning must be given concerning the fitting of capacitors in an attempt to reduce electrical interference when a radio is fitted. Never fit any capacitor between terminal 67 and earth or terminals 67 and 51, both on the generator and the regulator. If interference is being caused by the regulator it is a sign that it is failing and must be renewed. If a new regulator causes interference, a screened cable could be tried for the connection between the '67' terminals of the generator and regulator. The '67' terminal is the one on the frame of the generator and the '51' terminal is attached to the commutator end plate. **FIG 11 : 1** shows a sectioned side view and **FIG 11 : 2** the brush gear of the generator.

To dismantle the generator proceed as follows:
1 Remove the two long bolts which pass through the generator from end to end.
2 Ease the commutator end plate away just enough to hook the brush springs back from the brushes and then rest them against the side of each brush. This will prevent the brushes being thrown violently against the shaft when they clear the commutator.

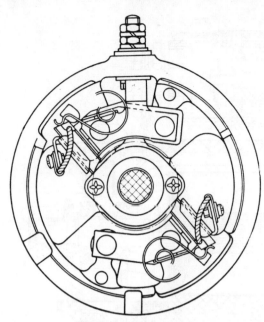

FIG 11 : 2   Brush gear, generator

FIG 11 : 3   Undercutting the commutator insulation

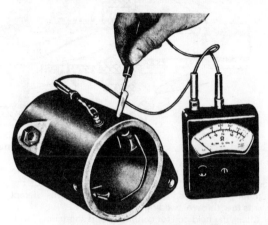

FIG 11 : 4   Checking the field coil

3 Remove the commutator end plate and take out the brushes.

4 Pull the drive end plate complete with the armature, fan and pulley out of the frame.

5 Undo the nut on the end of the armature shaft and remove the pulley and fan. Prise out the Woodruff key and extract the shaft from the ballrace.

6 If the bearing is slack or any roughness is apparent when it is rotated it may be easily replaced. Remove the four bolts holding the bearing covers to the end plate and press the bearing out. Keep the gaskets and retaining plates in order of removal and be careful to support the end plate properly when removing the bearing.

7 Wipe all components with a clean dry rag. Do not use any solvent or petrol on the armature or near the field coil in the frame.

Examine the brushes for chipping of the faces or cracks in the sides or ends. If they have worn so that the springs do not exert full pressure they must be renewed.

The armature must be inspected for signs of overheating of the winding and wear of the commutator. Check that the armature windings are not shorting to earth by putting an ohmmeter between the commutator and the shaft. There must be no movement of the needle. If the commutator surface is evenly worn with a dull smooth finish but the copper segments are flush with the mica insulating strip, then the commutator may be skimmed in a lathe to restore its efficiency. Set the armature up between centres and check that the shaft is running truly. Use medium speed, fine feed and a very sharp tool, remove the minimum amount of metal from the commutator to enable it to just clean up. Do not polish the commutator with emerycloth or sandpaper. The mica must be undercut to a depth of .04 inch (1 mm) with a hacksaw blade or the special tool shown in **FIG 11 : 3**.

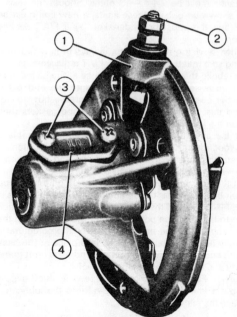

FIG 11 : 5   Generator lubricator

Key to Fig 11 : 5   1 End frame   2 Positive terminal
3 Screws   4 Cover

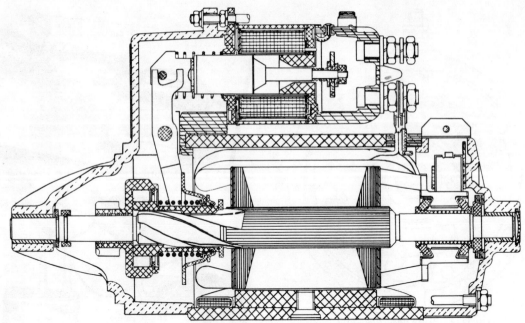

FIG 11 : 6   Sectioned view of starter

If the commutator has a bad burn at one or more segments such that they are below the surface of the adjoining segments, reject the armature. This defect points to a 'thrown' winding.

Check the field coil for continuity and shortcircuit with an ohmmeter as shown in **FIG 11 : 4.** At 68°F (20°C) the resistance must be $7 + 1 - .3$ ohms. Should the resistance shown be outside these limits, a new coil must be fitted and this must be undertaken by a FIAT Service Station.

When servicing the generator always fit new brushes, making sure that they are genuine FIAT replacements.

To rebuild the generator, commence at the ballbearing and if necessary press a new one into the end plate. Pack the bearing with FIAT Jota 3 grease but do not overdo this. Refit the retaining plates and gaskets then tighten the four bolts securely.

Fit the armature through the ballbearing and replace the Woodruff key. Mount the fan and pulley tightening the retaining nut hard home. Slide the end plate complete with the armature assembly into the frame.

Fit the new brushes so that they are high enough up in their boxes to clear the commutator as the end plate is assembled. Position the brush springs at the side of each brush to hold them in position. Enter the end plate in the frame and when the brushes are over the commutator carefully hook the springs up and into place at the back of each brush. Push the commutator end plate right home then fit and tighten the two through-bolts.

Refer to **FIG 11 : 5,** remove the screws 3, lift off plate 4 and put a few drops of FIAT VE oil into the lubricator. Replace the plate and screws.

11 : 4 The regulator

This unit is sealed by the manufacturer not only to prevent tampering but also to keep out moisture. The sealing is very important and is carried out at a controlled temperature after the unit has been operated for a given time. All the functions of the regulator are tested on a special FIAT test bench and the resetting and adjustments when necessary are carried out to critical limits. For these reasons it is not practical for the private owner to repair or adjust this unit. An exchange can be made at a FIAT Service Station for a guaranteed replacement.

11 : 5 Servicing the starter motor

Before commencing work on the starter motor, disconnect both the battery cables.

Remove the starter by disconnecting the leads at the solenoid then release the bolts holding the starter to the bellhousings, lift the unit forwards and lower it free of the vehicle.

FIG 11 : 6 shows a sectioned view of the starter motor and solenoid while **FIG 11 : 7** illustrates all the components in order of assembly. It must be noted that the the only repair work which the private owner can undertake will be the cleaning up of the commutator and the fitting of new brushes.

Fortunately, the starter can be dismantled to the following sub-assemblies, any of which are available from a FIAT Service Agent.

(a) Solenoid, complete.

(b) Commutator end frame and brush gear.

(c) Field frame (starter body).

(d) Armature.

(e) Pinion and clutch assembly.

(f) Pinion end frame.

Dismantling the starter:

1 Release the three nuts holding the through-bolts which retain the solenoid to the starter motor frame; disconnect the nut holding the field winding to the solenoid and withdraw the solenoid from the starter

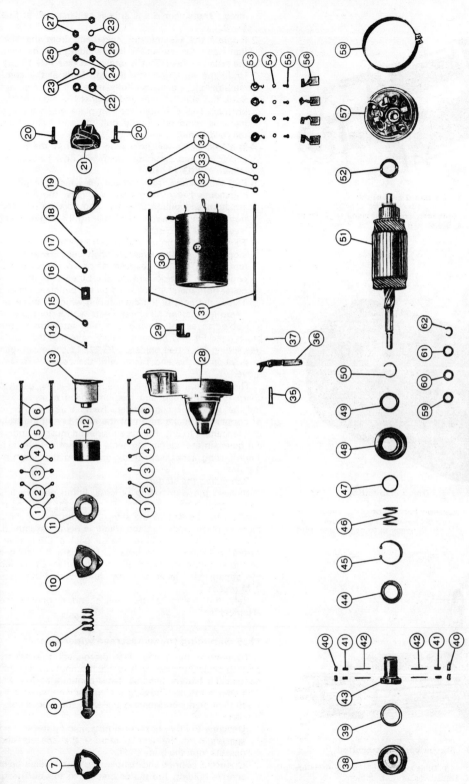

FIG 11:7 Starter motor components

Key to Fig 11:7 1 Solenoid-to-motor nuts 2 Washers 3 Through-bolt nuts 4 Lockwashers 5 Plain washers 6 Solenoid through-bolts 7 Gasket 8 Solenoid core
9 Core reaction spring 10 End plate 11 Gasket 12 Frame 13 Solenoid winding 14 Movable contact spring 15 Insulator 16 Movable contact 17 Insulating washer
18 Movable contact nut 19 Gasket 20 Solenoid stationary contacts 21 Point carrier 22 Plain washers 23 Lockwashers 24 Stationary contact-to-contact carrier nuts
25 Lockwasher 26 Plain washer 27 Nuts, fixing power cable from battery and field winding cable 28 Drive end head 29 Rubber block 30 Field frame, complete with
field winding 31 Through-bolts 32 Plain washers 33 Lockwashers 34 Through-bolt nuts 35 Lever pin 36 Drive shift lever 37 Cotter pin 38 Drive pinion
39 Ring 40 Drive rollers 41 Drive trunnions 42 Trunnion springs 43 Overrunning clutch hub 44 Disc 45 Snap ring 46 Sheave spring 47 Spring spacer 48 Drive
sheave 49 Stop disc 50 Snap ring 51 Armature 52 Armature backing plate 53 Brush pressure springs 54 Lockwashers 55 Brush terminal screws 56 Brushes
57 Commutator end head 58 Commutator end head band 59 Compensating washer 60 Washer 61 Stop ring 62 Snap ring

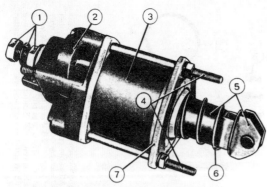

FIG 11:8   Solenoid assembly

Key to Fig 11:8   1 Stationary contact terminal   2 Point carrier   3 Frame   4 Bolts   5 Core   6 Return spring   7 End plate

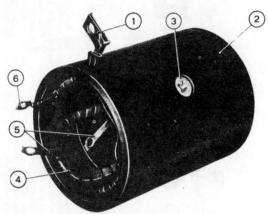

FIG 11:9   Field frame dismantled

Key to Fig 11:9   1 Solenoid connection   2 Field frame   3 Pole shoe screw to positive brushes   4 Field winding   5 Connection   6 Connection to negative brushes

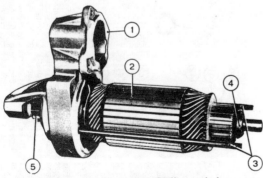

FIG 11:10   Starter partly dismantled

Key to Fig 11:10   1 Drive end frame   2 Armature   3 Through-bolts   4 Thrust washer   5 Pinion

motor. The solenoid will appear as illustrated at **FIG 11:8**.

2 Remove the commutator coverband from the field frame and disconnect the field winding terminal from the brush holders. This is terminal 6 (see **FIG 11:9**).

3 Undo the nuts from the through-bolts at the commutator end frame, carefully raise the brushes and hook the springs over and against the sides of the brushes. This will hold them in place when the end frame is removed. Gently pull the end frame from the field frame.

4 The field frame will now slide away from the pinion end frame and armature which will now be seen as shown at **FIG 11:10**.

5 Pull the splitpin from the pin on which the pinion engagement lever pivots and withdraw the pin. The armature and pinion assembly can now be released from the end frame by manoeuvring the engagement lever free of the clutch.

6 To release the pinion and clutch assembly press the stop collar on the armature shaft back towards the armature. This will expose a circlip. Release the circlip from its groove in the shaft then slide the stop collar from the shaft followed by the pinion assembly. This is the limit of the dismantling which is possible.

Thoroughly clean all components with a dry rag or if available, an air jet, paying particular attention to the brush gear. Fit new brushes, making sure that they are a free sliding fit in their holders. **FIG 11:11** shows a brush in position in the end frame with the commutator removed.

The commutator can be skimmed in a lathe, using a sharp tool, fine feed and medium speed as described for the generator commutator. Remove the minimum of copper and make sure that the shaft is running truly before starting to cut. The mica insulation must be undercut between the copper segments to a depth of .04 inch 1 mm) using a hacksaw blade ground to the width of the slot.

Rebuilding the starter.

Reverse the dismantling process, fitting new circlips and splitpins where necessary. To replace the brush gear, position the springs at the side of the brushes to hold them in place while the end frame is being assembled. Hook the springs over to rest on the back of the brushes before replacing the coverband. Lubricate the splines on the armature shaft and all bearing surfaces between the engagement lever and the clutch with FIAT Jota 2/M grease.

Refit the starter to the vehicle and reconnect the electrical leads.

11:6 Servicing the windscreen wiper motor

To remove the motor, first disconnect the battery positive cable and position it so that it cannot accidentally contact the battery terminal. Now continue as follows:

1 Remove the nuts holding the windscreen wiper arms to their pivots and remove the arms and blades complete.

2 Unscrew the thin hexagonal nuts holding the shaped spacers over the pivots, remove the spacers and gaskets from the body shell.

3 Open the bonnet and remove the four Phillips head screws holding the motor bracket to the bulkhead.

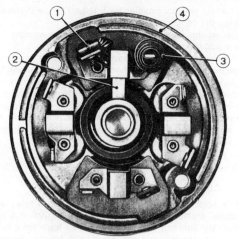

FIG 11:11   Starter brush gear

Key to Fig 11:11   1 Terminal   2 Brush   3 Spring
4 End plate

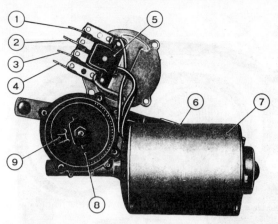

FIG 11:12   Wiper motor partly dismantled

Key to Fig 11:12   1 Terminal 31   2 Terminal C
3 Terminal INT   4 Terminal F   5 Automatic parking
switch   6 Pole shoe screw   7 Frame   8 Gear   9 Parking
switch cam

The motor junction block must be disconnected then the motor and the links can be lifted away from the bulkhead. Disconnect the motor crank arm from the links by releasing the circlip and the two nuts.

With the motor on the bench, wipe off all external dirt then remove the cover from the gearwheel (see **FIG 11:12**). Undo the centre nut and lift out the parking cam contact and the gearwheel. Release the through-bolts from the motor end cover and then the end cover can be eased back followed by the main body and the armature.

Clean the armature and the interior of the motor with a dry rag paying particular attention to removing carbon dust from the brush gear.

The only attention which can be given to the motor is to clean the commutator with fine emerycloth and if necessary, ease any sticky brushes. Beyond this the manufacturers recommend exchanging the complete unit for a reconditioned one.

Rebuild the motor by reversing the dismantling operations, lubricating the worm and gear with FIAT Jota grease. Make sure that the parking cam contact is in

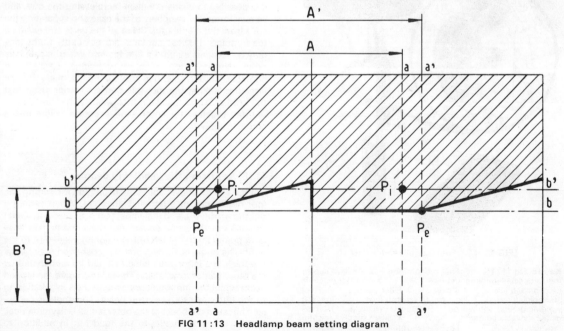

FIG 11:13   Headlamp beam setting diagram

Key to Fig 11:13   For dimensions see text

FIG 11:14 Headlamp cluster prepared for beam setting

Key to Fig 11:14   1 Trim mounting screw holes
2 Vertical beam setting screw   3 Horizontal beam setting
screws   4 Lamp unit retaining screws

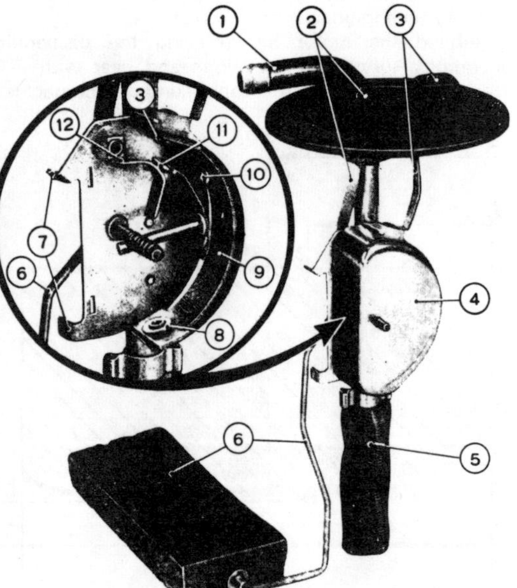

FIG 11:15 Fuel gauge sender unit

Key to Fig 11:15   1 Fuel suction tube   2 Reserve supply
indicator cable junction and inlet   3 Fuel gauge cable
junction and inlet   4 Cover   5 Filter gauze   6 Float
and holding rod   7 Float rod travel stop lugs   8 Rheostat
winding ground connection   9 Rheostat winding   10 Fuel
gauge movable contact   11 Reserve supply indicator
movable contact   12 Reserve supply indicator stationary
contact

the correct angular position with regard to the crank and
replace the cover.

Fitting the motor and its linkage to the vehicle is a
reversal of the removal process.

Reconnect the battery and run the motor for a few
seconds, then switch off. Check that the motor crank has
stopped at the 'park' position. Refit the wiper arms and
blades so that when looking from the front to the back of
the vehicle, the lefthand blade is near the lower edge of
the windscreen without fouling the rubber moulding and
the righthand blade is between $\frac{24}{32}$ inch to $1\frac{3}{16}$ inch
(2 to 3 cm) above the lefthand blade.

11:7 Checking and adjusting the horns

The horns are supplied with current via a relay unit
mounted on the engine compartment wing valance just
behind the ignition coil. Two makes of horn have been
fitted, the Marelli and the Mixo but for all practical
purposes they may be considered as of similar design.

If the horn note is not well tuned it may be adjusted
by the screw at the back of the horn casing; screw it in or
out until a satisfactory note is emitted.

Should the horns fail altogether, check that current is
reaching their terminals by connecting a jumper wire
from the battery (after disconnecting the existing feed
cable) to the terminal. If the horns now operate, system-
atically check back through the circuit. First examine the
fuse; this is No. 7, 16 amp, coloured green and it also
protects the cigar lighter. See that current is reaching the
relay, if it is, then the relay has failed and must be renewed, no repair is possible. Check the horn ring contacts
at the steering wheel and also the block connector
contacts.

If the horns are receiving current but still fail to operate,
it is possible to dismantle them by releasing the nuts and
screws round the periphery of the case and separating the
coils from the diaphragm. Clean all the parts and examine
the contacts. If these contacts are not badly burnt they
may be cleaned up with a fine file and wiped clean. Any
other damage such as burnt windings, badly worn
contacts, seized solenoid core or marks made by the
armature striking the movable contact carrier mean that
the horn must be renewed. It is unlikely that both horns
will fail together for any reason except a failure in the
current supply.

11:8 Adjusting the headlamp beams

FIG 11:13 shows the aiming pattern for setting the
four headlamps of a lefthand drive car. When setting a
righthand drive car headlamps (such as used in Great
Britain) use the same pattern but draw the angled lines
from points Pe to the left of the diagram instead of to the
right. The angle is 15 deg. and the unshaded area below
the thick line is the area which should be illuminated by
the outer pair of headlamps. These lamps give the dipped
beam while the inner pair are switched on in addition to
to the outer pair to give main beam. The angle is necessary because the beam of the outer lamps is asymmetrical,
that is, it is not parallel to the road but in addition to
being directed downwards is also swept up towards the

nearside kerb. The great advantage is that road signs, etc. at the edge of the road can be seen without dazzling oncoming traffic when the vehicle is travelling on dipped beam only.

The inner and outer headlamp units are not interchangeable; inner units have a letter 'R' on the lens while the outer units have the letter 'C' on the lens.

To prepare the vehicle for beam setting, first undo the two screws which hold the trim panel over the lamps at each side of the vehicle. A headlamp cluster will now look as illustrated at **FIG 11 : 14**. The screws 2, are for vertical adjustment and the screws 3, for horizontal adjustment.

Set the beams as follows:

1 Inflate the tyres to the recommended pressures.
2 Set the car on a level floor at right angles to and 16 feet 5 inch (5 metres) from a vertical surface, preferably light in colour.
3 Bounce the car up and down two or three times to settle the suspension.
4 Draw two pairs of vertical lines a—a and a'—a' equally spaced from the centre line of the car. The inner pair of lines must be $39\frac{32}{64}$ inch (100.6 cm) apart and the outer pair $49\frac{3}{8}$ inch (125.4 cm) apart.
5 Measure the exact height from the centre of the lamps to the floor and call this dimension 'C'. Draw the thick line b at height 'C' minus $4\frac{21}{64}$ inch (11 cm) for a new car or a car with new suspension units, but if the car has run more mileage than its first service voucher, draw line b at minus $3\frac{35}{64}$ inch (9 cm) from height 'C'.
6 Draw the thin line 'b' above the thick line at a height of dimension 'C' minus 1 inch (2.5 cm) for both new and used vehicles. Draw the angle of 15 deg. from point Pe either to the left for vehicles which operate on the left of the road or as shown in **FIG 11 : 13** for vehicles which operate on the right of the road.
7 Switch on dipped beam (outer lamps only) and adjust the two screws on each lamp until the beams light up the area under the thick line b and approximate closely to the angle of the line.
8 Switch on main beam (all four lamps) and adjust the screws on both inner lamps until the centres of intensity of the inner lamps fall at points P1.

Note that it is allowable for the dipped and main beams to diverge by not more than 3 deg. This means that the dimensions for A and A' can be increased by up to $10\frac{19}{64}$ inch (26 cm).

Switch off the lamps and replace the trim panels.

11 : 9 The fuel gauge

This is a sealed unit which cannot be repaired. **FIG 11 : 15** shows the main features of the sender unit which is mounted in the fuel tank. It will be seen that the unit is welded to the main fuel supply pipe and to the flange which locates it in the tank. Before dismantling the tank check that any failure does not lie with the wiring to the unit or a failure of the instrument panel gauge. A wiring diagram is included in the **Appendix** of this manual. A quick check of the sender unit may be made if an ohmmeter is available. The resistance between terminal 'T' on the tank unit and the vehicle body should vary from 3 to 8 ohms with an empty tank and 86 to 91 ohms

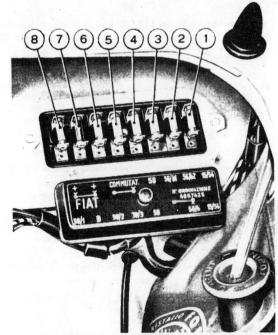

FIG 11 : 16   Fuse box, 116.000 and 115.000 engines

Key to Fig 11 : 16   1 Fuse No. 15/54   2 Fuse No. 56/b2
3 Fuse No. 56/b1   4 Fuse No. 58   5 Fuse No. 30/3
6 Fuse No. 30/2   7 Fuse B   8 Fuse No. 30/1

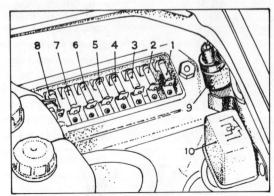

FIG 11 : 17   Fuse box, 116C.000 and 115C.000 engines

Key to Fig 11 : 17   1 Fuse No. 15/54   2 Fuse No. 56/b2
3 Fuse No. 56/b1   4 Fuse No. 30   5 Fuse No. 30/3
6 Fuse No. 30/2   7 Fuse No. 58/1   8 Fuse No. 58/2
9 Tubular sheath for 16-amp fuse   10 High beam relay
switch

for a full tank. Terminal 'W' on the tank unit is the reserve supply warning lamp contact connection.

If the unit has to be renewed take great care to disconnect the battery, extinguish all naked lights and avoid striking metal surfaces together in case of a spark. A dangerous petrol/air vapour will be present when the unit is removed. Use a new gasket when refitting the flange to the tank and tighten the bolts evenly.

11 :10 Fuses

Vehicles fitted with the 116.000 and 115.000 engines have the electrical circuits protected by a fuse box as illustrated at **FIG 11 :16**. The values of the fuses and the circuits they protect are given in the following table:

	FUSES	ELECTRICAL CIRCUITS
1	15/54 (8A)*	Ignition indicator light. Low oil pressure warning light. Temperature gauge. Fuel gauge and reserve supply indicator light. Rear stoplights. Choke warning light. Parking brake warning light. Directional signal and indicator lights. Instrument cluster light. Glove compartment light.
2	56/b2 (8A)*	Righthand low beam.
3	56/b1 (8A)*	Lefthand low beam.
4	58 (8A)*	Engine compartment lights. Blower motor. Windscreen wiper.
5	30/3 (8A)*	Lefthand high beam. High beam indicator light. Righthand front parking light. Lefthand tail light. Righthand license plate light.
6	30/2 (8A)*	Righthand high beam. Righthand tail light. Lefthand license plate light. Lefthand front parking and indicator light. Reversing light. Boot light. Cigar lighter spotlight.
7	B (16A) (green coloured)	Horns. Cigar lighter.
8	30/1 (8A)	Courtesy light. Roof light.

*With ignition on.

Later vehicles with 116C.000 and 115C.000 engines are protected as shown in **FIG 11 :17** and the related table which follows:

	FUSES	PROTECTED CIRCUITS
1	15/54 (8A)*	Parking brake warning light. Fuel gauge and reserve supply indicator. Choke warning light. Ignition indicator. Low oil pressure indicator. Temperature gauge. Glove compartment light. Electromagnetic fan (Model 1500 only).
2	56/b2 (8A)*	Righthand side low beam.
3	56/b1 (8A)*	Lefthand side low beam.
4	30 (8A)*	Windshield wiper. Directional signal lights and indicator. Stoplights. Instrument cluster lights. Blower motor. Engine compartment lights.
5	30/3 (8A)*	Lefthand side high beam. High beam indicator.
6	30/2 (8A)*	Righthand side high beam.
7	58/1 (8A)*	Lefthand side front parking light. Parking light indicator. Righthand side tail light. Lefthand side license plate light. Boot light (S.W. excluded). Cigar lighter spotlight. Reversing lights.
8	58/2 (8A)*	Righthand side front parking light. Lefthand side tail light. Righthand side license plate light.
9	Separate fuse (16A)	Horns. Cigar lighter. Unipolar power socket. Rear view mirror map light. Roof lights.

*With ignition on

11:11 Fault diagnosis

(a) Discharged battery

1 Generator failure
2 Regulator failure
3 Open circuit between generator, regulator or battery
4 Excessive short journeys at night
5 Shortcircuit to earth from some part of the circuit

(b) Ignition light remains on

1 Open circuit between terminals 67 (see wiring diagram)
2 Oxidized contacts in control box
3 Control box internal connections broken at terminals 67 or 51
4 Control box cut-out relay failure
5 Open circuit in generator field winding
6 Armature in generator shorted to earth
7 Open circuit in armature
8 Shortcircuit to earth in field winding
9 Worn generator brushes or dirty commutator

(c) Ignition light will only extinguish at high speed

1 Shortcircuit in field winding furthest away from pole core
2 Armature partly shortcircuited between windings
3 Dirty contacts in control box

(d) Ignition light does not appear

1 Blown bulb
2 Open circuit between generator terminal 51 and plug in connector of red indicator on instrument cluster
3 Open circuit between red indicator and plug in connector
4 Open circuit as at 3 and 15/54 connection on fuse box
5 Open circuit between 15/54 on fuse box and ignition switch
6 Defective ignition switch
7 Open circuit between terminal 30 of ignition switch and plug in coneector 30 of fuse box

(e) Ignition light glows at high speed

1 Faulty bulb, resistance of filament too low

(f) Battery overcharging

1 Voltage regulator set at too high a value
2 Voltage regulator winding or resistor failing
3 Shortcircuit between generator positive terminal and field winding
4 Poor earth connection, generator or regulator
5 Voltage or current regulator contacts welded together

(g) Battery undercharging

1 Break in charging circuit
2 High resistance in battery
3 Wrongly set voltage or current regulators
4 Oxidized contacts in regulators

(h) Startor turns slowly

1 Discharged battery
2 Armature coils shorted
3 Worn bushes in end frame
4 Bent armature shaft
5 Worn brushes

(j) Starter will not turn

1 Pinion jammed in mesh
2 Armature winding earthed
3 Field winding earthed
4 Broken brushes
5 Solenoid coils failed or contacts oxidized

(k) Fuel gauge reads full at all times

1 Open circuit in tank unit
2 Open circuit between tank unit and gauge
3 Poor earth connection between tank unit and body shell

(l) Fuel gauge reads empty at all times

1 Tank unit shorted to earth
2 Seizure of float arm in tank unit

(m) Windscreen wiper will not park

1 Switch cam on motor gear not making contact with switch

CHAPTER 12

THE BODYWORK

12:1 Description

The bodywork used for the 1300 and 1500 models is identical for all practical purposes of maintenance and repair and throughout this Section no distinction is made between the two.

The main shell is of unitary construction to provide strength and stiffness with minimum weight. The bonnet and boot lids, doors and bumpers together with the decorative chrome strips are the only major items which can be separated from the body shell. **FIG 12:1** gives a good idea of the amount of pressings included in this main structure.

FIAT service agents carry a stock of body panels which in the event of damage to the vehicle can be used to renew the affected parts; the private owner is unlikely to require these since such damage should be repaired by a specialist who can if necessary check the alignment of the body on the proper FIAT jigs.

The bodywork should be cleaned with a soft brush or sponge under a copious supply of water; leathered dry and polished with a soft clean cloth. The paint finish can be further protected by the application of any good quality vehicle polish. Do not apply polish in hot sunshine or when the vehicle is not completely dry.

12:2 Removing the door trim

Before any work can be carried out on the window regulator or door lock the trim panel must be removed. Proceed as follows:

1 Remove the two screws and lift off the arm rest.

2 Refer to **FIG 12:2**. With a screwdriver, carefully lever the trim panel away from the window regulator handle. This handle is held by a concealed spring clip which in the illustration is shown just emerging from the handle boss. The special tool illustrated can be replaced by a piece of stout wire such as a bicycle spoke bent to a hook at the end. With the clip removed the handle can be pulled from the regulator shaft. The door lock remote control handle is held by a screw which enters the end of the shaft. Remove the screw and this handle will be free.

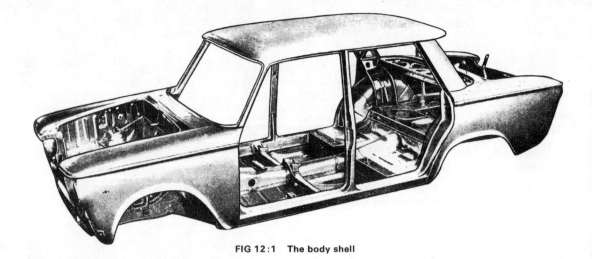

FIG 12:1   The body shell

3 With a wide bladed screwdriver carefully prise the trim panel away from the door. Work all round the edge of the panel applying the screwdriver as near as possible to the clips.

To replace the door trim reverse the preceding instructions.

12:3 Positioning the doors

To prevent draughts and rattles as well as ensuring the easy closing of the doors, some movement of each door relative to the body shell is possible. **FIG 12:3** shows the recommended gap between each side of the doors which the draught sealing strip can accommodate.

To remove a door, first scribe a line round each hinge leaf on the door pillar. This will show how much and in which direction the door is moved.

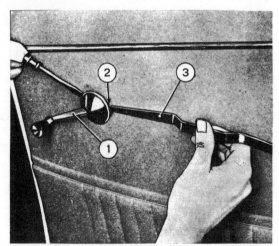

FIG 12:2   Removing the window regulator handle

Key to Fig 12:2   1 Regulator handle   2 Spring clip
3 Tool A78007

Slacken the hinge screws just enough to free the door then with the aid of an assistant, lift or lower the door, move it back or forth keeping a watch on the scribed lines while doing so. Tighten the screws and check the alignment. Repeat as necessary. The striker plate on the body pillar can be moved up or down, in or out to suit the door latch.

12:4 Removing door sliding window

Refer to **Section 12:2** and release the door trim panel. Wind the window right up then remove the nut and washer holding the front channel to the door (see **FIG 12:4**). The channel will now pull downwards and out through the large aperture in the door inner skin. Undo the four screws which hold the window regulator mechanism to the door, tilt it so that the roller disengages from the window channel and extract it from the door as illustrated at **FIG 12:5**. Be careful that the glass does not fall when the regulator is removed. Lower the glass and remove from the door as shown at **FIG 12:6**.

To replace the window, reverse the dismantling process. A light smear of grease in the regulator channel will help the mechanism to operate smoothly.

12:5 Removing the quarter lights

The door sliding window must first be removed as described in **Section 12:4**. Now push the inner weatherstrip assembly away from the door (see **FIG 12:7**). This strip is retained in the door by clips. Detach the window outer trim, by pulling it upwards as shown in **FIG 12:8**.

Undo the screw holding the bottom of the door sliding window rear channel to the door frame and remove the channel. Remove the front and rear upper channels for the sliding window.

Release the two screws (see **FIG 12:9**), indicated by the arrows and tilt the quarter light frame to the rear. It can now be lifted clear of the door. A new quarter light can be installed by reversing the dismantling process.

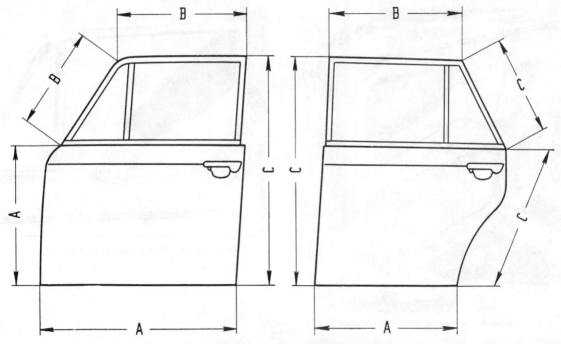

FIG 12:3   Door alignment diagram

Key to Fig 12:3   **A** .213 inch (5.4 mm)   **B** .177 inch (4.5 mm)   **C** .158 inch (4 mm)

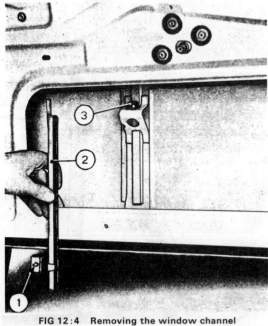

FIG 12:4   Removing the window channel

Key to Fig 12:4   1 Stud   2 Window channel   3 Glass buffer block

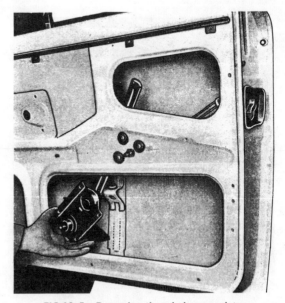

FIG 12:5   Removing the window regulator

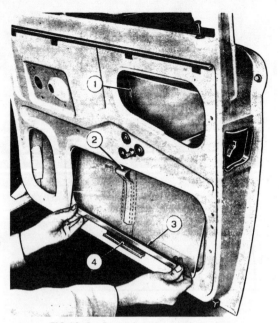

FIG 12:6   Removing the window glass

Key to Fig 12:6   1 Glass   2 Buffer block   3 Rubber strip
4 Regulator channel

FIG 12:8   Removing door outer trim strip

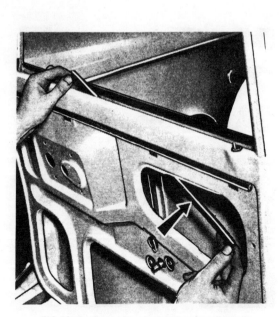

FIG 12:7   Removing door inner weatherstrip

FIG 12:9   Releasing the quarter light frame

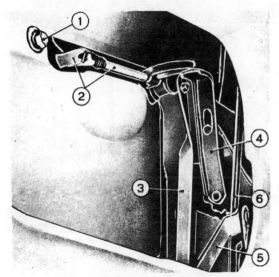

FIG 12:10 The door lock mechanism

Key to Fig 12:10 1 Handle mounting bolt 2 Release handle 3 Link 4 Pushrod 5 Relay arm 6 Safety button rod

12:6 Renewing a door lock

It is not wise to attempt to repair a door lock. When wear or damage show in the mechanism a new unit should be installed.

To remove the lock first obtain access to the inside of the door by removing the trim panel (see **Section 12:2**). Unscrew the safety catch pushbutton and remove the bush. Refer to **FIG 12:10** and disconnect link 3 from the door handle. Release bolt 1 and the screw which passes into the door handle from the outside edge of the door. Lift the outer handle away.

Refer to **FIG 12:11** and remove the three screws 3, which hold the latch plate and lock to the door.

Undo the three screws which hold the remote control to the door panel and lower the remote control, link and lock out through the large aperture in the door panel.

To fit the new mechanism reverse the dismantling sequence lubricating where necessary with FIAT A5 grease.

12:7 Fitting a new windscreen

If a shattered windscreen is to be renewed be meticulously careful to clear away all particles of glass which may be trapped in corners or recesses in the car. Pay particular attention to the demister ducts; a sharp sliver of glass blown out when the heater fan is switched on could enter the eye of an occupant of the vehicle with very serious results.

Clean all traces of the old rubber weatherstrip from the edges of the aperture with petrol then continue as follows:

1 Remove the interior mirror and courtesy light.
2 Detach the padded surface between the facia and the windscreen. **FIG 12:12** shows the location of the

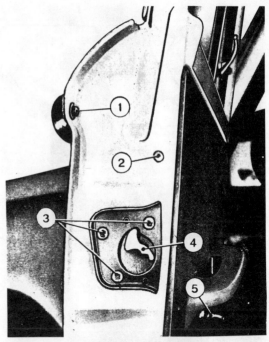

FIG 12:11 Latch plate

Key to Fig 12:11 1 Door handle retaining screw 2 Rear glass channel retaining screw 3 Latch cover screws 4 Rotary cam 5 Remote control handle

FIG 12:12 Location points for panel padding

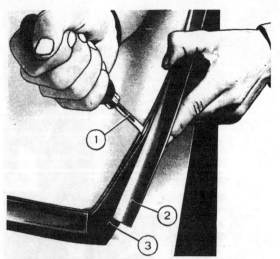

FIG 12:13   Fitting weatherstrip to windscreen

Key to Fig 12:13   1 Tool A78015 **2** Trim strip **3** Rubber weatherstrip

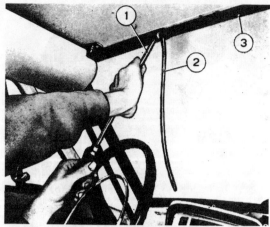

FIG 12:15   Fitting tensioner cord

Key to Fig 12:15   1 Tool A78014   **2** Tensioner cord
3 Weatherstrip

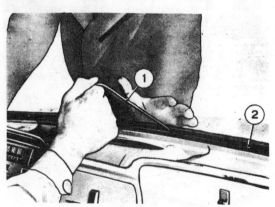

FIG 12:14   Windscreen ready for fitting

Key to Fig 12:14   1 Tensioner cord   **2** Rubber
weatherstrip   **3** Windscreen

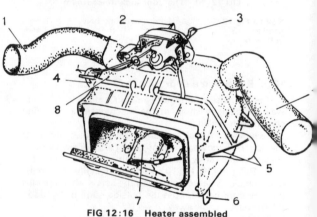

FIG 12:16   Heater assembled

Key to Fig 12:16   1 Demister hoses   **2** Water valve
control   **3** Air intake control   **4** Water valve   **5** Blower
leads   **6** Radiator drain plug   **7** Blower motor
8 Radiator case

screws but in addition remove the two screws which hold the glove box striker plate.

3 Apply a coating of petroleum jelly to the windscreen aperture in the body shell where the new weatherstrip will seat.

4 Fit the weatherstrip to the glass then press the trim strips and joint caps into the moulded slot using special FIAT Tool No. A78015 and petroleum jelly to ease into place. **FIG 12:13** shows the operation in progress.

5 Place clean newspaper or an old rug on the bench and lay the windscreen face downwards so that the curved ends are uppermost. Coat the inner slot in the weatherstrip with petroleum jelly and insert the tensioner cord. Arrange the cord as shown in **FIG 12:14**. Insert it in the weatherstrip at both sides and the bottom of the windscreen but leave it outside the weatherstrip at the top.

6 With the help of an assistant, fit the top edge of the windscreen to the car, locating the slot in the weatherstrip over the edge of the body aperture. Press the windscreen firmly towards the vehicle while the assistant inside the vehicle pulls the tensioner cord out of the weatherstrip. As the cord leaves the weatherstrip, the edges will slide over the edge of the aperture until the cord is finally removed and the windscreen is firmly located in the vehicle.

7 The tensioner cord must now be replaced in the grooves to lock the windscreen in place. A special tool, FIAT No. A78014 used as shown in **FIG 12:15** makes this a simple matter but a little ingenuity and a blunt screwdriver will achieve the same result although with more difficulty.

8 Replace the padded panel, glove box striker plate and the courtesy light. Clean the windscreen and weatherstrip with white spirit.

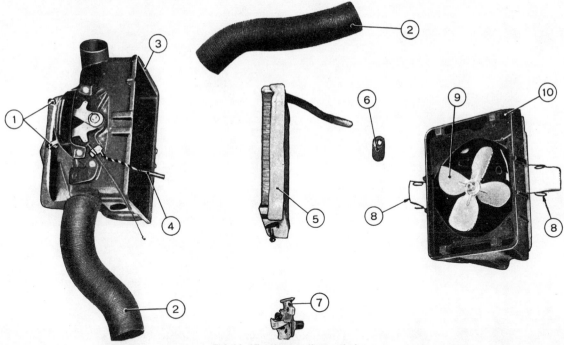

FIG 12:17   Heater dismantled

Key to Fig 12:17   1 Controls   2 Demister hoses   3 Radiator case   4 Cigar lighter earth lead   5 Radiator   6 Water outlet
pipe grommet   7 Water valve   8 Clips   9 Fan   10 Blower case

12:8 The heater

If a water leak develops in the heater or the blower fails to operate it may be necessary to remove the heater for servicing. Before doing this check all the hoses to see that they are not perished or have loose connecting clips and also make sure that the blower failure is not due to an external failure of the electrical supply. If the fuse has blown the windscreen wipers will also be inoperative as will the engine compartment light.

To remove the heater proceed as follows:
1 Drain the engine cooling system and also the heater radiator. The drain plug for the heater is located on the lower righthand side of the casing.
2 Loosen the water hose clips and the demister air hose clamps at the heater.
3 Disconnect the blower motor leads.
4 Remove the four mounting nuts (early cars, five mounting nuts, the fifth is on the righthand side of the heater case) and ease the heater downwards releasing the hoses at the same time. Lift from the car. The unit will appear as shown in FIG 12:16.

To service the heater, dismantle it into the components shown at FIG 12:17. Release the clips 8 and separate the blower case 10 from the radiator case 3. Disconnect the water valve control cable and remove the valve 7 by undoing the nuts. Lift out the radiator 5.

First check that the water valve closes properly when the lever is in the correct position. If it leaks it must be renewed. See that the air intake shutter operates freely and that the cable is not seized or fractured.

The motor can be tested on a 12-volt supply and if it fails to operate it may be dismantled. Release the nut which holds the fan to the motor spindle then remove the through-bolts in the motor casing. Service the motor generally as described in Chapter 11 for the generator, starter or windscreen wiper. Clean the commutator with a clean cloth slightly moistened with petroleum jelly then wipe dry. See that the brushes slide freely in their holders and are not excessively worn. Any other faults found mean that the motor must be renewed, no provision is made for further repair work.

If the radiator is leaking from anywhere in the core it should be renewed as it means that the water tubes are badly corroded. While the radiator is out of the vehicle the opportunity should be taken to flush it through with a good head of water to remove any loose deposits or scale. This is only worthwhile if the radiator is sound but the water flow and therefore the heat output seem restricted. In any case of doubt it is wisest to renew the radiator.

Refit the heater to the vehicle by reversing the dismantling and removal instructions. Use new adhesive tape for sealing the halves of the case and a new gasket under the water valve. If the water hoses are at all doubtful, renew them. Refill the engine cooling system and then run the engine for a few minutes with the heater water valve open. This means that the lower control lever on the heater case will correspond to the base of the red triangle marking. Stop the engine and top up the engine cooling system. This will ensure that the heater radiator is filled.

APPENDIX

TECHNICAL DATA

Engines	Fuel system	Ignition system	Cooling system
Clutch	Gearbox	Propeller shafts, rear axle and suspension	
Front suspension	Steering	Brakes	Electrical equipment
Capacities	Torque wrench settings		

WIRING DIAGRAMS

METRIC CONVERSION TABLE

HINTS ON MAINTENANCE AND OVERHAUL

GLOSSARY OF TERMS

INDEX

TECHNICAL DATA

Dimensions are in inches unless otherwise stated

ENGINES

	116.000 115.000	116C.000 115C.000
Bore and stroke	72 x 79.5 mm 77 x 79.5 mm	72 x 79.5 mm 77 x 79.5 mm
Compression ratio	8.8:1	9:1

Crankshaft:

Main journal diameter ...	2.479	2.479
Main journal clearance ...	.001 to .003	.001 to .003
Crankpin diameter	2.086	2.086
Big-end clearance	.0008 to .0026	.0008 to .0026
End float	.002 to .01	.002 to .01

Regrind main and crankpin journals by .01 steps to .04 maximum

Connecting rods:

Small-end bush I/D... ...	.8661	.8661
Gudgeon pin clearance in bush	.0002 to .0004	.0002 to .0004

Maximum misalignment of big-end and small-end axes ± .002

Pistons:

Type	Light alloy, slipper type	Light alloy, steel insert
Standard diameter ...	2.8303, 3.0272	2.8331, 3.0299
Clearance, top of skirt ...	.0039 to .0047	.0012 to .0020
Gudgeon pin diameter ...	.8658	.8658
Rings	3 compression—2 oil control	
Top ring, thickness	.0779 to .0783	
Top ring, gap	.012 to .018	
Top ring, clearance in groove	.0018 to .0028	
Second ring, oil control, thickness	.0779 to .0783	
Second ring, gap	.008 to .014	
Second ring, clearance in groove ...	.001 to .002	
Third ring, radial slotted, thickness	.1535 to .1547	
Third ring, gap	Ends butted	
Third ring, clearance in groove	.0011 to .0028	
Gudgeon pin fit in piston ...	.0001 to .0003 interference	.0002 to .0004 clearance

Camshaft:

Bearings, reamed in line, bore diameter:

Centre	1.8780 to 1.8785	1.8780 to 1.8788
Rear	1.8230 to 1.8235	1.8230 to 1.8238
Front bearing supplied finish bored to	1.4183 to 1.4198	

Journal diameters:

Front	1.4163 to 1.4173
Centre	1.8760 to 1.8770
Rear	1.8210 to 1.8220

Bearing to journal clearance:

Front	.001 to .0035
Centre	.001 to .0025
Rear	.001 to .0025
Cam lift, inlet and exhaust	.2256

Tappet clearance, inlet and exhaust:

Inlet...	.0079	.0079		.0079	.0079
Exhaust	.0079	.0079		.0079	.0098

Valves:

Face angle, inlet and exhaust		45 deg. 30' ± 5'
Seat angle, cylinder head		45 deg. ± 5'
Valve head diameter:		
Inlet	1.338	1.378
Exhaust	1.220	1.240
Stem diameter	.3144	.3144
Stem to guide clearance	.0011 to .0024	.0011 to .0024
Stem to guidance	.0011 to .0024	.0011 to .0024
Inside diameter of guide		.3161 to .3168
Spring, free length:		
Inner		1.543
Outer		1.968

Valve timing:

Inlet opens BTDC	9 deg.	9 deg.		9 deg.	25 deg.
Inlet closes ABDC	61 deg.	61 deg.		61 deg.	51 deg.
Exhaust opens BBDC	49 deg.	49 deg.		49 deg.	64 deg.
Exhaust closes ATDC	21 deg.	21 deg.		21 deg.	12 deg.

Oil pump:

Type	Spur gear
Oil pressure, engine warm	57 to 64 lb/sq. inch
Warning light glows when pressure drops to between 4 and 9 lb/sq. inch	
Clearance, drive shaft to bearings	.0006 to .0022
Clearance, radial, gear to body	.004 to .007
Gear backlash	.006
Gear face to bottom cover	.0006 to .0034
Pressure release valve:	
Clearance in housing	.0012 to .0044
Spring, free length	1.114
Spring, length loaded under 14 lb.	.787

Rocker gear:

Shaft diameter	.7069 to .7076
Rocker arm bore diameter	.7089 to .7096
Rocker arm spring, free length	.2748
Tappet, diameter	.8653 to .8660
Tappet, clearance in crankcase	.0003 to .0017

COOLING SYSTEM

Thermostat:

Type	Bellows
Opens at	180°F (82°C)
Fully open at	203°F (95°C)

Water pump:

Type	Centrifugal impeller
Pulley flange to shaft fit	.0005 to .0024 interference
Impeller to shaft fit	.0007 to .0022 interference
Bearing to body fit	.0006 interference to .0006 clearance
Impeller vanes to body clearance	.0197 to .0394
Impeller to cover clearance	.0079 to .0098

FUEL SYSTEM

	28.36 DCD	28.36 DCD1
Fuel pump type	Mechanical	
Carburetter type	*Weber*	
Primary Venturi	.9449	.9843
Main jet	.0492	.0512
Idling jets:		
Primary	.0197	.0197
Secondary	.0276	.0276
Accelerator pump jet	.0276	.0276
Choke jet	.0591	.0591
Emulsion tubes	F30	F30
Air bleed jet:		
Primary	.0866	.0866
Secondary	.0787	.0709
Needle valve bore	.0689	.0689
Float level setting	.1969	.1969

Weber 34 DCHD:

Engine type	116C.000	115C.000
Bore	1.339	1.339
Venturi	.945	.984
Main jet:		
Primary	.047	.049
Secondary	.053	.055
Idling jet:		
Primary	.020	.020
Secondary	.020	.027
Air correction jet:		
Primary	.083	.083
Secondary	.083	.083
Starting jet	.059	.059
Accelerator pump jet	.027	.027
Needle valve housing	.069	.069

Solex C34 PA1A2:

Engine type	116C.000	115C.000
Bore	1.339	1.339
Venturi	.905	.945
Main jet:		
Primary	.043	.045
Secondary	.049	.051
Idling jet:		
Primary	.016	.016
Secondary	.020	.020
Air correction jet:		
Primary	.071	.067
Secondary	.079	.079
Starting jet	.047	.047
Accelerator pump jet	.027	.027
Needle valve housing	.069	.069

NOTE: A yellow paint mark identifies the Weber 34 DCHD or Solex C34 PA1A2 carburetter for use with the 116C.000 engine and a green paint mark for the 115C.000 engine.

IGNITION SYSTEM

Distributor type	S91A			
Static advance—Engines	116.000	116C.000	115.000	115C.000
	12 deg.	12 deg.	12 deg.	10 deg.
Vacuum advance	15 deg.	15 deg.	15 deg.	15 deg.
Centrifugal advance	20 deg.	20 deg.	20 deg.	20 deg.
Contact breaker gap	.016 to .018			
Capacitor	.20 to .25 µf			
Lubricant	FIAT VE Oil			
Coil type	BE 200B		TK 12A 17	G528
Primary winding resistance ...	3.1 to 3.4 ohms		3.1 to 3.4 ohms	2.9 to 3.2 ohms
Secondary winding resistance	6,700 to 8,300 ohms		7,200 to 8,000 ohms	7,200 to 8,000 ohms

Insulation resistance at 500 volts	Not below 50 megohms		
Sparking plugs...	Marelli	Champion	AC/Delco
1300 to engine No. 00117 ...	M14-12/240		
1500 to engine No. 000450	(CW 240 N)	L5	42F
1300 from engine No. 00118 ...	M14-19		
1500 from engine No. 000451 ...	(CW 240 LP)	N9Y	44 XL
Thread	14 mm	14 mm	14 mm
Gap	.020 to .024	.024 to .028	.024 to .028

CLUTCH

Type	Single dry plate			
	116.000	115.000	116C.000	115C.000
Friction plate O/D	7.25		7.874	
Friction plate I/D	5.00		5.590	
Springs:				
Wire diameter	.1732			
Outside diameter	1.3150			
Free length	2.2991			
Pedal free travel	$1\frac{37}{64}$			
Release lever tip height from flywheel face	1.764			
Master cylinder I/D	$\frac{3}{4}$			
Slave cylinder I/D	$\frac{3}{4}$			
Fluid type	FIAT blue label			

GEARBOX

Ratios:	
Top	1:1
Third	1.49:1
Second	2.30:1
First	3.75:1
Reverse	3.87:1
Gear backlash	.0039
First speed gear to gear bushing and second/third gear to main-shaft bore clearance	.002 to .004
Reverse shaft to reverse gear bush clearance	.002 to .004
Synchro sleeve guide groove to hub backlash	.003 to .006
Ballbearing radial play	.002
Ballbearing axial play	.020
Lubricating oil grade	SAE.90.EP

STEERING

Type	Worm and roller
Ratio	16.4 to 1
Number of steering wheel turns lock to lock	3
Worm shaft bearings	2, roller
Roller shaft bearings	2, bronze
Bearing adjustment	Shims
Roller shaft adjustment	Screw
Roller shaft bushes, bore diameter	1.1298 to 1.1307
Roller shaft diameter	1.1287 to 1.1295
Turning circle	34' 1½ inch
Turning angle:	
Inner wheel	35 deg.
Outer wheel	26 deg. 45'
Front wheels, toe-in	.118 ± .039
Steering box lubricant	SAE.90.EP

FRONT SUSPENSION

Type	Independent, hydraulic dampers and coil springs
Kingpin inclination	6 deg.
Caster	3 deg. 10' ± 15'
Camber	0 deg. 30' ± 20'
Loaded car, height from ground to chassis:	
Front	$9\frac{3}{16}$
Rear	$12\frac{3}{16}$
Coil spring:	
Wire diameter	.5
Inside diameter	3.988
Free length	16.34 approx.
Test load	1,213 lb.
Hub bearings	Taper roller
Hydraulic dampers:	
Stroke	4.429
Fluid grade	FIAT SA1
Length, compressed	9.31
Length, extended	14.13

PROPELLER SHAFTS, REAR AXLE AND SUSPENSION

Front shaft diameter	$1\frac{49}{64}$
Front shaft length	$19\frac{9}{16}$
Rear shaft diameter	$1\frac{49}{64}$
Rear shaft length	$32\frac{19}{32}$
Lubrication:	
Sliding joint	FIAT Jota 1 grease
Universal joints	FIAT Jota 1 grease
Rear axle, type	Hypoid, semi-floating
Ratio	4.1:1
Pinion bearing preload	57.9 to 115.7 ft/lb.
Differential preload (cap movement)	.0051
Crownwheel to pinion backlash	.0031 to .0047
Lubrication	SAE.90.EP
Rear suspension, type	Leaf spring
Number of leaves	4

Camber under 350 lb. load:
Car 4.763
Station wagon 4.787
Rate:
Car ... ... 1.3744 in % lbs
Station wagon ... ... 1.1960 in % lbs
Hydraulic dampers:
Stroke 7.322
Fluid grade ... ... FIAT SA1
Length, compressed 12.1654
Length, extended 19.4882

BRAKES

Type:

Front ... ... Disc
Rear... ... ... Drum

Rear ... ...
Disc diameter 9.2913
Drum diameter... ... ... 9.8425
Total friction area:
Front ... ... 22 sq. inch
Rear... ... ... 70.7 sq. inch
Rear shoe to drum clearance ... ... .004 to .006
Master cylinder diameter ... ... $\frac{3}{4}$
Inner half caliper piston diameter 1.891
Outer half caliper piston diameter 1.335
Rear wheel cylinder diameter ... ... $\frac{3}{4}$
Maximum refacing allowed each side of disc ... ... .0197
Maximum reboring of rear drum ... ... .0315
Minimum thickness of front pads ... ... .1575
Minimum thickness of rear brake linings ... ... .0591
Master cylinder pushrod to piston clearance ... ... .0039 to .0118
Pedal free travel approx. ... ... $\frac{1}{2}$
Hydraulic fluid... ... ... FIAT blue label

ELECTRICAL EQUIPMENT

Battery:
Type 12-volt
Polarity ... ... Negative earth
Capacity (at 20 hr discharge rate) ... ... 45 amp/hr
Generator:
Type ... ... FIAT D 115/12/28/4
Voltage 12
Current (continuous) ... ... 28 amps
Current maximum ... ... 35 amps
Poles 2
Field winding ... ... Shunt
Initial charging speed ... ... 1,400 rev/min
28 amp output ... ... 2,500 rev/min
35 amp output ... ... 2,900 rev/min
Maximum steady speed ... ... 10,200 rev/min
Rotation, from drive end ... ... Clockwise
Brush, Part No. 4042681
Brush spring pressure ... ... 27 oz.
Commutator undercutting, maximum depth ... ... .04

Regulator:

Type	GN 2/12/28
Cut-out relay:	
Closing voltage	12.6
Reverse current	Not above 16 amps
Air gap, contacts closed	.0138
Contact gap	.0177
Voltage regulator:	
Air gap	.039 to .0437
Current regulator:	
Air gap	.039 to .0437
Regulating resistor	105 ohms
Voltage regulator series resistor	17 ohms

Starter motor:

Type	FIAT E 100—1.5/12 Var. 1
Voltage	12
Power	1.5 KW
Brushes, Part No.	4045771
Solenoid coil resistance	.399 to .409 ohms
Shunt field resistance	1.96 to 2.04 ohms
Series field resistance	.0039 to .0041 ohms
Brush spring pressure	2.2 lb.
Armature shaft end float	.004 to .0275
Commutator undercutting, maximum depth	.04
Solenoid core stroke	.5039 to .622

CAPACITIES

Fuel Tank	9.9 gallons
Radiator including heater	1.47 gallons
Sump (engine)	6 pints
Gearbox	$2\frac{1}{4}$ pints
Rear axle	$1\frac{1}{2}$ pints
Steering box	$\frac{1}{3}$ pint
Clutch and brake hydraulic reservoir	1 pint
Front hydraulic damper	$\frac{1}{4}$ pint
Rear hydraulic damper...	$\frac{1}{3}$ pint
Windscreen washer reservoir	$1\frac{3}{4}$ pints

TORQUE WRENCH SETTINGS

Measures are in lb. ft. unless otherwise stated

	115.000 116.000	115C.000 116C.000
Main bearing cap bolt	75	75
Connecting rod cap bolt	47	47
Cylinder head bolts	65	50
Flywheel bolts	58	58
Camshaft sprocket bolt	50	36
Rocker shaft pedestal bolts	16	14
Crankshaft pulley bolt	101	101
Sparking plugs	26	18
Bellhousing bolts	54	54
Bellhousing to gearbox bolts	40	40
Mainshaft front bearing bolt	69	69
Yoke flange to mainshaft nut	58	58
Gearbox sump nuts	7	7
Crossmember to gearbox nut	24	24
Propeller shaft nuts	37	37
Front propeller shaft, rear flange nut	144	144
Differential carrier to axle nuts	16	16
Brake backplate bolts, rear	21	21
Spring U-bolt nuts	22	22
Road wheel studs	58	58
Drop arm nut	173	173
Steering wheel nut	36	36
Brake caliper mounting bolts	72	72
Ball joint nut	21	21
Front suspension upper arm	43	43
Front suspension upper arm bracket	39	39
Kingpin ball joint nut	65	65
Front wheel stub axle nut	21 lb. ft. and release $\frac{1}{6}$ turn	
Rear brake cylinder nuts	4 to 5 lb. ft.	

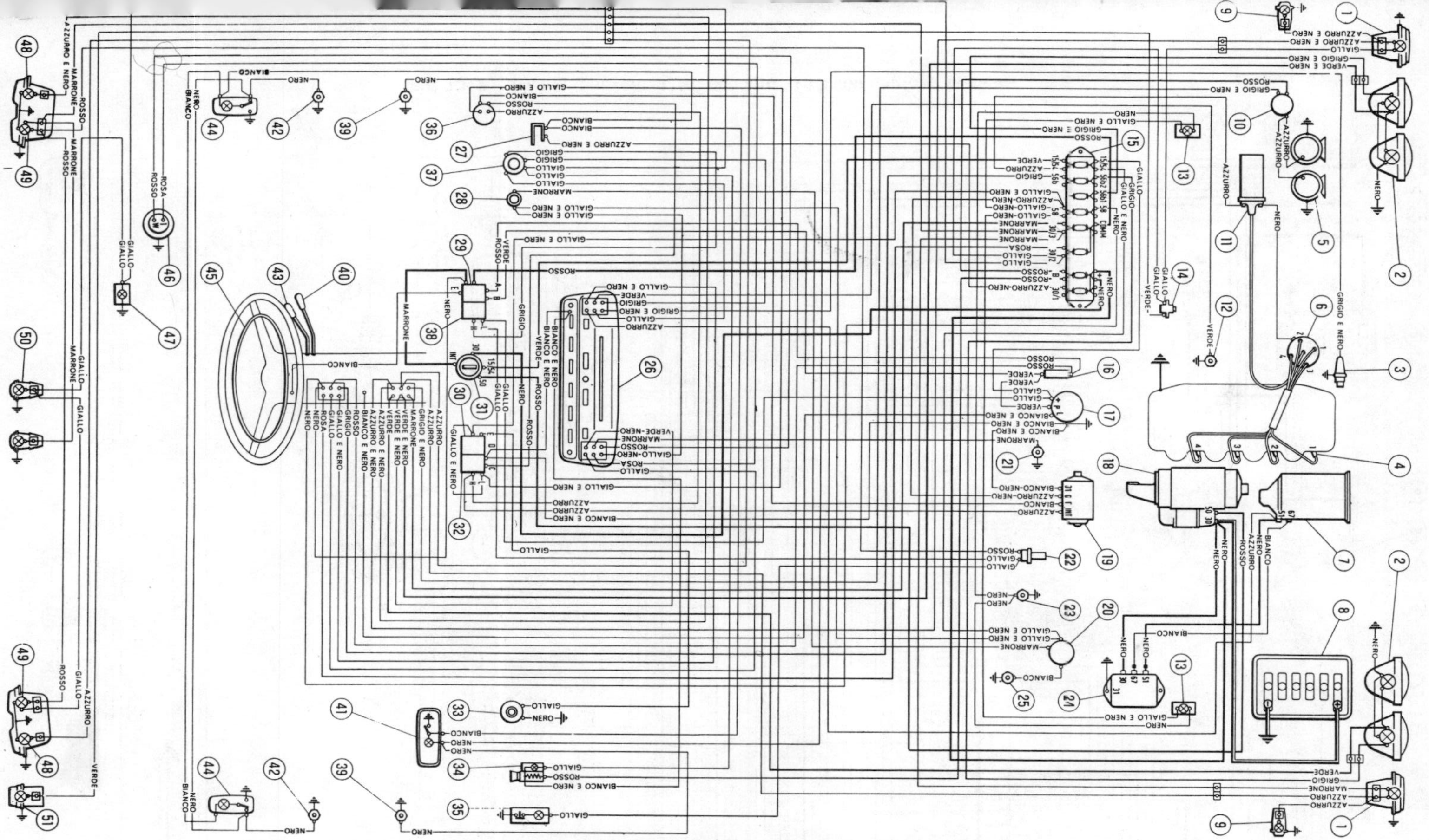

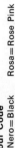

Key to Fig 13:1 1 Front parking and directional signal lights 2 High and low beam dual headlights 3 Low oil pressure indicator sending unit 4 Spark plugs 5 Horns 6 Ignition distributor 7 Generator 8 Battery 9 Side directional signal lights 10 Horn relay switch 11 Ignition coil 12 Temperature gauge sending unit 13 Engine compartment lights 14 Reversing lamp switch 15 Fuses 16 Directional signal indicator light dimming resistor 17 Directional signal light flasher unit 18 Starting motor 19 Windshield wiper motor 20 Manual brake warning light flasher unit 21 Choke warning light switch 22 Stoplight switch 23 Engine compartment light switch 24 Generator regulator 25 Manual brake warning light switch 26 Instrument cluster 27 Trouble light receptacle 28 Manual brake blinking warning light 29 Master light switch 30 Heater fan switch 31 Ignition, lighting and starting key-operated switch 32 Windshield wiper switch 33 Heater fan switch 34 Electric cigar lighter 35 Glove compartment light, with built-in button switch 36 Windshield wiper and washer operating pedal 37 Instrument cluster light and parking light indicator rheostats 38 Instrument cluster light switch 39 Rear view mirror courtesy light front quarter door switches 40 Front light beam shifting switch lever 41 Courtesy light rheostat and switch, built-in rear view mirror 42 Roof light rear quarter door switches 43 Directional signal switch lever 44 Roof lights, with switch built-in 45 Horn ring 46 Fuel gauge 47 Boot compartment light 48 Boot compartment light 49 Tail and stoplights 50 License plate lights 51 Reversing lamp sending unit NOTE—The wiring diagram to suit the Station Wagon differs only for the absence of the boot light (47)

Cable Colour Code

Rosa = Rose Pink	Rosso = Red	Grigio = Grey	Marrone = Brown	

Key to Cable Colour Code Azzurro = Blue Bianco = White Giallo = Yellow Nero = Black
Verde = Green INT Comm = Switch

FIG 13:1 Wiring diagram, 115.000 and 116.000 engined vehicles

FIAT 1300/1500

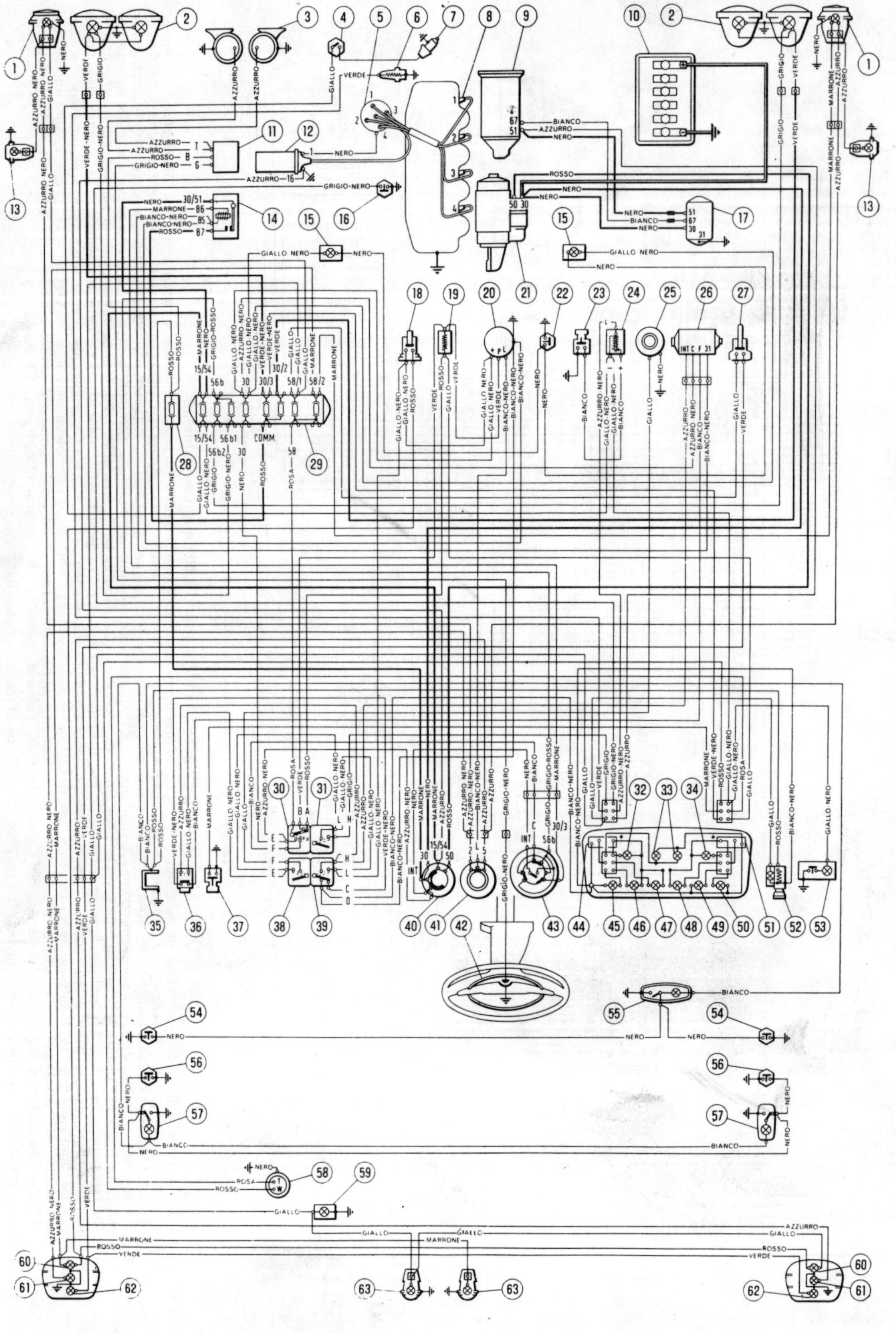

FIG 13:2 Wiring diagram, 115C.000 and 116C.000 engined vehicles

Key to Fig 13:2 1 Front parking and directional signal lights 2 High and low beam dual headlights 3 Horns 4 Electromagnetic fan thermal switch 5 Ignition distributor 6 Temperature gauge sending unit 7 Electromagnetic fan 8 Spark plugs 9 Generator 10 Battery 11 Horn relay switch 12 Ignition coil 13 Side directional signal lights 14 High beam relay switch 15 Engine compartment lights 16 Low oil pressure indicator sending unit 17 Generator regulator 18 Stoplight switch 19 Directional signal indicator light dimming resistor 20 Directional signal light flasher unit 21 Starting motor 22 Engine compartment light switch 23 Parking brake warning light switch 24 Parking brake warning light flasher unit 25 Blower 26 Wiper motor 27 Reversing light switch 28 16-amp fuse 29 8-amp fuses 30 Outer lighting master switch 31 Instrument cluster light switch 32 Low oil pressure indicator (red light) 33 Instrument cluster lights 34 Fuel reserve supply indicator (red light) 35 Trouble light receptacle 36 Windshield washer wiper pedal switch 37 Choke warning light switch 38 Blower switch 39 Windshield wiper switch 40 Key type ignition switch, also energizing warning lights and starting circuits 41 Directional signal switch 42 Horn control ring 43 Change-over switch for outer lighting and light flashes 44 Water temperature gauge 45 Parking light indicator (green light) 46 No-charge indicator (red light) 47 Parking brake warning light (red, blinking) 48 Choke warning light, (orange-yellow) 49 High beam indicator (blue light) 50 Directional signal indicator (green light) 51 Fuel gauge 52 Electric cigar lighter 53 Glove compartment light, with switch built-in 54 Courtesy light switches on front quarter doors 55 Rear view mirror map light and switch 56 Roof light switches on rear quarter doors 57 Roof lights with toggle switch built in 58 Fuel gauge tank unit 59 Boot compartment light 60 Tail and stoplights 61 Rear d rectional signal lights 62 Reversing lights 63 License plate lights

Cable Colour Code

Key to Cable Colour Code Bianco=White Giallo=Yellow Azzurro=Blue Rosso=Red Rosa=Pink Nero=Black Marrone=Brown Verde=Green Grigio=Grey Bianco-Nero=Black and White Giallo-Nero=Black and Yellow Azzurro-Nero=Black and Yellow Grigio-Nero=Black and Grey Verde-Nero=Black and Green Grigio-Rosso=Red and Grey COMM-INT.=Switch

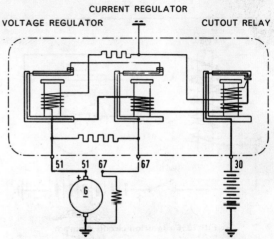

FIG 13:3 GN2/12/28 regulator circuit diagram

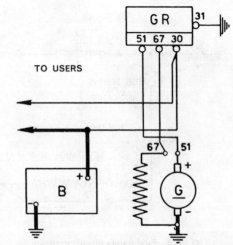

FIG 13:4 Regulator and generator charging circuit

Key to Fig 13:4 GR=Regulator B=Battery G=Generator

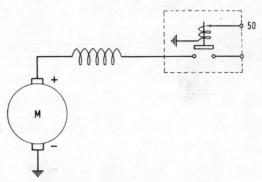

FIG 13:5 Starter motor circuit diagram

FIAT 1300/1500

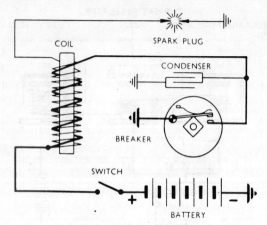

FIG 13:6 Ignition circuit diagram

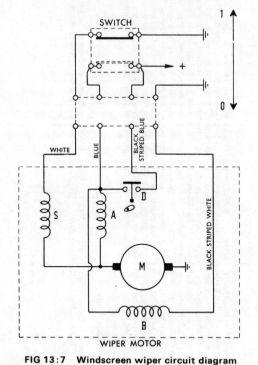

FIG 13:7 Windscreen wiper circuit diagram

Key to Fig 13:7   **A** Series winding   **B** Shunt winding
D Parking switch   **M** Motor   **S** Extra winding

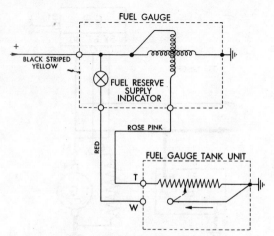

FIG 13:8 Fuel gauge circuit diagram

Inches	Decimals	Milli-metres	Inches to Millimetres: Inches	mm	Millimetres to Inches: mm	Inches
1/64	.015625	.3969	001	.0254	.01	.00039
1/32	.03125	.7937	.002	.0508	.02	.00079
3/64	.046875	1.1906	.003	.0762	.03	.00118
1/16	.0625	1.5875	.004	.1016	.04	.00157
5/64	.078125	1.9844	.005	.1270	.05	.00197
3/32	.09375	2.3812	.006	.1524	.06	.00236
7/64	.109375	2.7781	.007	.1778	.07	.00276
1/8	.125	3.1750	.008	.2032	.08	.00315
9/64	.140625	3.5719	.009	.2286	.09	.00354
5/32	.15625	3.9687	.01	.254	.1	.00394
11/64	.171875	4.3656	.02	.508	.2	.00787
3/16	.1875	4.7625	.03	.762	.3	.01181
13/64	.203125	5·1594	.04	1.010	.4	.01575
7/32	.21875	5.5562	.05	1.270	.5	.01969
15/64	.234375	5.9531	.06	1.524	.6	.02362
1/4	.25	6.3500	.07	1.778	.7	.02756
17/64	.265625	6.7469	.08	2.032	.8	.03150
9/32	.28125	7.1437	.09	2.286	.9	.03543
19/64	.296875	7.5406	.1	2.54	1	.03937
5/16	.3125	7.9375	.2	5.08	2	.07874
21/64	.328125	8.3344	.3	7.62	3	.11811
11/32	.34375	8.7312	.4	10.16	4	.15748
23/64	.359375	9.1281	.5	12.70	5	.19685
3/8	.375	9.5250	.6	15.24	6	.23622
25/64	.390625	9.9219	.7	17.78	7	.27559
13/32	.40625	10.3187	.8	20.32	8	.31496
27/64	.421875	10.7156	.9	22.86	9	.35433
7/16	.4375	11.1125	1	25.4	10	.39370
29/64	.453125	11.5094	2	50.8	11	.43307
15/32	.46875	11.9062	3	76.2	12	.47244
31/64	.484375	12.3031	4	101.6	13	.51181
1/2	.5·	12.7000	5	127.0	14	.55118
33/64	.515625	13.0969	6	152.4	15	.59055
17/32	.53125	13.4937	7	177.8	16	.62992
35/64	.546875	13.8906	8	203.2	17	.66929
9/16	.5625	14.2875	9	228.6	18	.70866
37/64	.578125	14.6844	10	254.0	19	.74803
19/32	.59375	15.0812	11	279.4	20	.78740
39/64	.609375	15.4781	12	304.8	21	.82677
5/8	.625	15.8750	13	330.2	22	.86614
41/64	.640625	16.2719	14	355.6	23	.90551
21/32	.65625	16.6687	15	381.0	24	.94488
43/64	.671875	17.0656	16	406.4	25	.98425
11/16	.6875	17.4625	17	431.8	26	1.02362
45/64	.703125	17.8594	18	457.2	27	1.06299
23/32	.71875	18.2562	19	482.6	28	1.10236
47/64	.734375	18.6531	20	508.0	29	1.14173
3/4	.75	19.0500	21	533.4	30	1.18110
49/64	.765625	19.4469	22	558.8	31	1.22047
25/32	.78125	19.8437	23	584.2	32	1.25984
51/64	.796875	20.2406	24	609.6	33	1.29921
13/16	.8125	20.6375	25	635.0	34	1.33858
53/64	.828125	21.0344	26	660.4	35	1.37795
27/32	.84375	21.4312	27	685.8	36	1.41732
55/64	.859375	21.8281	28	711.2	37	1.4567
7/8	.875	22.2250	29	736.6	38	1.4961
57/64	.890625	22.6219	30	762.0	39	1.5354
29/32	.90625	23.0187	31	787.4	40	1.5748
59/64	.921875	23.4156	32	812.8	41	1.6142
15/16	.9375	23.8125	33	838.2	42	1.6535
61/64	.953125	24.2094	34	863.6	43	1.6929
31/32	.96875	24.6062	35	889.0	44	1.7323
63/64	.984375	25.0031	36	914.4	45	1.7717

UNITS	Pints to Litres	Gallons to Litres	Litres to Pints	Litres to Gallons	Miles to Kilometres	Kilometres to Miles	Lbs. per sq. In. to Kg. per sq. Cm.	Kg. per sq. Cm. to Lbs. per sq. In.
1	.57	4.55	1.76	.22	1.61	.62	.07	14.22
2	1.14	9.09	3.52	.44	3.22	1.24	.14	28.50
3	1.70	13.64	5.28	.66	4.83	1.86	.21	42.67
4	2.27	18.18	7.04	.88	6.44	2.49	.28	56.89
5	2.84	22.73	8.80	1.10	8.05	3.11	.35	71.12
6	3.41	27.28	10.56	1.32	9.66	3.73	.42	85.34
7	3.98	31.82	12.32	1.54	11.27	4.35	.49	99.56
8	4.55	36.37	14.08	1.76	12.88	4.97	.56	113.79
9		40.91	15.84	1.98	14.48	5.59·	.63	128.00
10		45.46	17.60	2.20	16.09	6.21	.70	142.23
20				4.40	32.19	12.43	1.41	284.47
30				6.60	48.28	18.64	2.11	426.70
40				8.80	64.37	24.85		
50					80.47	31.07		
60					96.56	37.28		
70					112.65	43.50		
80					128.75	49.71		
90					144.84	55.92		
100					160.93	62.14		

UNITS	Lb ft to kgm	Kgm to lb ft	UNITS	Lb ft to kgm	Kgm to lb ft
1	.138	7.233	7	.967	50.631
2	.276	14.466	8	1.106	57.864
3	.414	21.699	9	1.244	65.097
4	.553	28.932	10	1.382	72.330
5	.691	36.165	20	2.765	144.660
6	.829	43.398	30	4.147	216.990

HINTS ON MAINTENANCE AND OVERHAUL

There are few things more rewarding than the restoration of a vehicle's original peak of efficiency and smooth performance.

The following notes are intended to help the owner to reach that state of perfection. Providing that he possesses the basic manual skills he should have no difficulty in performing most of the operations detailed in this manual. It must be stressed, however, that where recommended in the manual, highly-skilled operations ought to be entrusted to experts, who have the necessary equipment, to carry out the work satisfactorily.

Quality of workmanship:

The hazardous driving conditions on the roads to-day demand that vehicles should be as nearly perfect, mechanically, as possible. It is therefore most important that amateur work be carried out with care, bearing in mind the often inadequate working conditions, and also the inferior tools which may have to be used. It is easy to counsel perfection in all things, and we recognize that it may be setting an impossibly high standard. We do, however, suggest that every care should be taken to ensure that a vehicle is as safe to take on the road as it is humanly possible to make it.

Safe working conditions:

Even though a vehicle may be stationary, it is still potentially dangerous if certain sensible precautions are not taken when working on it while it is supported on jacks or blocks. It is indeed preferable not to use jacks alone, but to supplement them with carefully placed blocks, so that there will be plenty of support if the car rolls off the jacks during a strenuous manoeuvre. Axle stands are an excellent way of providing a rigid base which is not readily disturbed. Piles of bricks are a dangerous substitute. Be careful not to get under heavy loads on lifting tackle, the load could fall. It is preferable not to work alone when lifting an engine, or when working underneath a vehicle which is supported well off the ground. To be trapped, particularly under the vehicle, may have unpleasant results if help is not quickly forthcoming. Make some provision, however humble, to deal with fires. Always disconnect a battery if there is a likelihood of electrical shorts. These may start a fire if there is leaking fuel about. This applies particularly to leads which can carry a heavy current, like those in the starter circuit. While on the subject of electricity, we must also stress the danger of using equipment which is run off the mains and which has no earth or has faulty wiring or connections. So many workshops have damp floors, and electrical shocks are of such a nature that it is sometimes impossible to let go of a live lead or piece of equipment due to the muscular spasms which take place.

Work demanding special care:

This involves the servicing of braking, steering and suspension systems. On the road, failure of the braking system may be disastrous. Make quite sure that there can be no possibility of failure through the bursting of rusty brake pipes or rotten hoses, nor to a sudden loss of pressure due to defective seals or valves.

Problems:

The chief problems which may face an operator are:
1 External dirt.
2 Difficulty in undoing tight fixings
3 Dismantling unfamiliar mechanisms.
4 Deciding in what respect parts are defective.
5 Confusion about the correct order for reassembly.
6 Adjusting running clearances.
7 Road testing.
8 Final tuning.

Practical suggestion to solve the problems:

1 Preliminary cleaning of large parts—engines, transmissions, steering, suspensions, etc.,—should be carried out before removal from the car. Where road dirt and mud alone are present, wash clean with a high-pressure water jet, brushing to remove stubborn adhesions, and allow to drain and dry. Where oil or grease is also present, wash down with a proprietary compound (Gunk, Teepol etc.,) applying with a stiff brush—an old paint brush is suitable—into all crevices. Cover the distributor and ignition coils with a polythene bag and then apply a strong water jet to clear the loosened deposits. Allow to drain and dry. The assemblies will then be sufficiently clean to remove and transfer to the bench for the next stage.

On the bench, further cleaning can be carried out, first wiping the parts as free as possible from grease with old newspaper. Avoid using rag or cotton waste which can leave clogging fibres behind. Any remaining grease can be removed with a brush dipped in paraffin. If necessary, traces of paraffin can be removed by carbon tetrachloride. Avoid using paraffin or petrol in large quantities for cleaning in enclosed areas, such as garages, on account of the high fire risk.

When all exteriors have been cleaned, and not before, dismantling can be commenced. This ensures that dirt will not enter into interiors and orifices revealed by dismantling. In the next phases, where components have to be cleaned, use carbon tetrachloride in preference to petrol and keep the containers covered except when in use. After the components have been cleaned, plug small holes with tapered hard wood plugs cut to size and blank off larger orifices with grease-proof paper and masking tape. Do not use soft wood plugs or matchsticks as they may break.

2 It is not advisable to hammer on the end of a screw thread, but if it must be done, first screw on a nut to protect the thread, and use a lead hammer. This applies particularly to the removal of tapered cotters. Nuts and bolts seem to 'grow' together, especially in exhaust systems. If penetrating oil does not work, try the judicious application of heat, but be careful of starting a fire. Asbestos sheet or cloth is useful to isolate heat.

Tight bushes or pieces of tail-pipe rusted into a silencer can be removed by splitting them with an open-ended hacksaw. Tight screws can sometimes be started by a tap from a hammer on the end of a suitable screwdriver. Many tight fittings will yield to the judicious use of a hammer, but it must be a soft-faced hammer if damage is to be avoided, use a heavy block on the opposite side to absorb shock. Any parts of the steering system which have been damaged should be renewed, as attempts to repair them may lead to cracking and subsequent failure, and steering ball joints should be disconnected using a recommended tool to prevent damage.

3 If often happens that an owner is baffled when trying to dismantle an unfamiliar piece of equipment. So many modern devices are pressed together or assembled by spinning-over flanges, that they must be sawn apart. The intention is that the whole assembly must be renewed. However, parts which appear to be in one piece to the naked eye, may reveal close-fitting joint lines when inspected with a magnifying glass, and, this may provide the necessary clue to dismantling. Left-handed screw threads are used where rotational forces would tend to unscrew a right-handed screw thread.

Be very careful when dismantling mechanisms which may come apart suddenly. Work in an enclosed space where the parts will be contained, and drape a piece of cloth over the device if springs are likely to fly in all directions. Mark everything which might be reassembled in the wrong position, scratched symbols may be used on unstressed parts, or a sequence of tiny dots from a centre punch can be useful. Stressed parts should never be scratched or centre-popped as this may lead to cracking under working conditions. Store parts which look alike in the correct order for reassembly. Never rely upon memory to assist in the assembly of complicated mechanisms, especially when they will be dismantled for a long time, but make notes, and drawings to supplement the diagrams in the manual, and put labels on detached wires. Rust stains may indicate unlubricated wear. This can sometimes be seen round the outside edge of a bearing cup in a universal joint. Look for bright rubbing marks on parts which normally should not make heavy contact. These might prove that something is bent or running out of truth. For example, there might be bright marks on one side of a piston, at the top near the ring grooves, and others at the bottom of the skirt on the other side. This coul well be the clue to a bent connecting rod. Suspected cracks can be proved by heating the component in a light oil to approximately 100°C, removing, drying off, and dusting with french chalk, if a crack is present the oil retained in the crack will stain the french chalk.

4 In determining wear, and the degree, against the permissible limits set in the manual, accurate measurement can only be achieved by the use of a micrometer. In many cases, the wear is given to the fourth place of decimals; that is in ten-thousandths of an inch. This can be read by the vernier scale on the barrel of a good micrometer. Bore diameters are more difficult to determine. If, however, the matching shaft is accurately measured, the degree of play in the bore can be felt as a guide to its suitability. In other cases, the shank of a twist drill of known diameter is a handy check.

Many methods have been devised for determining the clearance between bearing surfaces. To-day the best and simplest is by the use of Plastigage, obtainable from most garages. A thin plastic thread is laid between the two surfaces and the bearing is tightened, flattening the thread. On removal, the width of the thread is compared with a scale supplied with the thread and the clearance is read off directly. Sometimes joint faces leak persistently, even after gasket renewal. The fault will then be traceable to distortion, dirt or burrs. Studs which are screwed into soft metal frequently raise burrs at the point of entry. A quick cure for this is to chamfer the edge of the hole in the part which fits over the stud.

5 **Always check a replacement part with the original one before it is fitted.**

If parts are not marked, and the order for reassembly is not known, a little detective work will help. Look for marks which are due to wear to see if they can be mated. Joint faces may not be identical due to manufacturing errors, and parts which overlap may be stained, giving a clue to the correct position. Most fixings leave identifying marks especially if they were painted over on assembly. It is then easier to decide whether a nut, for instance, has a plain, a spring, or a shakeproof washer under it. All running surfaces become 'bedded' together after long spells of work and tiny imperfections on one part will be found to have left corresponding marks on the other. This is particularly true of shafts and bearings and even a score on a cylinder wall will show on the piston.

6 Checking end float or rocker clearances by feeler gauge may not always give accurate results because of wear. For instance, the rocker tip which bears on a valve stem may be deeply pitted, in which case the feeler will simply be bridging a depression. Thrust washers may also wear depressions in opposing faces to make accurate measurement difficult. End float is then easier to check by using a dial gauge. It is common practice to adjust end play in bearing assemblies, like front hubs with taper rollers, by doing up the axle nut until the hub becomes stiff to turn and then backing it off a little. Do not use this method with ballbearing hubs as the assembly is often preloaded by tightening the axle nut to its fullest extent. If the splitpin hole will not line up, file the base of the nut a little.

Steering assemblies often wear in the straight-ahead position. If any part is adjusted, make sure that it remains free when moved from lock to lock. Do not be surprised if an assembly like a steering gearbox, which is known to be carefully adjusted outside the car, becomes stiff when it is bolted in place. This will be due to distortion of the case by the pull of the mounting bolts, particularly if the mounting points are not all touching together. This problem may be met in other equipment and is cured by careful attention to the alignment of mounting points.

When a spanner is stamped with a size and A/F it means that the dimension is the width between the jaws and has no connection with ANF, which is the designation for the American National Fine thread. Coarse threads like Whitworth are rarely used on cars to-day except for studs which screw into soft aluminium or cast iron. For this reason it might be found that the top end of a cylinder head stud has a fine thread and the lower end a coarse thread to screw into the cylinder block. If the car has mainly UNF threads then it is likely that any coarse threads will be UNC, which are not the same as Whitworth. Small sizes have the same number of threads in Whitworth and UNC, but in the $\frac{1}{2}$ inch size for example, there are twelve threads to the inch in the former and thirteen in the latter.

7 After a major overhaul, particularly if a great deal of work has been done on the braking, steering and suspension systems, it is advisable to approach the problem of testing with care. If the braking system has been overhauled, apply heavy pressure to the brake pedal and get a second operator to check every possible source of leakage. The brakes may work extremely well, but a lead could cause complete failure after a few miles.

Do not fit the hub caps until every wheel nut has been checked for tightness, and make sure the tyre pressures are correct. Check the levels of coolant, lubricants and hydraulic fluids. Being satisfied that all is well, take the car on the road and test the brakes at once. Check the steering and the action of the handbrake. Do all this at moderate speeds on quiet roads, and make sure there is no other vehicle behind you when you try a rapid stop.

Finally, remember that many parts settle down after a time, so check for tightness of all fixings after the car has been on the road for a hundred miles or so.

8 It is useless to tune an engine which has not reached its normal running temperature. In the same way, the tune of an engine which is stiff after a rebore will be different when the engine is again running free. Remember too, that rocker clearances on pushrod operated valve gear will change when the cylinder head nuts are tightened after an initial period of running with a new head gasket.

Trouble may not always be due to what seems the obvious cause. Ignition, carburation and mechanical condition are interdependent and spitting back through the carburetter, which might be attributed to a weak mixture, can be caused by a sticking inlet valve.

For one final hint on tuning, never adjust more than one thing at a time or it will be impossible to tell which adjustment produced the desired result.

GLOSSARY OF TERMS

Allen key Cranked wrench of hexagonal section for use with socket head screws.

Alternator Electrical generator producing alternating current. Rectified to direct current for battery charging.

Ambient temperature Surrounding atmospheric temperature.

Annulus Used in engineering to indicate the outer ring gear of an epicyclic gear train.

Armature The shaft carrying the windings, which rotates in the magnetic field of a generator or starter motor. That part of a solenoid or relay which is activated by the magnetic field.

Axial In line with, or pertaining to, an axis.

Backlash Play in meshing gears.

Balance lever A bar where force applied at the centre is equally divided between connections at the ends.

Banjo axle Axle casing with large diameter housing for the crownwheel and differential.

Bendix pinion A self-engaging and self-disengaging drive on a starter motor shaft.

Bevel pinion A conical shaped gearwheel, designed to mesh with a similar gear with an axis usually at 90 deg. to its own.

bhp Brake horse power, measured on a dynamometer.

bmep Brake mean effective pressure. Average pressure on a piston during the working stroke.

Brake cylinder Cylinder with hydraulically operated piston(s) acting on brake shoes or pad(s).

Brake regulator Control valve fitted in hydraulic braking system which limits brake pressure to rear brakes during heavy braking to prevent rear wheel locking.

Camber Angle at which a wheel is tilted from the vertical.

Capacitor Modern term for an electrical condenser. Part of distributor assembly, connected across contact breaker points, acts as an interference suppressor.

Castellated Top face of a nut, slotted across the flats, to take a locking splitpin.

Castor Angle at which the kingpin or swivel pin is tilted when viewed from the side.

cc Cubic centimetres. Engine capacity is arrived at by multiplying the area of the bore in sq cm by the stroke in cm by the number of cylinders.

Clevis U-shaped forked connector used with a clevis pin, usually at handbrake connections.

Collet A type of collar, usually split and located in a groove in a shaft, and held in place by a retainer. The arrangement used to retain the spring(s) on a valve stem in most cases.

Commutator Rotating segmented current distributor between armature windings and brushes in generator or motor.

Compression The ratio, or quantitative relation, of the total volume (piston at bottom of stroke) to the unswept volume (piston at top of stroke) in an engine cylinder.

Condenser See capacitor.

Core plug Plug for blanking off a manufacturing hole in a casting.

Crownwheel Large bevel gear in rear axle, driven by a bevel pinion attached to the propeller shaft. Sometimes called a 'ring wheel'.

'C'-spanner Like a 'C' with a handle. For use on screwed collars without flats, but with slots or holes.

Damper Modern term for shock-absorber, used in vehicle suspension systems to damp out spring oscillations.

Depression The lowering of atmospheric pressure as in the inlet manifold and carburetter.

Dowel Close tolerance pin, peg, tube, or bolt, which accurately locates mating parts.

Drag link Rod connecting steering box drop arm (pitman arm) to nearest front wheel steering arm in certain types of steering systems.

Dry liner Thinwall tube pressed into cylinder bore

Dry sump Lubrication system where all oil is scavenged from the sump, and returned to a separate tank.

Dynamo See Generator.

Electrode Terminal, part of an electrical component, such as the points or 'Electrodes' of a sparking plug.

Electrolyte In lead-acid car batteries a solution of sulphuric acid and distilled water.

End float The axial movement between associated parts, end play.

EP Extreme pressure. In lubricants, special grades for heavily loaded bearing surfaces, such as gear teeth in a gearbox, or crownwheel and pinion in a rear axle.

Fade	Of brakes. Reduced efficiency due to overheating.
Field coils	Windings on the polepieces of motors and generators.
Fillets	Narrow finishing strips usually applied to interior bodywork.
First motion shaft	Input shaft from clutch to gearbox.
Fullflow filter	Filters in which all the oil is pumped to the engine. If the element becomes clogged, a bypass valve operates to pass unfiltered oil to the engine.
FWD	Front wheel drive.
Gear pump	Two meshing gears in a close fitting casing. Oil is carried from the inlet round the outside of both gears in the spaces between the gear teeth and casing to the outlet, the meshing gear teeth prevent oil passing back to the inlet, and the oil is forced through the outlet port.
Generator	Modern term for 'Dynamo'. When rotated produces electrical current.
Grommet	A ring of protective or sealing material. Can be used to protect pipes or leads passing through bulkheads.
Grubscrew	Fully threaded headless screw with screwdriver slot. Used for locking, or alignment purposes.
Gudgeon pin	Shaft which connects a piston to its connecting rod. Sometimes called 'wrist pin', or 'piston pin'.
Halfshaft	One of a pair transmitting drive from the differential.
Helical	In spiral form. The teeth of helical gears are cut at a spiral angle to the side faces of the gearwheel.
Hot spot	Hot area that assists vapourisation of fuel on its way to cylinders. Often provided by close contact between inlet and exhaust manifolds.
HT	High Tension. Applied to electrical current produced by the ignition coil for the sparking plugs.
Hydrometer	A device for checking specific gravity of liquids. Used to check specific gravity of electrolyte.
Hypoid bevel gears	A form of bevel gear used in the rear axle drive gears. The bevel pinion meshes below the centre line of the crownwheel, giving a lower propeller shaft line.
Idler	A device for passing on movement. A free running gear between driving and driven gears. A lever transmitting track rod movement to a side rod in steering gear.
Impeller	A centrifugal pumping element. Used in water pumps to stimulate flow.
Journals	Those parts of a shaft that are in contact with the bearings.
Kingpin	The main vertical pin which carries the front wheel spindle, and permits steering movement. May be called 'steering pin' or 'swivel pin'.
Layshaft	The shaft which carries the laygear in the gearbox. The laygear is driven by the first motion shaft and drives the third motion shaft according to the gear selected. Sometimes called the 'countershaft' or 'second motion shaft.'
lb ft	A measure of twist or torque. A pull of 10 lb at a radius of 1 ft is a torque of 10 lb ft.
lb/sq in	Pounds per square inch.
Little-end	The small, or piston end of a connecting rod. Sometimes called the 'small-end'.
LT	Low Tension. The current output from the battery.
Mandrel	Accurately manufactured bar or rod used for test or centring purposes.
Manifold	A pipe, duct, or chamber, with several branches.
Needle rollers	Bearing rollers with a length many times their diameter.
Oil bath	Reservoir which lubricates parts by immersion. In air filters, a separate oil supply for wetting a wire mesh element to hold the dust.
Oil wetted	In air filters, a wire mesh element lightly oiled to trap and hold airborne dust.
Overlap	Period during which inlet and exhaust valves are open together.
Panhard rod	Bar connected between fixed point on chassis and another on axle to control sideways movement.
Pawl	Pivoted catch which engages in the teeth of a ratchet to permit movement in one direction only.
Peg spanner	Tool with pegs, or pins, to engage in holes or slots in the part to be turned.
Pendant pedals	Pedals with levers that are pivoted at the top end.
Phillips screwdriver	A cross-point screwdriver for use with the cross-slotted heads of Phillips screws.
Pinion	A small gear, usually in relation to another gear.
Piston-type damper	Shock absorber in which damping is controlled by a piston working in a closed oil-filled cylinder.
Preloading	Preset static pressure on ball or roller bearings not due to working loads.
Radial	Radiating from a centre, like the spokes of a wheel.

Radius rod   Pivoted arm confining movement of a part to an arc of fixed radius.

Ratchet   Toothed wheel or rack which can move in one direction only, movement in the other being prevented by a pawl.

Ring gear   A gear tooth ring attached to outer periphery of flywheel. Starter pinion engages with it during starting.

Runout   Amount by which rotating part is out of true.

Semi-floating axle   Outer end of rear axle halfshaft is carried on bearing inside axle casing. Wheel hub is secured to end of shaft.

Servo   A hydraulic or pneumatic system for assisting, or, augmenting a physical effort. See 'Vacuum Servo'.

Setscrew   One which is threaded for the full length of the shank.

Shackle   A coupling link, used in the form of two parallel pins connected by side plates to secure the end of the master suspension spring and absorb the effects of deflection.

Shell bearing   Thinwalled steel shell lined with anti-friction metal. Usually semi-circular and used in pairs for main and big-end bearings.

Shock absorber   See 'Damper'.

Silentbloc   Rubber bush bonded to inner and outer metal sleeves.

Socket-head screw   Screw with hexagonal socket for an Allen key.

Solenoid   A coil of wire creating a magnetic field when electric current passes through it. Used with a soft iron core to operate contacts or a mechanical device.

Spur gear   A gear with teeth cut axially across the periphery.

Stub axle   Short axle fixed at one end only.

Tachometer   An instrument for accurate measurement of rotating speed. Usually indicates in revolutions per minute.

TDC   Top Dead Centre. The highest point reached by a piston in a cylinder, with the crank and connecting rod in line.

Thermostat   Automatic device for regulating temperature. Used in vehicle coolant systems to open a valve which restricts circulation at low temperature.

Third motion shaft   Output shaft of gearbox.

Threequarter floating axle   Outer end of rear axle halfshaft flanged and bolted to wheel hub, which runs on bearing mounted on outside of axle casing. Vehicle weight is not carried by the axle shaft.

Thrust bearing or washer   Used to reduce friction in rotating parts subject to axial loads.

Torque   Turning or twisting effort. See 'lb ft'.

Track rod   The bar(s) across the vehicle which connect the steering arms and maintain the front wheels in their correct alignment.

UJ   Universal joint. A coupling between shafts which permits angular movement.

UNF   Unified National Fine screw thread.

Vacuum servo   Device used in brake system, using difference between atmospheric pressure and inlet manifold depression to operate a piston which acts to augment brake pressure as required. See 'Servo'.

Venturi   A restriction or 'choke' in a tube, as in a carburetter, used to increase velocity to obtain a reduction in pressure.

Vernier   A sliding scale for obtaining fractional readings of the graduations of an adjacent scale.

Welch plug   A domed thin metal disc which is partially flattened to lock in a recess. Used to plug core holes in castings.

Wet liner   Removeable cylinder barrel, sealed against coolant leakage, where the coolant is in direct contact with the outer surface.

Wet sump   A reservoir attached to the crankcase to hold the lubricating oil.

INDEX

THE AUTOBOOK SERIES OF WORKSHOP MANUALS

Make				Author	Title
ALFA ROMEO					
1600 Giulia TI 1961–67	..	..	..	Ball	Alfa Romeo Giulia 1962–70 Autobook
1600 Giulia Sprint 1962–68	..	..	..	Ball	Alfa Romeo Giulia 1962–70 Autobook
1600 Giulia Spider 1962–68	..	..	..	Ball	Alfa Romeo Giulia 1962–70 Autobook
1600 Giulia Super 1965–70	..	..	..	Ball	Alfa Romeo Giulia 1962–70 Autobook
ASTON MARTIN					
All models 1921–58	..	..	..	Coram	Aston Martin 1921–58 Autobook
AUSTIN					
A30 1951–56	..	..	..	Ball	Austin A30, A35, A40 Autobook
A35 1956–62	..	..	..	Ball	Austin A30, A35, A40 Autobook
A40 Farina 1957–67	..	..	..	Ball	Austin A30, A35, A40 Autobook
A40 Cambridge 1954–57	..	..	..	Ball	BMC Autobook Three
A50 Cambridge 1954–57	..	..	..	Ball	BMC Autobook Three
A55 Cambridge Mk 1 1957–58	..	..	..	Ball	BMC Autobook Three
A55 Cambridge Mk 2 1958–61	..	..	..	Ball	Austin A55 Mk 2, A60 1958–69 Autobook
A60 Cambridge 1961–69	..	..	..	Ball	Austin A55 Mk 2, A60 1958–69 Autobook
A99 1959–61	..	..	..	Ball	BMC Autobook Four
A110 1961–68	..	..	..	Ball	BMC Autobook Four
Mini 1959–70	..	..	..	Ball	Mini 1959–70 Autobook
Mini Clubman 1969–70	..	..	..	Ball	Mini 1959–70 Autobook
Mini Cooper 1961–70	..	..	..	Ball	Mini Cooper 1961–70 Autobook
Mini Cooper S 1963–70	..	..	..	Ball	Mini Cooper 1961–70 Autobook
1100 Mk 1 1963–67	..	..	..	Ball	1100 Mk 1 1962–67 Autobook
1100 Mk 2 1968–70	..	..	..	Ball	1100 Mk 2, 1300 Mk 1, 2, America 1968–71 Autobook
1300 Mk 1, 2 1968–71	..	..	..	Ball	1100 Mk 2, 1300 Mk 1, 2, America 1968–71 Autobook
America 1968–71	..	..	..	Ball	1100 Mk 2, 1300 Mk 1, 2, America 1968–71 Autobook
1800 Mk 1, 2 1964–71	..	..	..	Ball	1800 1964–71 Autobook
1800 S 1969–71	..	..	..	Ball	1800 1964–71 Autobook
Maxi 1500 1969–71	..	..	..	Ball	Austin Maxi 1969–71 Autobook
Maxi 1750 1970–71	..	..	..	Ball	Austin Maxi 1969–71 Autobook
AUSTIN HEALEY					
100/6 1956–59	..	..	..	Ball	Austin Healey 100/6, 3000 1956–68 Autobook
Sprite 1958–70	..	..	..	Ball	Sprite, Midget 1958–70 Autobook
3000 Mk 1, 2, 3 1959–68	..	..	..	Ball	Austin Healey 100/6, 3000 1956–68 Autobook
BEDFORD					
CA Mk 1 and 2 1961–69	..	..	..	Ball	Vauxhall Victor 1, 2 FB 1957–64 Autobook
Beagle HA 1964–66	..	..	..	Ball	Vauxhall Viva HA 1964–66 Autobook
BMW					
1600 1966–70	..	..	..	Ball	BMW 1600 1966–70 Autobook
1600–2 1966–70	..	..	..	Ball	BMW 1600 1966–70 Autobook
1600TI 1966–70	..	..	..	Ball	BMW 1600 1966–70 Autobook
1800 1964–70	..	..	..	Ball	BMW 1800 1964–70 Autobook
1800TI 1964–67	..	..	..	Ball	BMW 1800 1964–70 Autobook
2000 1966–70	..	..	..	Ball	BMW 2000, 2002 1966–70 Autobook
2000A 1966–70	..	..	..	Ball	BMW 2000, 2002 1966–70 Autobook
2000TI 1966–70	..	..	..	Ball	BMW 2000, 2002 1966–70 Autobook
2000CS 1967–70	..	..	..	Ball	BMW 2000, 2002 1966–70 Autobook
2000CA 1967–70	..	..	..	Ball	BMW 2000, 2002 1966–70 Autobook
2002 1968–70	..	..	..	Ball	BMW 2000, 2002 1966–70 Autobook
CITROEN					
DS19 1955–65	..	..	..	Ball	Citroen DS19, ID19 1955–66 Autobook
ID19 1956–66	..	..	..	Ball	Citroen DS19, ID19 1955–66 Autobook

FIAT 1300/1500

Make				Author	Title

COMMER

Cob Series 1, 2, 3 1960–65	..	..	..	Ball	Hillman Minx 1 to 5 1956–65 Autobook
Imp Vans 1963–68	..	..	..	Smith	Hillman Imp 1963–68 Autobook
Imp Vans 1969–71	..	..	..	Ball	Hillman Imp 1969–71 Autobook

DE DION BOUTON

One-cylinder 1899–1907	..	..	..	Mercredy	De Dion Bouton Autobook One
Two-cylinder 1903–1907	..	..	..	Mercredy	De Dion Bouton Autobook One
Four-cylinder 1905–1907	..	..	..	Mercredy	De Dion Bouton Autobook One

DATSUN

1300 1968–70	..	..	..	Ball	Datsun 1300, 1600 1968–70 Autobook
1600 1968–70	..	..	..	Ball	Datsun 1300, 1600 1968–70 Autobook

FIAT

500 1957–61	..	..	..	Ball	Fiat 500 1957–69 Autobook
500D 1960–65	..	..	..	Ball	Fiat 500 1957–69 Autobook
500F 1965–69	..	..	..	Ball	Fiat 500 1957–69 Autobook
500L 1968–69	..	..	..	Ball	Fiat 500 1957–69 Autobook
600 633cc 1955–61	..	..	..	Ball	Fiat 600, 600D 1955–69 Autobook
600D 767cc 1960–69	..	..	..	Ball	Fiat 600, 600D 1955–69 Autobook
850 Sedan 1964–70	..	..	..	Ball	Fiat 850 1964–70 Autobook
850 Coupé 1965–70	..	..	..	Ball	Fiat 850 1964–70 Autobook
850 Roadster 1965–70	..	..	..	Ball	Fiat 850 1964–70 Autobook
850 Family 1965–70	..	..	..	Ball	Fiat 850 1964–70 Autobook
850 Sport 1968–70	..	..	..	Ball	Fiat 850 1964–70 Autobook
124 Saloon 1966–70	..	..	..	Ball	Fiat 124 1966–70 Autobook
124S 1968–70	..	..	..	Ball	Fiat 124 1966–70 Autobook
124 Spyder 1966–70	..	..	..	Ball	Fiat 124 Sport 1966–70 Autobook
124 Coupé 1967–69	..	..	..	Ball	Fiat 124 Sport 1967–70 Autobook

FORD

Anglia 100E 1953–59	..	..	..	Ball	Ford Anglia Prefect 100E Autobook
Anglia 105E 1959–67	..	..	..	Smith	Ford Anglia 105E, Prefect 107E 1959–67 Autobook
Anglia Super 123E 1962–67	..	..	..	Smith	Ford Anglia 105E, Prefect 107E 1959–67 Autobook
Capri 109E 1962	..	..	..	Smith	Ford Classic, Capri 1961–64 Autobook
Capri 116E 1962–64	..	..	..	Smith	Ford Classic, Capri 1961–64 Autobook
Capri 1300, 1300GT 1968–71	..	..	..	Ball	Ford Capri 1300, 1600 1968–71 Autobook
Capri 1600, 1600GT 1968–71	..	..	..	Ball	Ford Capri 1300, 1600 1968–71 Autobook
Classic 109E 1961–62	..	..	..	Smith	Ford Classic, Capri 1961–64 Autobook
Classic 116E 1962–63	..	..	..	Smith	Ford Classic, Capri 1961–64 Autobook
Consul Mk 1 1950–56	..	..	..	Ball	Ford Consul, Zephyr, Zodiac 1, 2 1950–62 Autobook
Consul Mk 2 1956–62	..	..	..	Ball	Ford Consul, Zephyr, Zodiac 1, 2 1950–62 Autobook
Corsair Straight Four 1963–65	..	..	..	Ball	Ford Corsair Straight Four 1963–65 Autobook
Corsair Straight Four GT 1963–65	..	..	..	Ball	Ford Corsair Straight Four 1963–65 Autobook
Corsair V4 3004E 1965–68	..	..	..	Smith	Ford Corsair V4 1965–68 Autobook
Corsair V4 GT 1965–66	..	..	..	Smith	Ford Corsair V4 1965–68 Autobook
Corsair V4 1663cc 1969–70	..	..	..	Ball	Ford Corsair V4 1969–70 Autobook
Corsair 2000, 2000E 1966–68	..	..	..	Smith	Ford Corsair V4 1965–68 Autobook
Corsair 2000, 2000E 1969–70	..	..	..	Ball	Ford Corsair V4 1969–70 Autobook
Cortina 113E 1962–66	..	..	..	Smith	Ford Cortina 1962–66 Autobook
Cortina Super 118E 1963–66	..	..	..	Smith	Ford Cortina 1962–66 Autobook
Cortina Lotus 125E 1963–66	..	..	..	Smith	Ford Cortina 1962–66 Autobook
Cortina GT 118E 1963–66	..	..	..	Smith	Ford Cortina 1962–66 Autobook
Cortina 1300 1967–68	..	..	..	Smith	Ford Cortina 1967–68 Autobook
Cortina 1300 1969–70	..	..	..	Ball	Ford Cortina 1969–70 Autobook
Cortina 1500 1967–68	..	..	..	Smith	Ford Cortina 1967–68 Autobook
Cortina 1600 (including Lotus) 1967–68	..	..	..	Smith	Ford Cortina 1967–68 Autobook
Cortina 1600 1969–70	..	..	..	Ball	Ford Cortina 1969–70 Autobook
Escort 100E 1955–59	..	..	..	Ball	Ford Anglia Prefect 100E Autobook
Escort 1100 1967–71	..	..	..	Ball	Ford Escort 1967–71 Autobook

Make				Author	Title
Escort 1300 1967–71 ..	..	..	..	Ball	Ford Escort 1967–71 Autobook
Prefect 100E 1954–59	..	..	..	Ball	Ford Anglia Prefect 100E Autobook
Prefect 107E 1959–61	..	..	..	Smith	Ford Anglia 105E, Prefect 107E 1959–67 Autobook
Popular 100E 1959–62	..	..	..	Ball	Ford Anglia Prefect 100E Autobook
Squire 100E 1955–59 ..	..	..	..	Ball	Ford Anglia Prefect 100E Autobook
Zephyr Mk 1 1950–56	..	..	..	Ball	Ford Consul, Zephyr, Zodiac 1, 2 1950–62 Autobook
Zephyr Mk 2 1956–62	..	..	..	Ball	Ford Consul, Zephyr, Zodiac 1, 2 1950–62 Autobook
Zephyr 4 Mk 3 1962–66	..	..	..	Ball	Ford Zephyr, Zodiac Mk 3 1962–66 Autobook
Zephyr 6 Mk 3 1962–66	..	..	..	Ball	Ford Zephyr, Zodiac Mk 3 1962–66 Autobook
Zodiac Mk 3 1962–66..	..	..	..	Ball	Ford Zephyr, Zodiac Mk 3 1962–66 Autobook
Zodiac Mk 1 1953–56..	..	..	..	Ball	Ford Consul Zephyr, Zodiac 1, 2 1950–62 Autobook
Zodiac Mk 2 1956–62..	..	..	..	Ball	Ford Consul, Zephyr, Zodiac 1, 2 1950–62 Autobook
Zephyr V4 2 litre 1966–70	..	..	..	Ball	Ford Zephyr V4, V6, Zodiac 1966–70 Autobook
Zephyr V6 2 5 litre 1966–70	..	..	..	Ball	Ford Zephyr V4, V6, Zodiac 1966–70 Autobook
Zodiac V6 3 litre 1966–70	..	..	..	Ball	Ford Zephyr V4, V6, Zodiac 1966–70 Autobook

HILLMAN

Make				Author	Title
Avenger 1970–71	..	..	..	Ball	Hillman Avenger 1970–71 Autobook
Avenger GT 1970–71 ..	..	..	..	Ball	Hillman Avenger 1970–71 Autobook
Hunter GT 1966–70 ..	..	..	..	Ball	Hillman Hunter 1966–70 Autobook
Minx series 1, 2, 3 1956–59 ..	..	..	..	Ball	Hillman Minx 1 to 5 1956–65 Autobook
Minx series 3A, 3B, 3C 1959–63	..	..	..	Ball	Hillman Minx 1 to 5 1956–65 Autobook
Minx series 5 1963–65	..	..	..	Ball	Hillman Minx 1 to 5 1956–65 Autobook
Minx series 6 1965–67	..	..	..	Ball	Hillman Minx 1965–67 Autobook
New Minx 1500, 1725 1966–70	..	..	..	Ball	Hillman Minx 1966–70 Autobook
Imp 1963–68 ..	..	..	..	Smith	Hillman Imp 1963–68 Autobook
Imp 1969–71 ..	..	..	..	Ball	Hillman Imp 1969–71 Autobook
Husky series 1, 2, 3 1958–65 ..	..	..	..	Ball	Hillman Minx 1 to 5 1956–65 Autobook
Husky Estate 1969–71	..	..	..	Ball	Hillman Imp 1969–71 Autobook
Super Minx Mk 1, 2, 3 1961–65	..	..	..	Ball	Hillman Super Minx 1961–65 Autobook
Super Minx Mk 4 1965–67	..	..	..	Ball	Hillman Minx 1965–67 Autobook

HUMBER

Make				Author	Title
Sceptre Mk 1 1963–65	..	..	..	Ball	Hillman Super Minx 1961–65 Autobook
Sceptre Mk 2 1965–67	..	..	..	Ball	Hillman Minx 1965–67 Autobook
Sceptre 1967–70	..	..	..	Ball	Hillman Hunter 1966–70 Autobook

JAGUAR

Make				Author	Title
XK 120 1948–54	..	..	..	Ball	Jaguar XK 120, 140, 150 Mk 7, 8, 9 1948–61 Autobook
XK 140 1954–57	..	..	..	Ball	Jaguar XK 120, 140, 150 Mk 7, 8, 9 1948–61 Autobook
XK 150 1957–61	..	..	..	Ball	Jaguar XK 120, 140, 150 Mk 7, 8, 9 1948–61 Autobook
XK 150S 1959–61	..	..	..	Ball	Jaguar XK 120, 140, 150 Mk 7, 8, 9 1948–61 Autobook
Mk 7, 7M, 8, 9 1950–61	..	..	..	Ball	Jaguar XK 120, 140, 150 Mk 7, 8, 9 1948–61 Autobook
2.4 Mk 1, 2 1955–67 ..	..	..	..	Ball	Jaguar 2.4, 3.4, 3.8 Mk 1, 2 1955–69 Autobook
3.4 Mk 1, 2 1957–67	..	..	..	Ball	Jaguar 2.4, 3.4, 3.8 Mk 1, 2 1955–69 Autobook
3.8 Mk 2 1959–67	..	..	..	Ball	Jaguar 2.4, 3.4, 3.8 Mk 1, 2 1955–69 Autobook
240 1967–69 ..	..	..	..	Ball	Jaguar 2.4, 3.4, 3.8 Mk 1, 2 1955–69 Autobook
340 1967–69	..	..	..	Ball	Jaguar 2.4, 3.4, 3.8 Mk 1, 2 1955–69 Autobook
E Type 3.8 1961–65	..	..	..	Ball	Jaguar E Type 1961–70 Autobook
E Type 4.2 1964–69	..	..	..	Ball	Jaguar E Type 1961–70 Autobook
E Type 4.2 2+2 1966–70	..	..	..	Ball	Jaguar E Type 1961–70 Autobook
E Type 4.2 Series 2 1969–70 ..	..	..	..	Ball	Jagua E Type 1961–70 Autobook
S Type 3.4 1963–68	..	..	..	Ball	Jaguar S Type and 420 1963–68 Autobook
S Type 3.8 1963–68 ..	..	..	..	Ball	Jaguar S Type and 420 1963–68 Autobook
420 1963–68 ..	..	..	..	Ball	Jaguar S Type and 420 1963–68 Autobook
XJ6 2.8 litre 1968–70 ..	..	..	..	Ball	Jaguar XJ6 1968–70 Autobook
XJ6 4.2 litre 1968–70 ..	..	..	..	Ball	Jaguar XJ6 1968–70 Autobook

FIAT 1300/1500

Make				Author	Title

JOWETT

Make				Author	Title
Javelin PA 1947–49	..	..	..	Mitchell	Jowett Javelin Jupiter 1947–53 Autobook
Javelin PB 1949–50	..	..	..	Mitchell	Jowett Javelin Jupiter 1947–53 Autobook
Javelin PC 1950–51	..	..	..	Mitchell	Jowett Javelin Jupiter 1947–53 Autobook
Javelin PD 1951–52	..	..	..	Mitchell	Jowett Javelin Jupiter 1947–53 Autobook
Javelin PE 1952–53	..	..	..	Mitchell	Jowett Javelin Jupiter 1947–53 Autobook
Jupiter Mk 1 SA 1949–52	..	..	..	Mitchell	Jowett Javelin Jupiter 1947–53 Autobook
Jupiter Mk 1A SC 1952–53	..	..	..	Mitchell	Jowett Javelin Jupiter 1947–53 Autobook

LANDROVER

Series 1 1948–58	..	..	..	Ball	Landrover 1, 2 1948–61 Autobook
Series 2 1997 cc 1959–61	..	..	..	Ball	Landrover 1, 2 1948–61 Autobook
Series 2 2052 cc 1959–61	..	..	..	Ball	Landrover 1, 2 1948–61 Autobook
Series 2 2286 cc 1959–61	..	..	..	Ball	Landrover 2, 2A 1959–70 Autobook
Series 2A 2286 cc 1961–70	..	..	..	Ball	Landrover 2, 2A 1959–70 Autobook
Series 2A 2625 cc 1967–70	..	..	..	Ball	Landrover 2, 2A 1959–70 Autobook

MG

TA 1936–39	..	..	..	Ball	MG TA to TF 1936–55 Autobook
TB 1939	..	..	..	Ball	MG TA to TF 1936–55 Autobook
TC 1945–49	..	..	..	Ball	MG TA to TF 1936–55 Autobook
TD 1950–53	..	..	..	Ball	MG TA to TF 1936–55 Autobook
TF 1953–54	..	..	..	Ball	MG TA to TF 1936–55 Autobook
TF 1500 1954–55	..	..	..	Ball	MG TA to TF 1936–55 Autobook
Midget 1961–70	..	..	..	Ball	Sprite, Midget 1958–70 Autobook
Magnette ZA, ZB 1955–59	..	..	..	Ball	BMC Autobook Three
MGA 1500, 1600 1955–62	..	..	..	Ball	MGA, MGB 1955–68 Autobook
MGA Twin Cam 1958–60	..	..	..	Ball	MGA, MGB 1955–68 Autobook
MGB 1962–68	..	..	..	Ball	MGA, MGB 1955–68 Autobook
MGB 1969–71	..	..	..	Ball	MG MGB 1969–71 Autobook
1100 Mk 1 1962–67	..	..	..	Ball	1100 Mk 1 1962–67 Autobook
1100 Mk 2 1968	..	..	..	Ball	1100 Mk 2, 1300 Mk 1, 2, America 1968–71 Autobook
1300 Mk 1, 2 1968–71	..	..	..	Ball	1100 Mk 2, 1300 Mk 1, 2, America 1968–71 Autobook

MERCEDES-BENZ

190B 1959–61	..	..	..	Ball	Mercedes-Benz 190 B, C, 200 1959–68 Autobook
190C 1961–65	..	..	..	Ball	Mercedes-Benz 190 B, C, 200 1959–68 Autobook
200 1965–68	..	..	..	Ball	Mercedes-Benz 190 B, C, 200 1959–68 Autobook
220B 1959–65	..	..	..	Ball	Mercedes-Ben 220 1959–65 Autobook
220SB 1959–65	..	..	..	Ball	Mercedes-Benz 220 1959–65 Autobook
220SEB 1959–65	..	..	..	Ball	Mercedes-Benz 220 1959–65 Autobook
220SEBC 1961–65	..	..	..	Ball	Mercedes-Benz 220 1959–65 Autobook
230 1965–67	..	..	..	Ball	Mercedes-Benz 230 1963–68 Autobook
230 S 1965–68	..	..	..	Ball	Mercedes-Benz 230 1963–68 Autobook
230 SL 1963–67	..	..	..	Ball	Mercedes-Benz 230 1963 68 Autobook
250 S 1965–68	..	..	..	Ball	Mercedes-Benz 250 1965–67 Autobook
250 SE 1965–67	..	..	..	Ball	Mercedes-Benz 250 1965–67 Autobook
250 SE BC 1965–67	..	..	..	Ball	Mercedes-Benz 250 1965–67 Autobook
250 SL 1967	..	..	..	Ball	Mercedes-Benz 250 1965–67 Autobook

MORGAN

Four wheelers 1936–69	..	..	..	Clarke	Morgan 1936–69 Autobook

MORRIS

Oxford 2, 3 1954–59	..	..	..	Ball	BMC Autobook Three
Oxford 5, 6 1959–69	..	..	..	Ball	Morris Oxford 5, 6 1959–70 Autobook
Minor series 2 1952–56	..	..	..	Ball	Morris Minor 1952–71 Autobook
Minor 1000 1957–71	..	..	..	Ball	Morris Minor 1952–71 Autobook
Mini 1959–70	..	..	..	Ball	Mini 1959–70 Autobook
Mini Clubman 1969–70	..	..	..	Ball	Mini 1959–70 Autobook
Mini Cooper 1961–70	..	..	..	Ball	Mini Cooper 1961–70 Autobook

Make				Author	Title
Mini Cooper S 1963–70	..	..	..	Ball	Mini Cooper 1961–70 Autobook
1100 Mk 1 1962–67 ..	..	..	..	Ball	1100 Mk 1 1962–67 Autobook
1100 Mk 2 1968–70 ..	..	..	..	Ball	1100 Mk 2, 1300 Mk 1, 2, America 1968–71 Autobook
1300 Mk 1, 2 1968–71	..	..	..	Ball	1100 Mk 2, 1300 Mk 1, 2, America 1968–71 Autobook
1800 Mk 1, 2 1966–71	..	..	..	Ball	1800 1964–71 Autobook
1800 S 1968–71 ..	..	..	..	Ball	1800 1964–71 Autobook

NSU

Prinz 1000 L, LS 1963–67	..	..	..	Ball	NSU 1000 1963–70 Autobook
Prinz TT, TTS 1965–70	..	..	..	Ball	NSU 1000 1963–70 Autobook
1000 C 1967–70 ..	..	..	..	Ball	NSU 1000 1963–70 Autobook
TYP 110 1966–67 ..	..	..	..	Ball	NSU 1000 1963–70 Autobook
110 SC 1967 ..	..	..	..	Ball	NSU 1000 1963–70 Autobook
1200, C, TT 1967–70 ..	..	..	..	Ball	NSU 1000 1963–70 Autobook

OPEL

Kadett 993 cc 1962–65	..	..	..	Ball	Opel Kadett, Olympia 993 cc, 1078 cc 1962–70 Autobook
Kadett 1078 cc 1965–70	..	..	..	Ball	Opel Kadett, Olympia 993 cc and 1078 cc 1962–70 Autobook
Kadett 1492 cc 1967–70	..	..	..	Ball	Opel Kadett, Olympia 1492 cc, 1698 cc and 1897 cc 1967–70 Autobook
Kadett 1698 cc 1967–70	..	..	..	Ball	Opel Kadett, Olympia 1492 cc, 1698 cc and 1897 cc 1967–70 Autobook
Kadett 1897 cc 1967–70	..	..	..	Ball	Opel Kadett, Olympia 1492 cc, 1698 cc and 1897 cc 1967–70 Autobook
Olympia 1078 cc 1967–70	..	..	..	Ball	Opel Kadett, Olympia 993 cc and 1078 cc 1962–70 Autobook
Olympia 1492 cc 1967–70	..	..	..	Ball	Opel Kadett, Olympia 1492 cc, 1698 cc and 1897 cc 1967–70 Autobook
Olympia 1698 cc 1967–70	..	..	..	Ball	Opel Kadett, Olympia 1492 cc, 1698 cc and 1897 cc 1967–70 Autobook
Olympia 1897 cc 1967–70	..	..	..	Ball	Opel Kadett, Olympia 1492 cc, 1698 cc and 1897 cc 1967–70 Autobook
Rekord C 1.5, 1.7, 1.9 1966–70	..	..	..	Ball	Opel Rekord C 1966–70 Autobook

PEUGEOT

404 1960–69 ..	..	..	..	Ball	Peugeot 404 1960–69 Autobook

PLYMOUTH

Cricket 1971 ..	..	..	..	Ball	Hillman Avenger 1970–71 Autobook

PORSCHE

356A 1957–59	..	..	..	Ball	Porsche 356A, 356B, 356C 1957–65 Autobook
356B 1959–63	..	..	..	Ball	Porsche 356A, 356B, 356C 1957–65 Autobook
356C 1963–65	..	..	..	Ball	Porsche 356A, 356B, 356C 1957–65 Autobook
911 1964–67 ..	..	..	..	Ball	Porsche 911 1964–69 Autobook
911L 1967–68	..	..	..	Ball	Porsche 911 1964–69 Autobook
911S 1966–69	..	..	..	Ball	Porsche 911 1964–69 Autobook
911T 1967–69	..	..	..	Ball	Porsche 911 1964–69 Autobook
911E 1968–69	..	..	..	Ball	Porsche 911 1964–69 Autobook
912 1582 cc 1965–70 ..	..	..	..	Ball	Porsche 912 1965–70 Autobook

RENAULT

R4L 748 cc 845 cc 1961–65	..	..	..	Ball	Renault R4, R4L, 4 1961–70 Autobook
R4 845 cc 1962–66	..	..	..	Ball	Renault R4, R4L, 4 1961–70 Autobook
4 845 cc 1966–70	..	..	..	Ball	Renault R4, R4L, 4 1961–70 Autobook
6 1968–70 ..	..	..	..	Ball	Renault 6 1968–70 Autobook
R8 956 cc 1962–65	..	..	..	Ball	Renault 8, 10, 1100 1962–70 Autobook
8 956 cc 1108 cc 1965–70	..	..	..	Ball	Renault 8, 10, 1100 1962–70 Autobook
8S 1108 cc 1968–70 ..	..	..	..	Ball	Renault 8, 10, 1100 1962–70 Autobook

FIAT 1300/1500

Make						Author	Title
1100, 1108 cc 1964–69						Ball	Renault 8, 10, 1100 1962–70 Autobook
R10 1108 cc 1967–69						Ball	Renault 8, 10, 1100 1962–70 Autobook
10 1289 cc 1969–70						Ball	Renault 8, 10, 1100 1962–70 Autobook
16 1470 cc 1965–70						Ball	Renault R16 1965–70 Autobook
16TS 1565 cc 1968–70						Ball	Renault R16 1965–70 Autobook

RILEY

1.5 1957–65						Ball	BMC Autobook Three
Elf Mk 1, 2, 3 1961–70						Ball	Mini 1959–70 Autobook
1100 Mk 1 1965–67						Ball	1100 Mk 1 1962–67 Autobook
1100 Mk 2 1968						Ball	1100 Mk 2, 1300 Mk 1, 2 America 1968–71 Autobook
1300 Mk 1, 2 1968–71						Ball	1100 Mk 2, 1300 Mk 1, 2, America 1968–71 Autobook

ROVER

60 1953–59						Ball	Rover 60–110 1953–64 Autobook
75 1954–59						Ball	Rover 60–110 1953–64 Autobook
80 1959–62						Ball	Rover 60–110 1953–64 Autobook
90 1954–59						Ball	Rover 60–110 1953–64 Autobook
95 1962–64						Ball	Rover 60–110 1953–64 Autobook
100 1959–62						Ball	Rover 60–110 1953–64 Autobook
105R 1957–58						Ball	Rover 60–110 1953–64 Autobook
105S 1957–59						Ball	Rover 60–110 1953–64 Autobook
110 1962–64						Ball	Rover 60–110 1953–64 Autobook
2000 SC 1963–70						Ball	Rover 2000 1963–70 Autobook
2000 TC 1963–70						Ball	Rover 2000 1963–70 Autobook
3 litre Saloon Mk 1, 1A 1958–62						Ball	Rover 3 litre 1958–67 Autobook
3 litre Saloon Mk 2, 3 1962–67						Ball	Rover 3 litre 1958–67 Autobook
3 litre Coupé 1965–67						Ball	Rover 3 litre 1958–67 Autobook
3500, 3500S 1968–70						Ball	Rover 3500, 3500S 1968–70 Autobook

SAAB

95, 96, 1960–64						Ball	Saab 95, 96 Sport 1960–68 Autobook
95(5), 96(5) 1964–68						Ball	Saab 95, 96 Sport 1960–68 Autobook
Sport 1962–66						Ball	Saab 95, 96 Sport 1960–68 Autobook
Monte Carlo 1965–66						Ball	Saab 95, 96 Sport 1960–68 Autobook
99 1969–70						Ball	Saab 99 1969–70 Autobook

SIMCA

1000 1961–65						Ball	Simca 1000 1961–71 Autobook
1000 Special 1962–63						Ball	Simca 1000 1961–71 Autobook
1000 GL 1964–71						Ball	Simca 1000 1961–71 Autobook
1000 GLS 1964–69						Ball	Simca 1000 1961–71 Autobook
1000 GLA 1965–69						Ball	Simca 1000 1961–71 Autobook
1000 LS 1965–71						Ball	Simca 1000 1961–71 Autobook
1000 L 1966–68						Ball	Simca 1000 1961–71 Autobook
1000 Special 1968–71						Ball	Simca 1000 1961–71 Autobook
1100 LS 1967–70						Ball	Simca 1100 1967–70 Autobook
1100 GL, GLS 1967–70						Ball	Simca 1100 1967–70 Autobook
1204 1970						Ball	Simca 1100 1967–70 Autobook

SINGER

Chamois 1964–68						Smith	Hillman Imp 1963–68 Autobook
Chamois 1969–70						Ball	Hillman Imp 1969–71 Autobook
Chamois Sport 1964–68						Smith	Hillman Imp 1963–68 Autobook
Chamois Sport 1969–70						Ball	Hillman Imp 1969–71 Autobook
Gazelle series 2A 1958						Ball	Hillman Minx 1 to 5 1956–65 Autobook
Gazelle 3, 3A, 3B, 3C 1958–63						Ball	Hillman Minx 1 to 5 1956–65 Autobook
Gazelle series 5 1963–65						Ball	Hillman Minx 1 to 5 1956–65 Autobook
Gazelle series 6 1965–67						Ball	Hillman Minx 1965–67 Autobook

Make				Author	Title
New Gazelle 1500, 1725 1966–70	..		..	Ball	Hillman Minx 1966–70 Autobook
Vogue Mk 1 to 3 1961–65	..	..	..	Ball	Hillman Super Minx 1961–65 Autobook
Vogue series 4 1965–67	..	..	..	Ball	Hillman Minx 1965–67 Autobook
New Vogue 1966–70	..	..	..	Ball	Hillman Hunter 1966–70 Autobook

SKODA

440, 445, 450 1957–69	..	..	..	Skoda	Skoda Autobook One

SUNBEAM

Alpine series 1, 2, 3, 4 1959–65	..	..		Ball	Sunbeam Rapier Alpine 1955–65 Autobook
Alpine series 5 1965–67	..	..		Ball	Hillman Minx 1965–67 Autobook
Alpine 1969–70	..	..		Ball	Hillman Hunter 1969–70 Autobook
Rapier series 1, 2, 3, 3A, 4 1955–65	..	..		Ball	Sunbeam Rapier Alpine 1955–65 Autobook
Rapier series 5 1965–67	..			Ball	Hillman Minx 1965–67 Autobook
Rapier H.120 1967–70				Ball	Hillman Hunter 1966–70 Autobook
Imp Sport 1963–68	..	..	..	Smith	Hillman Imp 1963–68 Autobook
Imp Sport 1969–71	..	..		Ball	Hillman Imp 1969–71 Autobook
Stilletto 1967–68	..	..		Smith	Hillman Imp 1963–68 Autobook
Stilletto 1969–71	..	..		Ball	Hillman Imp 1969–71 Autobook
1250 1970–71	..	..		Ball	Hillman Avenger 1970–71 Autobook
1500 1970–71	..	..		Ball	Hillman Avenger 1970–71 Autobook

TOYOTA

Corolla 1100 1967–70	..	..		Ball	Toyota Corolla 1100 1967–70 Autobook
Corolla 1100 De luxe 1967–70	..	..		Ball	Toyota Corolla 1100 1967–70 Autobook
Corolla 1100 Automatic 1968–69	..	..		Ball	Toyota Corolla 1100 1967–70 Autobook
Corona 1500 Mk 1 1965–70	..	..		Ball	Toyota Corona 1500 Mk 1 1965–70 Autobook
Corona 1900 Mk 2 1969–71	..	..		Ball	Toyota Corona 1900 Mk 2 1969–71 Autobook

TRIUMPH

TR2 1952–55	..	..		Ball	Triumph TR2, TR3, TR3A 1952–62 Autobook
TR3, TR3A 1955–62	..	..		Ball	Triumph TR2, TR3, TR3A 1952–62 Autobook
TR4, TR4A 1961–67	..	..		Ball	Triumph TR4, TR4A 1961–67 Autobook
TR5 1967–69	..	..	..	Ball	Triumph TR5, TR250, TR6 1967–70 Autobook
TR6 1969–70	..	..	..	Ball	Triumph TR5, TR250, TR6 1967–70 Autobook
TR250 1967–69	..	..		Ball	Triumph TR5, TR250, TR6 1967–70 Autobook
1300 1965–70	..	..		Ball	Triumph 1300 1965–70 Autobook
1300TC 1967–70	..	..		Ball	Triumph 1300 1965–70 Autobook
2000 Mk 1 1963–69	..	..		Ball	Triumph 2000 Mk 1, 2.5 PI Mk 1 1963–69 Autobook
2000 Mk 2 1969–71	..	..		Ball	Triumph 2000 Mk 2, 2.5 PI Mk 2 1969–71 Autobook
2.5 PI Mk 1 1963–69	..	..		Ball	Triumph 2000 Mk 1, 2.5 PI Mk 1 1963–69 Autobook
2.5 PI Mk 2 1969–71	..	..		Ball	Triumph 2000 Mk 2, 2.5 PI Mk 2 1969–70 Autobook
Herald 948 1959–64	..	..		Smith	Triumph Herald 1959–68 Autobook
Herald 1200 1961–68	..	..		Smith	Triumph Herald 1959–68 Autobook
Herald 1200 1969–70	..	..		Ball	Triumph Herald 1969–71 Autobook
Herald 12/50 1963–67	..	..		Smith	Triumph Herald 1959–68 Autobook
Herald 13/60 1967–68	..	..		Smith	Triumph Herald 1959–68 Autobook
Herald 13/60 1969–71	..	..		Ball	Triumph Herald 1969–71 Autobook
Spitfire 1962–68	..	..		Smith	Triumph Spitfire Vitesse 1962–68 Autobook
Spitfire Mk 3 1969–70	..	..		Ball	Triumpn Spitfire Mk 3 1969–70 Autobook
Vitesse 1600 and 2 litre 1962–68	..	..		Smith	Triumph Spitfire Vitesse 1962–68 Autobook
Vitesse 2 litre 1969–70	..	..		Ball	Triumph GT6, Vitesse 2 litre 1969–70 Autobook
GT Six 2 litre 1966–68	..	..		Smith	Triumph Spitfire Vitesse 1962–68 Autobook
GT Six 1969–70	..	..		Ball	Triumph GT6, Vitesse 2 litre 1969–70 Autobook

VANDEN PLAS

3 litre 1959–64	..	..	..	Ball	BMC Autobook Four
1100 Mk 1 1963–67	..	..	..	Ball	1100 Mk 1 1962–67 Autobook
1100 Mk 2 1968	..	..	..	Ball	1100 Mk 2, 1300 Mk 1, 2, America 1968–71 Autobook
1300 Mk 1, 2, 1968–71	..	..	..	Ball	1100 Mk 2, 1300 Mk 1, 2, America 1968–71 Autobook

FIAT 1300/1500

VAUXHALL

Make	Author	Title
Victor 1 1957–59	Ball	Vauxhall Victor 1, 2 FB 1957–64 Autobook
Victor 2 1959–61	Ball	Vauxhall Victor 1, 2 FB 1957–64 Autobook
Victor FB 1961–64	Ball	Vauxhall Victor 1, 2 FB 1957–64 Autobook
VX4/90 FBH 1961–64	Ball	Vauxhall Victor 1, 2 FB 1957–64 Autobook
Victor FC 101 1964–67	Ball	Vauxhall Victor 101 1964–67 Autobook
VX 4/90 FCH 1964–67	Ball	Vauxhall Victor 101 1964–67 Autobook
Victor FD 1599cc 1967–71	Ball	Vauxhall Victor FD 1600, 2000 1967–71 Autobook
Victor FD 1975cc 1967–71	Ball	Vauxhall Victor FD 1600, 2000 1967–71 Autobook
VX 4/90 1969–71	Ball	Vauxhall Victor FD 1600, 2000 1967–71 Autobook
Velox, Cresta PA 1957–62	Ball	Vauxhall Velox Cresta 1957–70 Autobook
Velox, Cresta PB 1962–65	Ball	Vauxhall Velox Cresta 1957–70 Autobook
Cresta PC 1965–70	Ball	Vauxhall Velox Cresta 1957–70 Autobook
Viscount 1966–70	Ball	Vauxhall Velox Cresta 1957–70 Autobook
Viva HA (including 90) 1964–66	Ball	Vauxhall Viva HA 1964–66 Autobook
Viva HB (including 90 and SL90) 1966–70	Ball	Vauxhall Viva HB 1966–70 Autobook

VOLKSWAGEN

Make	Author	Title
1200 Beetle 1954–67	Ball	Volkswagen Beetle 1954–67 Autobook
1200 Beetle 1968–71	Ball	Volkswagen Beetle 1968–71 Autobook
1200 Karmann Ghia 1955–65	Ball	Volkswagen Beetle 1954–67 Autobook
1200 Transporter 1954–64	Ball	Volkswagen Transporter 1954–67 Autobook
1300 Beetle 1965–67	Ball	Volkswagen Beetle 1954–67 Autobook
1300 Beetle 1968–71	Ball	Volkswagen Beetle 1968–71 Autobook
1300 Karmann Ghia 1965–66	Ball	Volkswagen Beetle 1954–67 Autobook
1500 Beetle 1966–67	Ball	Volkswagen Beetle 1954–67 Autobook
1500 Beetle 1968–70	Ball	Volkswagen Beetle 1968–71 Autobook
1500 1961–65	Ball	Volkswagen 1500 1961–66 Autobook
1500N 1963–65	Ball	Volkswagen 1500 1961–66 Autobook
1500S 1963–65	Ball	Volkswagen 1500 1961–66 Autobook
1500A 1965–66	Ball	Volkswagen 1500 1961–66 Autobook
1500 Karmann Ghia 1966–67	Ball	Volkswagen Beetle 1954–67 Autobook
1500 Transporter 1963–67	Ball	Volkswagen Transporter 1954–67 Autobook
1500 Karmann Ghia 1968–70	Ball	Volkswagen Beetle 1968–71 Autobook
1600 TL 1965–70	Ball	Volkswagen 1600 Fastback 1965–70 Autobook
1600 Variant 1965–66	Ball	Volkswagen 1600 Fastback 1965–70 Autobook
1600 L 1966–67	Ball	Volkswagen 1600 Fastback 1965–70 Autobook
1600 Variant L 1966–70	Ball	Volkswagen 1600 Fastback 1965–70 Autobook
1600 T 1968–70	Ball	Volkswagen 1600 Fastback 1965–70 Autobook
1600 TA 1969–70	Ball	Volkswagen 1600 Fastback 1965–70 Autobook
1600 Variant A, M	Ball	Volkswagen 1600 Fastback 1965–70 Autobook

VOLVO

Make	Author	Title
121, 131, 221 1962–68	Ball	Volvo P120 1961–68 Autobook
122, 132, 222 1961–68	Ball	Volvo P120 1961–68 Autobook
123 GT 1967–68	Ball	Volvo P120 1961–68 Autobook
142, 142S 1967–69	Ball	Volvo 140 1966–70 Autobook
144, 144S 1966–70	Ball	Volvo 140 1966–70 Autobook
145, 145S 1968–71	Ball	Volvo 140 1966–70 Autobook

WOLSELEY

Make	Author	Title
1500 1959–65	Ball	BMC Autobook Three
15/50 1956–58	Ball	BMC Autobook Three
6/99 1959–61	Ball	BMC Autobook Four
6/110 1961–68	Ball	BMC Autobook Four
Hornet Mk 1, 2, 3 1961–70	Ball	Mini 1959–70 Autobook
1100 Mk 1 1965–67	Ball	1100 Mk 1 1962–67 Autobook
1100 Mk 2 1968	Ball	1100 Mk 2, 1300 Mk 1, 2, America 1968–71 Autobook
1300 Mk 1, 2 1968–71	Ball	1100 Mk 2, 1300 Mk 1, 2, America 1968–71 Autobook
18/85 Mk 1, 2 1967–71	Ball	1800 1964–71 Autobook
18/85 S 1969–71	Ball	1800 1964–71 Autobook